Springer Series in Cognitive Development

Series Editor
Charles J. Brainerd

Springer Series in Cognitive Development

Series Editor: Charles J. Brainerd

Sophie Haroutunian

Equilibrium in the Balance

A Study of Psychological Explanation

Springer-Verlag
New York Berlin Heidelberg Tokyo

Sophie Haroutunian
Education Center
Saint Xavier College
Chicago, Illinois 60655 U.S.A.

Series Editor
Charles J. Brainerd
Department of Psychology
University of Alberta
Edmonton, Alberta
Canada T6G 2E9

With 4 Figures

Library of Congress Cataloging in Publication Data
Haroutunian, Sophie.
Equilibrium in the balance.
(Springer series in cognitive development)
Bibliography: p.
Includes indexes.
1. Cognition in children. 2. Psychology—Philosophy.
3. Piaget, Jean, 1896–   . I. Title. II. Series.
[DNLM: 1. Psychological theory. 2. Cognition.
3. Phenotype. 4. Models, Biological. BF 311 H292e]
BF723.C5H36   1983   150′.1   83-4702

© 1983 by Springer-Verlag New York Inc.

This work contains previously copyrighted material reprinted by permission. Citations
appear on page xvii.

Typeset by Publishers Service, Bozeman, Montana.
Printed and bound by R.R. Donnelley & Sons, Harrisonburg, Virginia.
Printed in the United States of America.

9 8 7 6 5 4 3 2 1
ISBN 0-387-90834-X Springer-Verlag New York Berlin Heidelberg Tokyo
ISBN 3-540-90834-X Springer-Verlag Berlin Heidelberg New York Tokyo

In memory of my father, Joseph Haroutunian
1904–1968

Series Preface

For some time now, the study of cognitive development has been far and away the most active discipline within developmental psychology. Although there would be much disagreement as to the exact proportion of papers published in developmental journals that could be considered cognitive, 50% seems like a conservative estimate. Hence, a series of scholarly books devoted to work in cognitive development is especially appropriate at this time.

The *Springer Series in Cognitive Development* contains two basic types of books, namely, edited collections of original chapters by several authors, and original volumes written by one author or a small group of authors. The flagship for the Springer Series is a serial publication of the "advances" type, carrying the subtitle *Progress in Cognitive Development Research*. Each volume in the *Progress* sequence is strongly thematic, in that it is limited to some well-defined domain of cognitive-developmental research (e.g., logical and mathematical development, development of learning). All *Progress* volumes will be edited collections. Editors of such collections, upon consultation with the Series Editor, may elect to have their books published either as contributions to the *Progress* sequence or as separate volumes. All books written by one author or a small group of authors are being published as separate volumes within the series.

A fairly broad definition of cognitive development is being used in the selection of books for this series. The classic topics of concept development, children's thinking and reasoning, the development of learning, language development, and memory development will, of course, be included. So, however, will newer areas such as social-cognitive development, educational applications, formal modeling, and philosophical implications of cognitive-developmental theory. Although it is

anticipated that most books in the series will be empirical in orientation, theoretical
and philosophical works are also welcome. With books of the latter sort, hetero-
geneity of theoretical perspective is encouraged, and no attempt will be made to
foster some specific theoretical perspective at the expense of others (e.g., Piagetian
versus behavioral or behavioral versus information processing).

C. J. Brainerd

Foreword

It has been said about Piaget that he is a learning theorist without a learning theory. Sophie Haroutunian shows that this is so in a sense which goes far beyond what is usually contemplated under such a rubric. For the theory or theories that Piaget put forward during his long, active life surely cover areas of inquiry that involve learning on the part of the individual; yet in a curious sense Piaget has never emphasized learning. It is development that is the key notion in his approach to the subject, even if he was always anxious to distinguish developmental psychology from what he called "genetic epistemology." It is the notion of development too that makes biology the natural source for a model for the explanation of cognitive development so-called.

The concepts of accommodation and assimilation that are central Piagetian concepts are biological in their origin and they presuppose the idea of the individual adjusting to the environment or altering the environment to fit himself. That in turn presupposes that the goal of such interrelationships is equilibrium and the principle that it involves that of homeostasis. The balance once attained can be disrupted, setting up further processes of equilibration and leading in all probability to yet further states of balance. But how can such processes explain *development*? If there is a direction to the processes in question, as the reference to development suggests there must be, this must either be due, mysteriously, to chance encounters with the environment or be due to some inbuilt directional organization in the individual. Neither view seems to fit cognitive development and the question is whether there is any satisfactory view between these extremes. Dr. Haroutunian shows indeed that these problems affect the use of equilibrium principles in psychology in general.

Piaget took over from C. H. Waddington certain notions which might conceivably help in this respect—the notions of homeorhesis, of chreods and of epigenesis generally. The question remains whether such notions really help. Most recently, as Dr. Haroutunian emphasizes, Piaget has drawn elaborate parallels between cognitive development and evolutionary processes, parallels that are summed up in the principle of phenocopy, derived from R. B. Goldschmidt, to which I shall return later. The purpose of invoking such principles is to make clear how it is possible for the cognitive organism to proceed along lines of development, influenced in some way by the environment and without supposing that the lines of development are all innately determined.

Whether Piaget has succeeded in that aim is a major concern for Dr. Haroutunian, and she shows, to my mind quite clearly, that he has not. The biological theories in which Piaget sees the proper analogies to explain the growth of knowledge (though much that Piaget says implies that it is much more than an analogy) are theories which seek a middle way between preformationism and total plasticity in relation to the environment, or, as Piaget puts it sometimes, between neo-Darwinism and Lamarckianism. As far as concerns the growth of knowledge itself the middle way is between innatism and what Piaget calls "empiricism," construed as the thesis that what the individual becomes, cognitively speaking, is entirely what the environment makes him. There is a sense in which it is the latter extreme which Piaget has always been most anxious to avoid. It is evidently quite incompatible with any view that sees the existence of "stages" of cognitive development as quite universal and necessary, having nothing to do with environmental or cultural factors. And that is the essence of Piagetianism, a matter on which Dr. Haroutunian has much to say. It is arguable that innatism or nativism was initially less of a bogey for Piaget, because of the fact that something at least of what we are is inborn and because of the possibility of maturation as an explanation of some lines of development that take place.

Nevertheless, complete innatism has always been quite unacceptable to Piaget, and the importance of avoiding it received a new focus as the result of Chomsky's espousal of innate knowledge and capacities. The parallel with biology, however, suggests that even if something corresponding to preformationism is not acceptable there must be things about us that are innate and some account must be offered of how what *is* innate interacts with what is a function of the environment. Since it is *interaction* that we are thus concerned with, the obvious mechanism is a homeostatic one, with appeal to equilibrium principles. One thing that Dr. Haroutunian brings out, however, is that even if such a view, as applied to cognitive development, avoids the full rigors of a Chomskyan innatism, extended, as it must be once one enters this royal road, to everything, it still entails that the *possibilities* of all future development must be inborn. Which possibilities are actualized will be a function of the environment and seemingly chance encounters with it. Is that the way in which to conceive of the growth of human understanding where, as we ordinarily believe, genuinely new understanding can come about? Is learning merely a matter of possibilities that already exist in us being actualized as the result of the stimulus provided by the contingencies of experience?

This criticism suggests that the parallel with biology, even when something corresponding to preformationism is avoided, allows too much to what is innate. The second important criticism that Dr. Haroutunian brings forward is that which possibilities are actualized must, on this model, still be a matter of chance. Moreover, the principle of phenocopy which is invoked by Piaget in this connection does not really meet the objection. This principle is one according to which an initial phenotype is copied by a later genotype without this involving Lamarckianism. This is explained in terms of the idea that there comes about in the organic system a disequilibrium between "genetic programing" and "epigenetic innovation." Response to this disequilibrium along homeostatic lines takes the form of the genome "trying out variations" which are "canalized toward the areas of disequilibrium" (J. Piaget, *Behaviour and Evolution*, p. 76). Hence the genome is not directly changed by the environment but rather by its own responses to the state of disequilibrium that comes about in its relation with the environment. Dr. Haroutunian shows that this does not eliminate the role of chance. Even if the mechanism does not simply involve causal interaction with the environment it will not operate without that and the processes involved are in no sense directive, despite Piaget's use of the words "trying out."

When this is applied (by analogy?) to cognitive development the same criticisms apply and become more acute. Learning cannot simply be growth in whatever direction is determined by the contingencies of how the environment affects the individual and how the individual happens to react, whatever be the mechanism involved. Hence the mechanisms that Piaget suggests do not do justice to the facts to be explained, and if this means that equilibrium principles must be abandoned (and indeed with them the whole biological model) so much the worse for them.

Dr. Haroutunian's criticisms seem to me in this respect definitive, and it is good to see them worked through in such detail, much of which I have not space to mention. She concludes her work with a discussion of the question whether Piaget embraces his biological model because he accepts what Jerry Fodor has called the "Representational Theory of the Mind." Here she seems to me to be on thinner ice and the suggestions that she makes are certainly controversial. What is certain is that any interactional thesis of the kind that Piaget puts forward must, psychologically speaking, involve the thought that the individual brings to bear on the environment concepts, representations if you like, that are the individual's own contribution. In terms of the phenocopy principle it means "trying out variations," but in a literal, not metaphorical, sense of "trying out." Reflection on what that presupposes in the case of cognition has led Fodor to the notion of the "language of thought" and the suggestion that the individual must have innately a whole range of thoughts and forms of thought that he or she brings to bear on the environment; it is only because of this that learning is possible, learning being construed on the model of hypothesis formation and confirmation. The paradoxical character of that theory is, I suggest, enough to make one conclude that there is a misconception behind it. Learning cannot be like that and we cannot construe the growth of understanding in such interactionist terms.

How we *should* construe it is a further question. Dr. Haroutunian is certainly right to say that the Representational Theory of the Mind must be treated seriously, if only as something that must be circumvented if an acceptable account of cognitive development is to be arrived at. I suspect that we are still some distance from that. But Dr. Haroutunian has certainly shown that Piaget is not only a learning theorist without a learning theory (without a learning theory since he substitutes for that a theory of development), but a theorist who does not, properly speaking, confront learning at all. Moreover, the biological model takes us so far from that that "development" too seems the wrong word to use about what it deals with. For how *could* a theory that leaves to chance encounters with the environment and the organism's own reactions to what results from that which possibilities are realized be a theory of *development?*

Dr. Haroutunian's close examination of these points in general and of Piaget's use of the phenocopy principle in particular merits the attention of all concerned with Piagetian thinking. Since the phenocopy principle is the latest of the principles to which Piaget has appealed, and that towards the end of his long and fruitful life, it is important that it too should be thoroughly discussed. Dr. Haroutunian shows that it is no more successful than earlier principles. Her discussion of this issue adds a new dimension to Piagetian scholarship. More than that, she confronts anyone who wants to invoke equilibrium principles in psychology and genetic epistemology with an account of the limitations that such principles impose. Her discussion deserves every attention.

D.W. Hamlyn

Preface

The key of life is compensation, complement its vigour. Only with an infinite variation of unbalance can the harmony grow great and the pattern live. So it is with our human part of the pattern, with the smaller pattern within us, the meat of our bodies and the anxiety of its feeding. Here pain is the unbalance of peace, sorrow of satisfaction. How can peace be borne without pain, how can pain be borne without the certainty of peace? How can happiness dispense with sorrow, how can a life-time of sorrow be endured without the surmise of happiness? The principle of balance is the danger of disruption and its defeat of that danger. Life would not proceed but for these motors . . . they are its essence. (Sansom, 1948, pp. 44–45)

Why, after more than a century of systematic, experimental research, have we failed to generate a satisfactory account of behavior? Are we asking the wrong questions? Pursuing the wrong methods of investigation? Collecting inadequate data? Ignoring the wrong variables? Defending the wrong assumptions? All of these are possibilities. In the present work, I investigate still another which bears a relation to all of the above: Are we relying on explanatory principles in psychology that are inappropriate?

An explanatory principle is a rule which provides a framework for understanding phenomena. If the goal is to understand why behavior of certain sorts occurs, then some principle or model of explanation is invoked to generate an answer. The model provides rules for identifying variables to be investigated and for characterizing their effects. It prompts certain questions and motivates the investigator to seek particular types of data. To some extent, it dictates the nature of the experiments performed and the interpretation of results. Since the explanatory model sets parameters and procedures, the failures which the science encounters must at some point be examined in relation to the model.

In the present work, I analyze a principle which has dominated psychological explanation since the late nineteenth century, namely, equilibrium. Focusing on Jean Piaget's application of this model, I show how it saddled him with undesirable constraints—constraints he did not always recognize. I also consider conceptual limitations which arose from his use of equilibrium and explain why modifications in his accounts fail to eliminate them. More generally, I argue that some theoretical controversies in psychology find their source in this explanatory principle. I conclude by exploring why equilibrium seems so enticing in spite of the limitations which have arisen from its use.

There are many institutions and individuals who have assisted me in this work and to whom I express my sincere appreciation. To begin with, I owe a great debt to the National Science Foundation, History and Philosophy of Science Program, and the American Association of University Women. The NSF research grant (SOC 7825995), 1979-1981, and the AAUW Post-doctoral Fellowship, 1978-1979, made it possible for me to spend the academic year 1978-1979 as an Honorary Research Fellow in the department of philosophy, Birkbeck College, University of London, and to meet with the members of the Faculté de Psychologie et des Sciences de l'education, University of Geneva, in April of 1979. Much of the research was completed during this fellowship year. In addition, Saint Xavier College has greatly facilitated the project by allowing me a leave of absence in 1978-1979 and awarding Small Project Grants in 1979-1983. The University of London, and particularly Birkbeck College, was most generous in granting me library and other privileges during 1978-1979.

The following groups and individuals have helped enormously by providing criticism of my arguments: Members of the Midwest Cognitive Science Study Group and the Chicago History and Philosophy of Science Study Group; William Bechtel, Charles J. Brainerd, Guy Cellérier, Hubert L. Dreyfus, Norman Fischer, Owen Flanagan, Jerry A. Fodor, James Griesemer, Kenneth Kaye, Pierre Moessinger, Richard S. Peters, Hugh G. Petrie, Denis C. Phillips, Robert J. Richards, John R. Searle, Jacques Vonèche, John White, and George D. Wood. In addition to these persons, I especially wish to thank Stephen Toulmin, with whom I have been discussing these issues since 1974; Harvey Siegel, who has read and criticized the many drafts of the chapters in great detail; Gary S. Kahn, who has been especially perceptive about the limitations in the arguments; and David B. Klass, who has given the manuscript the benefit of his unique perspective. Finally, I owe deep gratitude to David W. Hamlyn, without whom this work might never have taken its present form. Professor Hamlyn met with me many times over the 1978-1979 academic year and has read countless versions of the arguments. His insights into both the issues and Piaget's theory have been of inestimable value.

As I say, the dialogue with and support of these persons have contributed enormously to the project. Where there are shortcomings in the analysis, however, I take full responsibility.

I conclude by thanking the fine secretaries who have assisted me so faithfully: Lorraine McPartlin, Ruth Strey, and, especially, Barbara Hansen.

Saint Xavier College   Sophie Haroutunian
May, 1983

Contents

Reprinted by Permission

1. The Problem

"A great day!" wrote Paul. I started skidding early—at seven o'clock—in fact as soon as I got up.". . . When he took a pace forward, that pace became three paces. It was simply that the soles of his feet slithered over the carpet, they seemed to have lost their frictional grip; he found himself balancing on the sides of his feet, walking at an incline, so that his whole body leaned dangerously. He moved across the bedroom like a sailboat keeling in the wind.

Added to this, at various intervals his knees suddenly crumpled beneath him—then sprang taut again in the same instant, in fact at the very point of collapse. He felt himself falling, yet he managed always to regain his balance at the extremity of danger. So it was with the angle of his body; it felt dangerous, as though he would overbalance completely at any moment, yet miraculously some complementary force maintained for him his equilibrium just at the point of overturning. (Sansom, 1948, pp. 9-10)

Although infrequently discussed, nearly all explanation in psychology makes some use of the equilibrium principle. The practice is evident in Dewey (1933), Erikson (1964), Freud (1923/1960), James (1890), Spencer (1892), and Watson (1929) and continues to the present day. The thesis of my book is that there is a direct connection between some widely acknowledged limitations in our psychological accounts and the use of this explanatory model. In the pages which follow, I attempt to substantiate the thesis.

My aim in the present chapter is to elaborate the basic claim about the equilibrium principle and outline the strategy I shall follow to defend it. In the first section, I define the principle of equilibrium and show briefly how Spencer, Dewey, Watson, Freud, Heider, and Festinger apply it. In the second section, I outline the discussion as it appears in the ensuing chapters, thereby sketching the fundamental argument I try to establish. I finish the section by discussing two controversial features of my strategy.

The Equilibrium Principle

To put it very simply, the equilibrium principle asserts a relation between a system (or an organism) and the environment in which it functions, such that if the environment changes, the organism will adjust its behavior to maintain certain desired conditions. Should the environment become modified, the system (be it living or nonliving) will vary its behavior so as to preserve itself.

One may express the principle of equilibrium with the following function:

$$(x) \ (x \text{ changes from } b_1 \text{ to } b_2 \text{ if } E_1 \text{ changes to } E_2)$$

Here, x is a system which survives in environment E_1 using behavior b_1; E_2 is the modified environment; and b_2 is the change in x's behavior which compensates for the change made by E_2. If environment E_1 is changed to E_2, then x will change its behavior from b_1 to b_2 so as to maintain itself.

The system-environment relation, as expressed here, is elaborated in biological, physical, chemical, social, and economic contexts. Theorists speak of static and dynamic equilibrium and of equilibrium between populations or individuals and their surrounding conditions. Sometimes, equilibrium characterizes the relation between two or more systems, each of which constitutes the environment to which the other must relate. While the model assumes somewhat different features in the various contexts, its focus is always upon optimizing the system's chances for survival in the face of changes in external conditions.[1]

With this definition in mind, we can get some idea of how equilibrium functions as an explanatory principle in psychology. Spencer (1892) uses it to explain how mental states arise in the mind. He argues that the features of our conscious states —the content of our images, beliefs, and ideas—depend upon what occurs in our surroundings. If one experiences mental state a, then the cause is the appearance of some element A in the environment. Furthermore, if two elements A and B frequently co-occur in the environment, the relation between the mental state a and state b that they cause will be strengthened. If A is frequently encountered and often followed by B, then state a will be followed by state b (1892, vol. I, pp. 408-409).

What will happen to the relation between a and b if B ceases to follow A? Spencer writes:

> If the strengths of the connexions between the internal states are not proportionate to the persistences of the relations between the answering external agents, there will be a failure of the correspondence—the inner order will disagree with the outer order. (p. 409)

In other words, if the relation between a and b does not correspond to the relation between A and B, then a discrepancy between inner states and outer events will occur. Spencer goes on to say that an adequate understanding of the world requires the elimination of such discrepancies (p. 410).

---

[1] Wimsatt (1971) distinguishes between equilibrium and feedback systems. While an equilibrium system need not employ feedback loops, the principle of equilibrium as defined here may be used to characterize the operation of both feedback and equilibrium mechanisms.

Here, then, is one application of the equilibrium principle. Spencer uses it as a basis for explaining the occurrence of mental states, arguing that if the conditions in the organism—the relation between mental states a and b—are not consistent with the relation between corresponding external elements, then equilibrium between the organism and the environment is upset. In this situation, the relation between the mental states must be modified if desired internal conditions are to be reached and equilibrium is to be reestablished.

Dewey (1933) employs the principle of equilibrium to explain how the mind reasons and solves problems. He gives the following example:

> Suppose you are walking along where there is no regular path. As long as everything goes smoothly, you do not have to think about your walking; your already formed habit takes care of it. Suddenly, you find a ditch in your way. You think you will jump it (supposition, plan); but to make sure, you survey it with your eyes (observation) and you find that it is pretty wide and that the bank on the other side is slippery (facts, data). You then wonder if the ditch may not be narrower somewhere else (idea), and you look up and down the stream (observation) to see how matters stand (test of idea by observation). You do not find any good place and so are thrown back upon forming a new plan. As you are casting about, you discover a log (fact again). You ask yourself whether you could not haul that to the ditch and get it across the ditch to use as a bridge (idea again). You judge that idea as worth trying, and so you get the log and manage to put it in place and walk across (test and confirmation by overt action). (p. 105)

In this example Dewey outlines five steps of reflective thinking which begin when there is a dilemma—a discrepancy between what is experienced in the environment and what the mind knows or understands. One eliminates the discrepancy as follows. First, suggestions "leap forward" in the mind—suggestions about possible solutions to the conflict. These suggestions are not under the control of the thinker but arise as the mind's first response to the changed environment. In order to determine which suggestions are appropriate and ought to be tried, the problem must be clearly defined. Once it is defined, one uses hypothetical answers to guide observations and collect relevant data. Given the data, one draws inferences about the soundness of the hypothesis. Finally, once the hypothetical reasoning is complete, one tests the hypothesis.

In short, reflective thinking occurs when one confronts a discrepancy in the environment, changes behavior to eliminate that discrepancy, and thereby returns to a point of equilibrium with the environment. The mind works naturally and more or less efficiently to carry out the process. For Dewey, as for Spencer, the equilibrium principle provides an objective for altering one's behavior, namely, eliminating discrepancy and hence disequilibrium between organism and environment.

Watson (1929) uses the equilibrium model to explain why all behaviors occur:

> We shall see that there are common factors running through all forms of human acts. In each adjustment there is always both a *response or act* and a *stimulus or situation* which calls out that response. Without going too far beyond our facts, it seems possible to say that the stimulus is always provided by the environment, external to the body, or by the movement of man's own muscles and the secretions will be changed through action or through cognitive reorganization. If a change is not possible, the state of imbalance will produce tension. (p. 39)

Clearly, the equilibrium principle provides the basis for Watson's stimulus-response ideas. Although the change (response) the organism makes in the face of the altered environment (stimulus) is not the consequence of conscious reflection as in Dewey's account, it occurs for the same reason, namely, to ensure the survival of the organism, given change in its situation. Alternative responses persist if they succeed in maintaining desirable internal conditions.

Freud, like Spencer, Dewey, and Watson, invokes the equilibrium principle. In speaking of psychosexual behavior, he writes (1923/1960):

> I am only putting forward a hypothesis . . . it seems a plausible view that this displaceable and neutral energy, which is no doubt active both in the ego and in the id, proceeds from the narcissistic store of libido—that it is desexualized Eros. (The erotic instincts appear to be altogether more plastic, more readily diverted and displaced than the destructive instincts.) From this we can easily go on to assume that this displaceable libido is employed in the service of the pleasure principle to obviate blockages and facilitate discharge. (pp. 34-35)

According to Freud, then, there is displaceable or free-flowing energy in the libido, which can be used "in the service of the pleasure principle," that is, to permit the satisfaction of needs and desires. The pleasure principle specifies the motivation for change. The desexualized energy provides the means by which change can occur. When there are blockages—when there are factors which prevent the organism from achieving pleasure—the desexualized energy is released in order to remove the blockages and permit pleasure to be felt.

Freud's explanation of the psyche is clearly based on the equilibrium principle. The achievement of pleasure is the achievement of equilibrium between the organism and the environment, and also between conflicting demands within the organism. In the face of these demands, the organism responds by energizing certain behaviors, which when performed relieve the conflicts and restore the state of equilibrium.

Equilibrium also forms the basis of more recent psychological theorizing. For example, within the field of social psychology, many use it to explain how attitude change occurs. In this case (in contrast to Watson and Freud) the balance between the system and its environment is regained by changing to a novel response rather than to an alternative already available in the repertoire of behaviors.

Consider Heider (1946/1967) and Festinger (1957), two of the most influential attitude theorists. Heider's thesis is that an attitude toward one event can influence attitudes toward other events or persons. If one has a positive attitude toward an occurrence, one will have a balanced attitude if one also has a positive attitude toward the person who caused the occurrence. He writes:

> A balanced state exists if all parts of a unit have the same dynamic character (i.e., if all are positive or negative), and if entities with different dynamic characters are segregated from each other. If no balanced state exists, then focus toward this state will arise. Either the dynamic characters will change, or the unit relations will be changed through action or through cognitive reorganization. If a change is not possible, the state of imbalance will produce tension. (p. 39)

According to Heider, a unit is a set of relations between two entities. PU_x can mean p owns x; p made x; x belongs to p. If any of the relations within the unit contradict the others (e.g., p made x, but x does not belong to p), a state of imbalance exists.[2] In the preceding example, the "dynamic characters"—the positive/negative relations between the entities within the unit—will change. If no modification occurs, then the state of imbalance created by the contradictions will produce tension.

Festinger (1957) argues similarly when he states:

> It has frequently been implied . . . that the individual strives toward consistency within himself. His opinions and attitudes, for example, tend to exist in clusters that are internally consistent. (p. 1)
> The existence of dissonance, being psychologically uncomfortable, will motivate the person to try to reduce the dissonance and achieve consonance. When dissonance is present, in addition to trying to reduce it, the person will actively avoid situations and information which would be likely to increase the dissonance. (p. 3)

Here, Festinger indicates that the existence of dissonance, or inconsistency between attitudes/opinions/beliefs ("knowledges," p. 9) will motivate change of some sort aimed at eliminating dissonance. Consonance (or balance) is regained when the attitudes/opinions/beliefs become consistent with one another again. Like Heider, Festinger argues that imbalance or dissonance may be eliminated with a novel occurrence—an attitude or belief which did not exist previously. Both invoke the equilibrium principle when they argue that imbalance, or conflicting attitudes, motivate change.

Unlike Heider (although not in contradiction to him), Festinger stresses that cognitive dissonance can occur when people have "knowledges" about reality (or the environment) which do not correspond to it:

> Persons frequently have cognitive elements which deviate markedly from reality, at least as we see it . . . *the reality which impinges on a person will exert pressures in the direction of bringing the appropriate cognitive elements into correspondence with reality.* . . . if the cognitive elements do not correspond within a certain reality which impinges, certain pressures must exist. (p. 11)

Festinger's use of equilibrium parallels Spencer's to the extent that both argue for an increasing correspondence between the environment and one's beliefs about it. In both cases, the system is motivated to change when discrepancy with the environment exists. The need for change is eliminated when the contradiction with the environment is eliminated.

Of modern theorists, the Swiss psychologist Jean Piaget makes perhaps the most explicit and detailed use of equilibrium. He takes a version of the model from biology and uses it to explain how the ability to reason and solve problems improves over time. Unlike Heider, Festinger, and Spencer, Piaget uses equilibrium to explain why the organism reaches successively improved states of operation, not just different ones. Much of the ensuing analysis will focus on Piaget's case.

Given the extensive use of equilibrium in psychology, and the limitations in our accounts of behavior, it behooves us to ask: Is this principle really suitable for

---

[2]Heider provides similar examples of contradiction. The contradiction arises not from the content of the claims but from coupling negative with positive relations within the unit.

explaining psychological phenomena? Unfortunately, this question is much too broad for a single work. A full resolution of the question would require investigating the consequences that have arisen from its diverse use in explaining various kinds of behavior. As a first step in the enterprise, I will address the narrower issue of whether or not equilibrium can satisfactorily explain how problem-solving ability improves. In the chapters that follow, I pursue this question by analyzing Piaget's use of the model to explain cognitive change.

I will focus on Piaget's equilibration account, for his enormously rich discussions provide an excellent basis for identifying consequences that arise from at least one application of the equilibrium principle. Because he consciously elaborates his model in great detail (e.g., 1967/1971, 1975/1977, 1976/1978, 1974/1980a), it is possible to describe its features in detail and see exactly how he uses it to construct his explanation. It is also possible to identify the constraints that the model places upon him, some conceptual limitations which arise because of it, and some questions he raises but cannot answer. In addition, one can see why Piaget's attempts to eliminate these difficulties—many of which he recognizes—ultimately fail. Furthermore, one can understand how his use of equilibrium creates a major controversy with Noam Chomsky, namely, whether he explains the origin of (linguistic) structures with an alternative to Chomsky's nativism. By examining Piaget's case in depth, I generate hypotheses about the consequences of using equilibrium which can be applied to other cases.

Outline of the Argument

The analysis proceeds as follows. In Chapter 2, I summarize equilibration and present some criticisms that have been raised about its conceptual features. The summary involves defining the terms *assimilation, accommodation,* and *equilibrium,* and explaining what Piaget means by *cognitive structure* and *stage.* There are five conceptual issues raised by critics which I consider: (1) Does Piaget provide an alternative to Chomsky's account of cognitive structures? (2) Does he make clear how cognitive structures cause or otherwise relate to behavior? (3) Does he use logical relations between cognitive stages as a basis for asserting causal or prerequisite relations between them? (4) Does he use the terms *assimilation* and *accommodation* ambiguously? (5) Is the equilibration account fundamentally incapable of explaining how children make the transition from one stage to another? In each case, I review the claims made by the critics and indicate whether the objections seem to be justified.

In Chapter 3, I develop a perspective from which to evaluate the origin of the problems identified in Chapter 2. I begin by defining the term *model* and argue that the equilibrium principle is used by Piaget as a model in a very specific sense, namely, as a theory-constitutive metaphor (Boyd, 1979). I then examine the biological version of the equilibrium principle which Piaget appropriates—a version formulated by the embryologist C. H. Waddington (1957)—known as genetic assimilation. Waddington's model asserts that to maintain equilibrium between the organism and the environment, change in the organism's phenotypic characteristics can be followed by change in its genotype. Piaget finds this version of equilibrium appealing, for he wants to show how change in behavior can precede change in cognitive structure. He therefore uses genetic assimilation as a theory-constitutive metaphor to construct an explanatory principle that suits his purposes.

In Chapter 4, I compare the principle of genetic assimilation to Piaget's principle of phenocopy—the model which he derives from genetic assimilation. I then return to the criticisms of equilibration raised in Chapter 2 and ask: Can Piaget's use of phenocopy help us to understand why these criticisms are justified and why these conceptual difficulties are present? I argue that in each instance Piaget's use of the phenocopy principle creates the problem.

In Chapter 5, I review some of the criteria that equilibration would have to meet in order to be successful. I argue that by using phenocopy as he does, Piaget constrains his equilibration account to meet certain functional criteria specified by Hamlyn (e.g., 1975). Piaget makes numerous attempts to satisfy these criteria, for example, with discussions of decentration, contradiction, and interaction. However, each attempt fails to give a satisfactory explanation, and consequently his fundamental objectives are not met. Unfortunately, his use of phenocopy dooms these efforts from the start.

In Chapter 6, I examine the question: Why does Piaget choose equilibrium for an explanatory principle and use it as he does if it creates all the problems that have been identified? The reason, I argue, is that he assumed a certain conception of mind—what Fodor (1981) calls the representational theory of the mind (RTM). Because Chomsky also assumes RTM, his account of linguistic structures has certain features also found in Piaget's account. As my claim is a strong one, I consider a number of objections to it and in so doing take up the following questions: Does the concept of steady state enable Piaget to explain the origins of cognitive structures in a way alternative to Chomsky's? Does extant empirical evidence help us to understand whether Piaget provides an alternative to Chomsky's claims, and if so, which is correct? These matters resolved, I then consider two general issues that are raised when one assumes RTM. First, must the representations presupposed by RTM be explicit representations? If so, what consequences for psychological explanation and use of explanatory models arise from the fact? Second, can theories of artificial intelligence help to explain how the mind, as conceived by Piaget and Chomsky, is capable of attributing meaning (i.e., intentionality)? I conclude by discussing whether equilibrium, if used as a theory-constitutive metaphor, is satisfactory for explaining how people learn to reason and solve problems. Having analyzed Piaget's case in depth, it is possible to hypothesize about the limitations that may beset others and begin to speculate about the adequacy of the equilibrium model for explaining psychological phenomena.

Let me briefly defend two strategies that I have adopted in the chapters that follow. First, there are many places where I provide lengthy quotations. My reason for so doing is that many of the arguments turn on interpretations of writings by Piaget and others. Where they do, I present the quotation, summarize its meaning, and then analyze the passage. While this is a lengthy procedure, it leaves the reader free to make counterinterpretations and evaluate the arguments. As Piaget's writing is both difficult and ambiguous, there is much room for disagreement about his claims. It is therefore necessary to quote him at length in some places.

A second strategy I have followed is to use wherever possible the English translations that are available. I have done this for two reasons. First, I found these translations to be generally satisfactory for my purposes. In the cases where they are inadequate, I provide a translation. Second, by using the English translations, I focus on the references that will be accessible to most readers. Some may object to my decision on the grounds that the interpretations of Piaget's theory would have been different had I focused upon French rather than English texts. I can only respond that my readings of the French and English versions lead me to conclude that this is not the case.

2. Limitations in Piaget's Equilibration Account

This time the ball flew to the ceiling and then paused at the point of bouncing. It seemed then to hang motionless in the air. For a long second it hung there— and throughout this time the ear awaited a rustling sound that never came, the ear stretched upwards for it, a sound that should have marked the friction of the ball with its shadow, the kiss of the ball's light fur spinning against the ceiling. But silently it hung there, spinning slowly at the peak of its momentum, slowly as though turning round for the descent, hesitating against its own dark shadow, whispering against the ceiling a soundless kiss, suspended and yet still suspended for a moment of held beauty, breathless . . . (how long could it hang there? Would the rustle never be heard?) . . . until abruptly it dropped on its straight line gravitating downwards. (Sansom, p. 18)

In order to understand the consequences of using the equilibrium principle to explain psychological phenomena, a case study is required. As argued in Chapter 1, Jean Piaget's account of the development of reasoning ability provides a very rich and suitable example. Once conceptual limitations in his account are clear, one may proceed to determine whether these limitations arise from his use of the equilibrium principle (Chapter 3). The purpose of the present chapter is, then, to review Piaget's account and identify some of its conceptual limitations. The chapter is divided into three major sections.

In the first section, I summarize Piaget's stage theory, together with the equilibration account—his attempt to explain how the transition is made from one developmental stage to the next. I discuss Piaget's explanation in terms of a well-elaborated empirical example which he himself provides.

In the second section, I describe the fundamental conceptual issue that Piaget's account raises, namely: Does it explain how children become capable of new behavior—behavior of which they were incapable at the start? As is shown, Piaget rejects Chomsky's resolution of this issue. The question is, does he provide an alter-ternative to Chomsky's explanation?

In the third section, I review several conceptual limitations in Piaget's account which exist because he explains the origin of behavior as he does. I raise the possi-bility that his concepts of stage, cognitive structure, and the processes of assimilation and accommodation may not permit him to provide an alternative to Chomsky's account, despite Piaget's claims to the contrary. I conclude the chapter by review-ing J. A. Fodor's criticism of Piaget and argue that an evaluation of this criti-cism will require us to examine Piaget's use of explanatory principles.

Piaget's Theory of Cognitive Development

Piaget wants to explain how children become capable of solving problems they cannot solve initially. In other words, he wants to show how new, more effective problem-solving behaviors become possible for children. He argues that the chil-dren grow into mature, adult thinkers by passing through a series of stages. Arrival at a new stage is indicated by performance on a given task. At each successive level, the children are able to solve problems they could not solve before.

For example, Inhelder and Piaget (1955/1958) discuss the performance of several subjects working with a balance mechanism, each arm of which contains 28 holes (p. 171). From the holes may be hung any or all of a series of ordered weights, each half as heavy as the next ($A < B < C < D$, etc.). The task for the subject is to demonstrate precise understanding of the formula $W/W' = L'/L$: When two unequal weights, W and W', are balanced at unequal distances, L' and L, from the axis, an equal amount of work is done on each side. Given unequal weights on the two arms, the subject must state the precise relation between weights and distances needed to achieve a balance. In order to become capable of correctly solving the balance prob-lem, children proceed through the following stages in the order given:

[Substage I-A]: Subjects cannot guarantee equilibrium simply by distribut-ing weights, but intrude in the working of the apparatus with their *own* actions, which they fail to distinguish from the actions of the *objects* that they are trying to control. (p. 166)

[Substage I-B]: From this point on the child understands that weight is needed on both sides to achieve a balance and even that the weights should be approximately equal. But he does not yet know how to proceed toward this equilization in a systematic way. (p. 168)

[Substage II-A]: From this point on, weights are equalized and added exactly, while distances are added and made symmetrical. But coordination between weights and distances as yet goes no further than intuitive regulations. The subject discovers by trial-and-error that equilibrium ... [with unequal weights and distances] is possible, but he does not yet draw general correspon-dences. (p. 169)

[Substage II-B]: The difference between these reactions and those of sub-stage II-A is clear. At the earlier stage, when the subject comes across two weights which do not come into equilibrium, he works mostly with substitutions—additions or subtractions. In this way, he achieves certain equilizations by displacement, but only exceptionally and by groping about (regulations). On the other hand, at the present stage the subject who comes to two unequal weights tries to balance them by means of an oriented displacement on the hypothesis that the same object "will weigh more" at a greater distance from the axis. . . . He is working toward the law, but without metrical proportions. (pp. 171-172)

[Stage III] : When the experiment proceeds by successive and alternate suspensions of the weights, the subject's attention turns to the inclinations and the distances in height to be covered; this may lead him to an explanation in terms of equal amounts of work (displacement of forces). (p. 173)

These descriptions of performance on the balance problem show that errors in reasoning recorded at one stage are corrected or compensated for at the next level. For example, in substage I-A, the subject fails to distinguish between the effects of the weights hung on the mechanism and his own weight applied to it. He therefore interferes with the mechanism by pulling one of its arms. At substage I-B, the subject has corrected this error and adjusts the balance by hanging different weights on the arms. Nevertheless, he still cannot add equal amounts of weight to both sides of the mechanism with systematic regularity. By substage II-A, the subject knows how to add equal weight to both sides, and thus has compensated for the error of the previous substage. He still, however, does not succeed in balancing unequal weights by placing them at different distances from the axis. By substage II-B he overcomes this limitation, although he cannot yet state the law of compensations between unequal weights and distances. It is not until stage III that he achieves this final resolution of the problem.

Use of a stage theory to explain the development of reasoning ability raises a theoretical problem: If children give a sequence of performances that occur in fixed order, how is it that the ability to give a higher stage performance develops? In other words, how do the children make the transition from one stage of performance to the next? What happens to 10-year-old children such that at age 12, they will give a very different performance on the balance problem? Piaget (1957) answers these questions by describing the process of *equilibration*.[1]

The hypothesis of equilibration consists in seeing in the problem posed (if it really is a problem) a perturbation introduced into the subject's prior schemata: the dual reaction to [this perturbation] will consist of *assimilating* to the extent possible the given perturbation to the prior schemata, and in modifying to the extent necessary these same schemata to fit the given [perturbation], which will differentiate [the old schemata]. From the point of view of assimilation, there is therefore a problem of equilibrium from the start—of equilibrium between assimilation and accommodation. (p. 108; my translation)

There are three points to note here. First, when Piaget says that the subject "assimilates . . . to prior schemata," he means that subjects interpret the problem in terms of the intellectual framework—the schemata—available to them. Thus, the features that the problem will have depend on the features that the children's schemata have at that point in time.

[1] Those who have treated equilibration as an explanation of the phenomena of stage transition include Bruner (1959), Cunningham (1972), Pascual-Leone (1970), Rotman (1977), and Russell (1978).

For example, children at the concrete operational stage take the balance problem to be resolved by finding unequal weights and distances which compensate one another. They do not try to solve the problem by formulating a law of compensation. Since the definition of the required solution depends upon the features of the schemata to which the problem is assimilated, and since the schemata do not yet provide principles of proportion, the assimilation of this problem to the schemata will not permit a solution in terms of ratio (Inhelder and Piaget, 1955/1958, pp. 174-175).

Second, when Piaget states that the children "modify to the extent necessary these same schemata to fit the given [perturbation]," he is describing the means by which interpretation of the problem changes: If a perturbation is introduced into the subjects' prior schemata, this means they do not understand some of the data that are present. Under such circumstances, accommodation of the schemata is required. The accommodation involves (a) modification according to the demands of the data (as perceived) and, consequently, (b) a reinterpretation of all the data in light of the modification. The accommodation permits a more adequate understanding of the problem.

Take the case of the balance problem. From the fact that the children at substage II-B can recognize how two unequal weights balance, whereas children at substage I-B cannot, Inhelder and Piaget infer that the schemata have been altered. According to the equilibration account, the change occurs because at substage I-B, subjects cannot assimilate or interpret some elements of the problem. This failure creates a perturbation, and the schemata have to be accommodated to the situation, that is, some of their features must be changed. Given the accommodation, the children at substage I-B deal more effectively with the problem than do those at substage I-A.

Third, when Piaget says "the dual reaction to [the perturbation] will consist in assimilating to the extent possible . . . and modifying to the extent necessary these same schemata," he suggests that the tendency to achieve equilibrium between the organism and the environment—the equilibration factor—stimulates this twofold response. If accommodation occurs as the situation demands, a state of equilibrium between assimilation and accommodation exists. If, on the other hand, assimilation to present schemata persists when accommodation is needed, the balance between assimilation and accommodation is upset. Consequently, "there is . . . a problem of equilibrium from the start . . . between assimilation and accomodation." If the balance between these phases of the adaptation process is upset, the schemata will not be altered as the situation requires and subjects will fail to solve the problem: they will be in a state of *disequilibrium* with respect to some aspects of the environment.

In summary, Piaget argues that the performance given depends upon the features of the cognitive schemata to which a problem is assimilated. The features that a performance has are determined by these schemata. If the schemata are insufficient to organize the data, then they are accommodated. When accommodation occurs, a new performance becomes possible and the children can reach a new stage of development.

In the process of change described by the equilibration account, the term *equilibration* refers to two kinds of phenomena (Inhelder and Piaget, 1955/1958, p. 281). First, it refers to a tendency to develop so that a stable state of equilibrium with the environment is achieved. In this stable state, one has what Piaget calls a *reversible intelligence.*

For example, subjects at lower stages of development cannot systematically establish combinations which balance the mechanism in the problem described above. They show no evidence of being able to reverse or return the mechanism to a former position once they set up a combination of weights. As a result, their understanding is said to be *irreversible,* and as such it is insufficient to solve the problem. At a somewhat higher stage, combinations are reversed, but in no systematic manner. By the final stage, the subjects reverse the combinations they set up on the basis of principles or laws. Their reasoning ability is said to be fully reversible, and an adequate solution is finally possible. What makes subjects accommodate their schemata and pass through the sequence of stages? It is the tendency to equilibrate—to reach a level of intellectual operation that permits problems to be solved.

In Piaget's account, the term *equilibration* also refers to the tendency of the mature intellect to solve the problems it encounters. That is, it is the tendency to modify one's understanding of situations until correct rather than incorrect interpretations of them are possible. When intelligence has developed so that schemata which permit adequate solutions are available, the tendency to equilibrate will ensure that these are applied so that problems are indeed resolved.

When subjects reach the final stage of cognitive development, the formal operational stage, intelligence is said to have reached a state of permanent equilibrium with the environment. At this point, the intelligence is fully equilibrated:

> If the initial field C is changed to C', the substructure of elements corresponding to C retains the same equilibrium as before; by contrast equilibrium is displaced if the new form of equilibrium which corresponds to C' differs from that which corresponded to C. (Piaget, 1957, p. 40; my translation)

Accordingly, when the intelligence is permanently equilibrated with the environment, one may solve a new problem without altering one's perspective. If the perspective must be modified in order to solve the problem, then final equilibrium has not been achieved, and development of the cognitive structures must continue. Once the final stage is reached, problem solving will proceed as described above.

Given this brief summary of Piaget's theory, we are now in a position to identify some of his basic assumptions and the issues that arise from them. We begin with the most fundamental, namely, Piaget's assumption about what must be present for cognitive development, as he describes it, to occur.

The Nativism Issue

It is clear that according to Piaget, cognitive structures, or schemata, make possible all perception, experience, and understanding of the world. Schemata have the same function in Piaget's theory as the forms of pure intuition (space, time) and categories of understanding have in Kant's, that is, they are used to organize situations and permit experience. Consequently, they are, logically speaking, prior to experience.

If cognitive structures are logically prior to experience then we may ask: How do the schemata arise? Where do they come from? With reference to the categories and the forms of pure intuition, this is not a question which particularly troubles Kant. He writes (1787/1929):

> We can, however, with regard to these concepts, as with regard to all knowledge, seek to discover in experience, if not the principle of their possibility, at least the occasioning causes of their production. The impressions of the senses supplying the first stimulus, the whole faculty of knowledge opens out to them, and experience is brought into existence. That experience contains two very dissimilar elements, namely, the *matter* of knowledge [obtained] from the senses, and a certain *form* for the ordering of this matter, [obtained] from the inner source of the pure intuition and thought, which, on occasion of the sense-impressions, are first brought into action and yield concepts. (p. 121)

Kant's concern is the origin of experience, not the origins of the categories and the forms of pure intuition. When Kant says that "experience contains . . . matter . . . and . . . form for the ordering of . . . matter, [obtained] from the inner source of the pure intuition and thought," he means that the form, which provides the structure for sense data, is necessary for experience, though not necessarily temporally prior to it. He maintains that when sense impressions occur, they yield concepts and experience because they are ordered by forms of the pure intuition, for example, space, time, categories. He does not take a stand on whether the forms of the intuition are present at birth, and in fact, seems to have little concern for their origins.

The question of where schemata come from is hardly benign for Piaget. Indeed, it spawned many years of research and reflection. He writes as follows (1980b):

> Fifty years of experience have taught us that knowledge does not result from a mere recording of observations without a structuring activity on the part of the subject. Nor do any a priori or innate cognitive structures exist in man; the functioning of intelligence alone is hereditary and creates structures only through an organization of successive actions performed on objects. Consequently, an epistemology conforming to the data of psychogenesis could be neither empiricist nor preformationist, but could consist only of a constructivism, with a continual elaboration of new operations and structures. The central problem, then, is to understand how such operations come about, and why, even though they result from nonpredetermined constructions, they eventually become logically necessary. (p. 23)

Here, as in many other places (e.g., Piaget, 1967/1971), Piaget rejects outright the possibility that cognitive structures are innate, or present from birth. It is impossible, for example, that people are born with the schemata of conservation, classification, causality, space, time, or even object permanence. No neonate has any of these cognitive structures. What are present are procedures for functioning (procedures for assimilating, accommodating, equilibrating) which create the schemata over a period of time. Piaget's enterprise is to describe how the structures gradually emerge, and in so doing, explain why reasoning becomes (logically) necessary.[2]

---

[2] For further discussion of the similarities and differences between the accounts given by Kant and Piaget, see Broughton (1981b), Hamlyn (1978), and Mischel (1969). The topic is also discussed further in Chapter 6 of this volume.

Has Piaget managed to account for the origins of specific cognitive structures without claiming that they are innate? Since the nativism issue is the most central issue in this book, a brief introduction to the concept of innateness is in order before proceeding. (The concept of innateness will be discussed further in Chapter 3, where I consider its meaning in biological contexts, and in Chapter 6, where I examine Stich's [1975] argument that there have been two nativist traditions in philosophy.)

When it is said that something (x) is innate, one may mean at least three things. First, one may mean that an organism is born with x as part of its constitution. Second, one may mean that one is born with the tendency to develop x under certain conditions. In this case, x will eventually appear as one of the organism's characteristics, given the fulfillment of certain conditions, because of the organism's constitution. Third, one may mean that x must be present for the organism to operate as desired, making no claims about how x got there. In the third case, the term *innate* makes no reference to the origins of x. The claim is only that x must be there for the organism to carry out its procedures.

In Chapter 6, I show that the distinction between the first two meanings of *innate* is not valid. At this point, let us raise the following question: Does Piaget explain the origins of schemata with an alternative to the claim that one is simply born with them? Or does he provide an account of the third sort, thus asserting that they must be present but giving no account of their origins? It will take the rest of this book to resolve the issue, for a complete response involves not just a review of Piaget's claims, but also a study of the explanatory model upon which he bases his account and an analysis of its limitations.

To begin this investigation, it is useful to contrast Piaget's account with that of Noam Chomsky. Once the comparison is made, we may then consider whether Piaget has developed a theoretical alternative to Chomsky's claim that one is born with specific cognitive/linguistic structures. If he fails to provide an alternative, we can then ask: Is the failure due to the principles of explanation upon which his constructivism is based?

Chomsky (1980a) summarizes his position on innateness:

We may think of a grammar, represented somehow in the mind, as a system that specifies the phonetic, syntactic, and semantic properties of an infinite class of potential sentences. The child knows the language so determined by the grammar he has acquired. This grammar is a representation of his "intrinsic competence." In acquiring language, the child also develops "performance systems" for putting this knowledge to use (for example, production and perception strategies). So little is known about the general properties of performance systems that one can only speculate as to the basis for their development. My guess would be that, as in the case of grammars, a fixed, genetically determined system of some sort narrowly constrains the forms that they can assume. I would also speculate that other cognitive structures developed by humans might profitably be analyzed along similar lines. (p. 35)

Here (as in Chomsky, 1980b, 1980c), Chomsky argues that children are born with a Universal Grammar which determines the features of the language they later acquire. The Universal Grammar, "a representation of . . . intrinsic-competence," consists of a set of constraints, or rules, which define the phonetic, syntactic, and semantic properties of the language that can be learned. While neonates cannot speak or understand language at birth, they have the potential, in the form of a specific set of constraints, for acquiring it. To actualize the potential, and thus to learn a particular language, they must learn "performance systems" (e.g., production and perception strategies). Chomsky hypothesizes that the forms which these production systems can take, like the structures of the Universal Grammar, are "narrowly constrained" by the genes.

Thus, while Piaget argues that no specific cognitive structures are innate, Chomsky believes that at least the Universal Grammar is innate in the sense indicated above, that is, present at birth and specified at the level of the genome. As Papert (1980) points out, and Chomsky agrees, the explicit issue between Piaget and Chomsky is not whether something has to be there from the beginning, "but rather, how much and what kind of something" (p. 268). The question then is whether what must be present at birth for cognitive structures to be constructed under Piaget's account is different from what Chomsky says is present at birth. Putnam (1980) believes that a difference may not be present:

> But if a maturational schedule *involving the development of concepts* is innate, and *concepts are essentially connected with language*, then Piaget's hypothesis would seem to imply Chomsky's; "constructivism" would entail "nativism." (p. 300)

Is Putnam correct? If constructivism entails nativism, then is Piaget committed to Chomsky's view of what must be present at birth, that is, that linguistic (and any other cognitive structures) are specified by the genome? Piaget (1980b) states that it is unnecessary to make such claims because:

> The "innate fixed nucleus" would retain all its properties of a "fixed nucleus" if it were not innate but constituted the "necessary" result of the constructions of sensori-motor intelligence, which is prior to language and results from those joint organic and behavioral autoregulations that determine this epigenesis. (p. 31)

Piaget argues that it is unnecessary to posit an "innate fixed nucleus" of linguistic structures because the latter can be understood to arise from the "constructions of sensori-motor intelligence"—the cognitive structures produced at the sensori-motor stage. This would mean, says Piaget, that the linguistic structures need not be specified by the genes but arise as necessary consequences of operating with the sensori-motor structures.

Acceptance of Piaget's argument depends upon whether the linguistic structures can be proven to arise from sensori-motor structures, and Chomsky argues that Piaget has not shown that they do (Piattelli-Palmarini, 1980, p. 170). If, however, Piaget demonstrates the truth of his claim, then he is justified in asserting that linguistic constraints need not be specified in the genome.

Piaget (Piattelli-Palmarini, 1980) pushes his argument further and urges that it is misguided to argue as Chomsky does for the following reason:

> What especially bothers me about the innateness hypothesis is that the current explanations of the neo-Darwinians concerning the formation of any new character trait in the organism are based solely on notions of mutation and selection. Now, a mutation necessarily occurs at random; therefore, if there were innate-

ness, reason and language would be the result of selected accidents, but selected subsequently, after the fact, whereas the formation itself would be the result of mutations and would therefore occur at random. I claim that in that case, it would be tantamount to shaking the solidity of the fixed nucleus, and generally speaking the solidity of knowledge, instead of consolidating it, as one might wish to do by invoking the innateness hypothesis. . . . I absolutely refuse, for my part, to think that logico-mathematical structures would owe their origin to chance; there is nothing fortuitous about them. These structures could not be formed by survival selection but by an exact and detailed adaptation to reality. (p. 59)

Here Piaget clearly expresses his passionate conviction that cognitive structures cannot be innate, and that therefore Chomsky's version of the innateness hypothesis is wrong. The problem is not that the innateness hypothesis results from an argument *ad ignorantiam* (although Piaget sometimes suggests that it does), or that it is impossible for an innate structure to define (or constrain) the features of behavior (or surface structures). Rather, Piaget objects because he believes Chomsky's hypothesis requires that the possibility of the complex structures of reasoning arises by chance. This, says Piaget, would mean that logico-mathematical structures would never have existed had some chance mutation not generated the possibility of their existence.

It may not be clear why Piaget finds this account of origins so objectionable. After all, it uses the principles of random variation and natural selection, which are well-accepted explanatory tools in many sciences. Why does Piaget find these principles unsatisfactory? There are two related points to be made here.

First, we must bear in mind that Piaget wants to explain how individuals form cognitive structures. He is not concerned with explaining how the human species becomes adapted so that individuals have the capacity to form cognitive structures. In other words, Piaget wants an ontogenetic rather than a phylogenetic account. As a result, he does not want to give an evolutionary story but rather one which explains how the things people do result in understanding of certain sorts. He claims that cognitive structures arise as a result of one's behaviors, and he wants to show how this occurs.

The second point is that because Piaget wishes to tell an ontogenetic story, he recoils from the assertion that cognitive structures have their origins in random variation and selection that occurs at the genetic level. While these evolutionary principles may explain how the competence to form cognitive structures arises, their actual formation in ontogenetic history results, Piaget believes, from an "exact and detailed adaptation to reality." Cognitive structures are so well adapted to the world, says Piaget, that an adequate ontogenetic story cannot begin with the assumption that their appearance had its origins in a chance occurrence. Consequently, principles of random variation and natural selection are not sufficient.

In contrast, Chomsky does not share Piaget's disdain for the role of chance in explaining origins, for he strives to contribute to a phylogenetic account. That is, Chomsky's objective is to determine the nature of the constraints on language acquisition that have proven adaptive and have survived the evolutionary process. He assumes, rather than eschews, the possibility that these constraints have arisen fortuitously.

In the remainder of this chapter, I begin the task of showing whether Piaget's constructivist account provides an ontogenetic story that does not locate the origins of cognitive structures in chance occurrence. Does it, then, offer an alternative to Chomsky's claim that (linguistic) structures must be specified by the genome? I start by examining some conceptual limitations in Piaget's account which pertain to this issue.

An Assessment of Piaget's Account

Piaget's attempt to explain change in cognitive structure suffers from a number of empirical and conceptual problems. Many of the empirical limitations have been identified (e.g., Siegel and Brainerd, 1978), and these will not be considered here. Some of the conceptual limitations will be reviewed for the following reason: My thesis is that these limitations arise from Piaget's use of certain principles of explanation. The principles were chosen because Piaget believed they permit an ontogenetic account which is not based on random mutation and natural selection principles. The conceptual limitations which arise from Piaget's use of his explanatory principles make clear that his explanation is inadequate in some respects and that it does not avoid recourse to random variation and selection principles, and thus to a fortuitous account of origins. The latter point is demonstrated fully in Chapters 3 and 4.

The Relation of Necessity Between Cognitive Stages

As has already been indicated, the most obvious feature of Piaget's account is its developmental perspective. He argues that the ability to reason and solve problems develops through a series of stages. At each new stage, subjects are capable of solving problems they could not solve previously. The reason for change in problem-solving behavior is that the cognitive structures, or schemata, which make behavior possible improve at every stage. That is, they acquire features they did not have before. The mechanism for change, namely, equilibration, ensures that the cognitive structures will reach a final or mature stage of development.

The developmental aspect of Piaget's account has come under attack. For example, Brainerd (1978), Feldman and Toulmin (1976), Kessen (1970), and Phillips and Kelley (1975) raise questions about the explanatory power of the concept of stage. The following issue has emerged from the debate: To what extent has Piaget shown that each stage in the sequence is a necessary consequence of the previous one(s) in the sequence? This is a significant question, as Piaget tries to show that such necessity does arise. He writes (1980b):

> The hypothesis naturally will be that this increasing necessity arises from auto-regulation and has a counterpart with the increasing, parallel equilibration of cognitive structures. Necessity then proceeds from their "interlocking." (p. 31)

But what, exactly, is *necessary* here? What is meant by necessity? And on what grounds does Piaget assert that the necessity in question arises? (Others, including Macnamara, 1976, have found Piaget's account of necessity problematic.)

Feldman and Toulmin (1976) distinguish between three types of necessity: logical, instrumental, and prerequisite. They write:

We are often tempted to talk as though actual, empirical *thinking processes* could be logical or illogical *in themselves*. But the only things that can be logical or illogical are either the propositional arguments in which the outcome of those processes may be expressed, or else the formal representation used by the psychologist in his *theoretical analysis* of processes (p. 465). If we claim to find necessities also in the *empirical* features of cognitive experience, these will be of other, *nonformal* kinds. . . . Thus, we may speak of two aspects (A and B) of a cognitive performance as being related in an empirically necessary manner if they are related together *instrumentally*—that is, if A is the only, the universal, or at least the typical means for bringing about B. Or, alternatively, we may speak of two different cognitive abilities (A and B) as related in an empirically necessary manner, if one is the *prerequisite* of the other—that is, if a prior command of ability A is an indispensable preliminary for embarking on the task of learning B. (p. 466)

Feldman and Toulmin go on to argue that the necessity which holds between Piaget's cognitive stages is one of pragmatic prerequisiteness, not logical necessity:

The abilities called into play when tackling any kind of task, during, say, the formal operational stage of development may well be ones that the child could even *begin* learning only if he had previously mastered the corresponding abilities on the previous concrete operational level—and similarly for the other stage transitions. (p. 467)

Thanks to the Feldman and Toulmin analysis, it is possible to sort out some of the necessity claims that Piaget makes and to identify the kind of necessity he asserts. Take, for example, his statement that "increasing necessity arises from autoregulation and has a counterpart with the increasing, parallel equilibration of cognitive structures" (Piaget, 1980b, p. 31). There is some ambiguity here: Is Piaget saying that given the arrival at one stage in the sequence, it is more likely (increasingly necessary) that the next stage will have certain particular features more likely than it was for the previous stage to have certain features? Or is he saying that each stage in the sequence will have greater internal coherence (increasing necessity) than the one previous to it in the sequence? In fact, Piaget makes both claims. The likelihood that each stage will have certain features increases at each subsequent stage in the sequence. Further, the principles of the reasoning at each stage become increasingly logically coherent, so that at the final stage, the relation between them is fully logical and consistent.

Given that both claims are made, we may set the second aside, for it is the first which is crucial to Piaget's contention that the cognitive structures need not be innate but may be constructed out of one another. What are Piaget's grounds for maintaining that the necessity of following certain principles of reasoning increases at each stage? In other words, if stage y is more likely to have certain features than was stage x, is this due to the definitions of x and y—the logical relation that obtains between them? Or is it because stage x is a prerequisite for y? If the latter, then did Piaget mean that once x is achieved, the possibility for y's having certain features is increased?

Feldman and Toulmin argue that Piaget should maintain only the prerequisite relation between stages, given the nature of his stage descriptions. They accuse him, however, of confounding pragmatic and logical necessity and of trying to derive the former from the latter:

> With respect to stage succession, Piaget and his followers seem to find the idea of basing all *pragmatic* necessities on underlying *formal* necessities irresistible. If the abilities characteristic of cognitive stage S_n are pragmatic prerequisites for learning those characteristics of the successive stage S_{n+1} (they insist), there is a deeper reason for that fact—namely, the fact that the cognitive structures associated with S_{n+1} logically include those associated with S_n. Yet it by no means follows from this that the pragmatic relationships between successive stages can be derived from the corresponding logical relationships (e.g., logical inclusion) in the formal theory. (p. 468)

Feldman and Toulmin argue that the logical inclusion of one stage description in another provides no grounds for inferring that reaching the first stage is a prerequisite for reaching the second. From the fact that one stage description includes the characteristics of the other, one cannot infer that x is the only, the universal or the typical means of bringing about y; nor can one infer that x is an indispensable preliminary for bringing about y, and thus must exist first in time. The logical and pragmatic relations are two separate relations, and neither has implication for the other.

Are Feldman and Toulmin correct in saying that Piaget confounds logical and pragmatic necessity? Piaget (1956) writes:

> Take logical or mathematical structures such as the system of whole numbers. When a child of seven or eight years has managed to construct a series of whole numbers, when he has understood the series 1, 2, 3, 4, etc., then this structure will remain in equilibrium (if you prefer another word I do not mind) until death unless the individual goes mad. Now this does not mean that there is any state of rest; the individual will all the time make use of these ideas in action on objects or in exchange with other individuals. This system will also be integrated into other systems; that is to say that after having learnt whole numbers the individual will discover fractions, irrational numbers, complex numbers, transfinite numbers, and so on. But whatever the new systems into which the system of whole numbers is integrated, this number system will not be changed any further (p. 93)

Here is an instance in which Piaget seems to argue as Feldman and Toulmin charge. Fractions, for example, are logically related to whole numbers, as a numerical fraction is part of a numerical whole. By the same token, complex and irrational numbers are also logically related to whole numbers. On the basis of logical relations, Piaget infers that after the set of whole numbers has been learned, the other sets to which it is logically related will be learned as well. When he writes, "This system [the set of whole numbers] will be integrated into other systems; that is to say, after having learned whole numbers, the subject will discover fractions, irrational numbers . . .", he is inferring the occurrence of actual, prerequisite relations between the sets of numbers in question. On what grounds does he draw this inference and assert the prerequisite relations? The only ones offered are the logical relations that obtain between the different sorts of numbers. But the logical relations afford no basis for such inferences.

The same kind of fallacious reasoning appears in the analysis by Inhelder and Piaget (1955/1958) of performance on the balance problem discussed previously:

The numerical quantification of the proportion is usually preceded by a qualitative schema based on a conception of logical product—i.e., by the idea that
two factors acting together are equivalent to the action of two other factors
added together. . . . These logical multiplications are outlined at substage II-B
. . . but the subjects fail to generalize to all possible cases. Where does the gen-
eralization found at substages III-A and III-B come from? Without doubt, this is
where the notions of compensation and reciprocity connected with the I N R C
group come in.

It is clear that when the subject at stage III becomes able to understand transformations by inversion (N) and reciprocity (R) and group them into a single
system (I, N, R, C and N R=C), by the same token he becomes able to make use
of the equality of products in a more general form than in the multiplication of
relations. (p. 177)

When Inhelder and Piaget write that "The numerical quantification of the proportion is usually preceded by a qualitative schema based on a conception of logical
product," they assert an empirical, in-time relation. The child has the qualitative
schema of logical product before he has the numerically quantified schema of proportion. The schema of a logical product can be characterized by the formal structure known as grouping VII. The quantification schema of proportions cannot be
expressed by the formal structure of grouping VII, but it can be formulated in terms
of a mathematical structure called the I N R C Group. The description of grouping
VII is logically included in that of the I N R C Group. As a consequence of the logical relation that obtains between these formal structures, Inhelder and Piaget infer
a prerequisite relation between cognitive structures, arguing that the schema of proportion is preceded, in time, by the qualitative schema of logical product. The latter
is a pragmatic prerequisite for the former. Thus they write: "Where does generaliz-
tion . . . come from? Without doubt, this is where notions of compensation and
reciprocity connected with the I N R C Group come in." The claim is that because
the I N R C Group stands in logical relation to grouping VII, one may infer that
ideas of compensation and reciprocity, which exist separately at the concrete operations stage, are united at the formal stage, and the cognitive structures required for
these stage performances stand in prerequisite relation to one another.

However, the logical relation between the I N R C Group and grouping VII is
irrelevant to the order in which cognitive structures come into existence. When
Inhelder and Piaget argue that the child acquires cognitive structures in a particular
order because the formal characterization of one stage is logically included in
another they argue fallaciously.

The Function of Cognitive Structures in the Solution of Problems

Let us turn now to perhaps the most fundamental concept in Piaget's theory,
namely, that of schema or cognitive structure. Many questions have been raised
about the function, origin, and ontological status of cognitive structures. (See, for
example, Kessen, 1970; Feldman & Toulmin, 1976.) With regard to function,
Bruner (1959) and Brainerd (1978) argue that in Piaget's account a description of cognitive structure is little more than a redescription of behavior. As Brainerd puts it:

> Since the only empirical phenomena studied in Piaget's research are behaviors that undergo age change, the structures are at most abstractions from behavior. (p. 177)

There is clear evidence, however, that Piaget intends the cognitive structures to function as more than a redescription of behavior. But what is their role in his account?

First, Beilin (1971) argues that schemata are not, strictly speaking, representations of behavior. Rather, they make representations of behavior and situations possible. Beilin is correct, as will be seen from Inhelder and Piaget's (1955/1958) analysis of the following performance on the balance problem. The schemata are said to provide the child with procedures for determining problem-solving strategies:

> Mas (7;7) begins with E_3 and D_3, then replaces them with G_3 and F_3 (thus equal distance and an attempt to find equal weights), adds two other weights, takes some off, then all, and finally weighs two equal weights (E) in his hands, counts equal number of holes (14) and places E 14 at each side. Afterwards he looks for other forms of equilibrium; he adds the weights, moves them, takes off some and finally has GED on one side and P_3 on the other: "That's it (empirical compensation of weights and distances). It's just like when there weren't any (when the arms were horizontal without weight); it's the same weight on each side." He predicts that unequal distances are necessary for two unequal weights, but he does not find the law: Heavier $\rightleftharpoons$ nearer. (p. 169)

About this performance, Inhelder and Piaget write:

> Thus, from this point on the subject can order serially the weights he comes across as well as determine whether they are equal. He can add them in a reversible manner and correctly compare one pair of weights with another pair. What is more, he knows how to make use of the transitiveness of the relations of equality or inequality of the weights. Moreover, all these operations reappear when he compares distances. . . .
>
> On the other hand, in the case of unequal weights A_1 and B_2 and of unequal distances L_x and L_y, coordination is not yet possible at substage II-A. Even when the subject discovers by experimentation that a large weight at a small distance to the right of the axis balances a small weight at a large distance to the left, he does not know how to invert these relations from one side to the other. (pp. 170-171)

Inhelder and Piaget indicate that Mas's schemata provide him with rules and procedures for determining his strategies. For example, since Mas proceeds to solve the problem by comparing weights, ordering them in terms of their effects on the balance beam, taking two equal ones and locating them equidistant from the fulcrum, and so forth, he is said to have the cognitive structure of seriation. Evidently, these strategies would be impossible without the seriation schema.

Inhelder and Piaget, likewise, argue that Mas cannot produce a solution which involves a proportional formula because he lacks the schema of ratio. Thus he cannot understand that an answer in terms of proportions is required. Only a child at the formal stage of reason who has the ratio schema can determine strategies that will yield a proportional formula.

Does Piaget intend to say that children somehow employ their schemata to produce problem-solving strategies?[3] Piaget's descriptions of Mas's performance suggest that he does intend to say so. Furthermore, by maintaining that cognitive structures are used to generate strategies, he can argue that change in performance results from change in cognitive structure. Indeed, if the schemata play no role in generating solutions, then Piaget cannot explain the improvement in children's performances by saying that their cognitive structures have been modified in certain ways.

There is a conceptual question here. If schemata function in the production of strategies, and if performance changes because cognitive structures change, then one must ask: In what ways do the cognitive structures change so that performances of various sorts become possible?

Piaget answers by describing changes in behavior using a logically inclusive set of formal structures and defining the changes in schemata in terms of the differences between the formal structures. Again his reasoning is fallacious. The fact that change in behavior can be represented with logically inclusive formalisms is no grounds for inferring that the cognitive structures, which make the behavior change possible, differ in the respects that the formalisms differ from one another. Indeed, there are no grounds at all for inferring what has changed in the schemata.

Nevertheless, by characterizing cognitive performance in terms of logico-mathematical structures and maintaining that the development of cognitive structures makes performance of various sorts possible, Piaget gives his empirical research direction. After describing behavior in formal terms, Piaget infers that the subjects have some cognitive structures rather than others, and therefore have knowledge or understanding of certain sorts. He then undertakes experiments and observations to test his inferences.

For example, Piaget attributes understanding of some reversing operations to Mas. The knowledge is attributed to Mas because Mas's solution can be analyzed in terms of grouping VII, and the knowledge is consistent with the properties of this formal grouping. Piaget conducts experiments to see if Mas knows the principles in question: Does he know that the effects of weight can be reversed by adjusting distance from the axis? If so, he is said to have certain cognitive structures and his behavior is explained with reference to these.

Although Piaget is unjustified in inferring change in schemata from differences between characterizations, there is no question that the latter provide him with hypotheses about the nature of the children's understanding. Thus in spite of the fallacious reasoning which undergirds his research, he discovered a great deal about what children do and do not comprehend at given points in time.

Ambiguities in Piaget's Use of Assimilation and Accommodation

Since Piaget asserts that change in performance on cognitive tasks results from change in schemata, the question becomes: How do the schemata change? This is

[3]Broughton (1981a) argues that Piaget is a realist, that he distinguishes formal structures mathematicians employ from cognitive structures "in the head," and that the latter "enter into performance in a fashion that makes [them] more or less indispensable" (p. 212). I think there is good evidence for Broughton's claim.

the same question as: How do children make the transition from one developmental stage to the next? According to Piaget, the transition to higher stages occurs because cognitive structures are modified in various respects. The process is described in terms of assimilation, accommodation, and equilibration. To what extent does the equilibration account for change in cognitive structure?

As argued previously (Haroutunian, 1978), there are ambiguities which confound Piaget's equilibration account. A review of these is in order at this time, as they directly affect the meaning and explanatory adequacy of his argument.

Let us begin with the concept of assimilation. To what does this term refer? Flavell (1963) and Mischel (1971) have different views on the issue. Flavell argues that according to Piaget, there is a fundamental analogy between biological and cognitive assimilation:

> The organism must and will transform the substances it takes in in order to incorporate their food values into its system. . . . The process of changing elements in the milieu in such a way that they can become incorporated into the structure of the organism is called *assimilation*, i.e., the elements are assimilated to the system. (p. 45)
> It is Piaget's argument that intellectual assimilation is not different in principle from a more primary biological assimilation: in both cases the essential process is that of bending a reality event to the templet of one's ongoing structure. (p. 48)

When Flavell says, "the process of changing elements in the milieu in such a way that they can become incorporated into the structure of the organism is called assimilation," it sounds as though the term *assimilation* refers to a physical alteration of elements in the environment. Surely a "bending of reality" could involve such physical alteration. It need not, however, and Mischel argues that cognitive assimilation does not refer to a process of physical change. Mischel writes:

> [Biological] analogies obscure crucial differences between physiological and cognitive "structures," they slur over the very different senses in which physical and mental "organizations" can be said to "assimilate" . . . . We are not dealing with a physical or biological process of compensation. For what influences behavior is not feedback from physical stimuli, but only the subject's cognitive assimilation of it; what he responds to is his construal of the external intrusion, and he is also the one who interprets the outcome of his compensatory activities. Equilibration thus depends, from start to finish, on the subject's *cognitive* schemas. (pp. 323-324)

If "what [the subject] responds to is his construal of the external intrusion," the cognitive assimilation cannot mean the conversion of one substance to another. Rather, it means comparing one representation to another. Thus, cognitive assimilation involves treating one's representations of situations as if they had certain features and comparing the results of the treatment to expected outcomes. The assimilation of data alters the data only in the sense that they are understood in one way rather than another. If they fit the pattern provided by the schemata, that is, if the results are as expected, they are understood accordingly.

Mischel's definition of the term *assimilation* is compelling. Flavell might well take the point that cognitive assimilation need not involve physical change in the environment. However, an ambiguity remains. For there is evidence in Piaget's writing that cognitive assimilation does refer to a physical modification, not of the environment, but of one's representations of it. Consider, again, Piaget (1957):

> The hypothesis of equilibration consists in seeing in the problem posed (if it really is a problem) a perturbation introduced into the systems of the subject's prior schemata: the dual reaction to [this perturbation] will consist of *assimilating* to the extent possible the given perturbation to the prior schemata, and in modifying to the extent necessary these same schemata to fit the given [perturbation], which will differentiate [the old schemata]. (p. 108; my translation)

This passage may presuppose that a conception or view of the elements, rather than the elements themselves, is assimilated. If this is the meaning, then a perturbation is a representation of elements which does not match the expected view of them. The perturbation could have arisen if the representation had been compared to the expected situation and a preponderance of differences between the two had been detected. Accommodation of the assimilatory structure would then have been required.

However, this same passage could presuppose that a representation of the elements in the environment was assimilated by altering it—the representation—in terms of procedures provided by the schemata. The representation would have been altered "to the extent possible" so as to resemble the expected outcome more closely. Inability to alter it sufficiently could have created a perturbation which, again, would require the accommodation of the schemata.

From the above passage, it is not clear whether the process of assimilation refers to the act of comparing or converting representations. When Flavell notes the case of digestion and states, "In Piaget's argument, intellectual assimilation is not different in principle from a more primary biological assimilation," he may grant that cognitive assimilation treats representations rather than the physical objects, yet maintain that both cognitive and biological assimilation involve the conversion of properties. Mischel eschews the biological analogy, arguing that comparison rather than conversion is the process to which cognitive assimilation refers. Piaget leaves the matter unclear.

The process of accommodation is also central to Piaget's equilibration account. What is the nature of this process? Flavell writes:

> The essence of accommodation is precisely this process of adapting oneself to the variegated requirements or demands which the world of objects imposes upon one. And once again, Piaget underscores the essential continuity between biological accommodation, on the one hand, and cognitive accommodation, on the other: a receptive and accommodating mouth and digestive system are not really different in principle from a receptive and accommodating cognitive system. (p. 48)

According to Flavell, cognitive accommodation is like the physiological process of digestion. In both cases, the systems adjust themselves to receive and then utilize elements of the environment to meet their needs. In both cases, the goal of accommodating is to achieve adaptation.

The digestive system accommodates by selecting an alternate behavior from the repertoire of possibilities when the pressure to adapt dictates. The alternative is selected so that the body can maintain desirable physiological conditions. The behavior is not a novel one. It has been performed many times previously and is selected now to reverse existing conditions. Hence, the mouth may accommodate to a need for nourishment by opening (rather than closing) in the presence of food. The behaviors of which the mouth is capable are repeated over and over as conditions in the body necessitate.

Is one to assume that cognitive accommodation means the selection of alternative cognitive structures from an existing repertoire of possibilities? If so, it would appear that it cannot result in novel performances. Kaye (1982) answers the question in this way:

> At the level of simple assimilation, we do not see lasting accommodation of schemas. There may be momentary adjustments that fit a schema to the requirements of a situation (e.g., adjusting sucking to the shape and stiffness of a rubber nipple), but we reserve the word *accommodation* for adaptations that actually change the schema. Only when the sucking response changes as a result of experience, so that it becomes suited to either a narrower or a wider range of nipples than was the case at first, would we say that it has accommodated. An accommodation is therefore a representation of the world. (p. 165)

Kaye maintains that both he and Piaget take accommodation to mean change which permits novel behavior. Thus accommodated schemata will allow behaviors not available to the system previously. Kaye also suggests that one cannot explain how change in schemata occurs with the same principles used to explain the adjustment of bodily organs.

What does Piaget say about the process of accommodation?

> There can be no doubt either, that mental life is also *accommodation* to the environment. Assimilation can never be pure because by incorporating new elements into its earlier schemata the intelligence constantly modifies the latter in order to adjust them to new elements. . . . In short, intellectual adaptation, like every other kind, consists of putting an assimilatory mechanism and a complementary accommodation into progressive equilibrium. The mind can only be adapted to a reality if perfect accommodation exists, that is to say, if nothing, in that reality, intervenes to modify the subject's schemata. But, inversely, adaptation does not exist if the new reality has imposed motor or mental attitudes contrary to those which were adopted on contact with other earlier given data: adaptation only exists if there is coherence, hence assimilation. (Piaget, 1936/1952, pp. 6-7)

In this passage from *The Origins of Intelligence in Children*, it is not clear whether accommodation results in the ability to perform a novel act, or the selection of an existing, alternative structure. Intellectual adaptation occurs where cognitive schemata can assimilate the environment and satisfactory assimilation becomes possible after either sort of change. Thus in some circumstances assimilation may resume when alternative structures are applied, just as in the organic case. However, there are instances when existing alternatives cannot permit satisfactory assimilation. Does cognitive accommodation occur in this case, in the previous one, or in both? Piaget's discussion leaves the referent for accommodation ambiguous.

The question here is whether the term *accommodation* refers to a process in which the features of schemata are modified. If it does, Piaget's account faces a serious dilemma. The dilemma is characterized by J. A. Fodor. Fodor (1975) writes:

Suppose, e.g., that you are a stage one child trying to learn the concept C. Well, the least you have to do is to learn the conditions under which something is an instance of (falls under) C. So, presumably, you have to learn something of the form (x) (x is C iff x is F) where F is some concept that applies whenever C does. Clearly, however, a necessary condition on being able to learn *that* is that one's conceptual system should contain F. So now consider the case where C is, as it were, a stage *two* concept. If something is a stage two concept, then it must follow that it is not co-extensive with any stage *one* concept: otherwise, the difference between stages wouldn't be a difference in the expressive power of the conceptual systems that characterize the stages. But if the stage one child can't represent the extension of C in terms of some concept in the system available to him, he can't represent it at all since, be definition, his conceptual system just *is* the totality of representational devices that he can use for cognitive processing. And if he can't *represent* the extension of C, then he can't *learn* C since, by hypothesis, concept learning involves projecting and confirming biconditionals which determine the extension of the concept being learned. So, either the conditions on applying a stage two concept *can* be represented in terms of some stage one concept, in which case there is no obvious sense in which the stage two conceptual system is more powerful than the stage one conceptual system, or there are stage two concepts whose extension *cannot* be represented in the stage one vocabulary, in which case there is no way for the stage one child to learn them. (p. 90)

The present point is that . . . what is conspicuously lacking in the Piagetian version is a theory that explains *how* the organism manages to differentiate its schemata *in the right direction*; i.e., in a direction that, in general, *increases* the correspondence between the picture of the environment that the schemata imply and the properties that the environment actually has. If I am right in what I said above, Piaget's views *preclude* him presenting such a theory since, on the one hand, he wants the characteristic difference between levels of equilibration (i.e., between stages of development) to consist in the expressive power of the "logics" they invoke, and on the other, he wants the mechanism of equilibration to be learning. As we have seen, these two desiderata cannot be simultaneously satisfied. (p. 91)

What then is Piaget's dilemma? Fodor reads Piaget to say that one can learn a new concept when one can recognize the circumstances under which a given case is an instance of that concept. I can learn the concept of democracy (C), for example, only insofar as I can determine whether a given case of government fulfills the criteria of a democracy. I must have a representation of those criteria (viz., F) to make such judgments. Given F, I can learn C by comparing the features of specific cases (x) to see if they fit F and thus qualify as cases of C.

Thus, if C is a concept for which one has no representation of criteria (F), then one cannot learn C. For without F, there is no way of evaluating possible instances of C. Hence the dilemma: If C is a stage one concept, it can be learned by the child who is at stage one; if C is a stage two concept, there is no way for the child to learn it because the criteria required for its acquisition are lacking.

Piaget's system, says Fodor, presents no means for altering the criteria that are present so that they will be adequate. While concepts and, *ipso facto*, schemata, can change by accommodating, they cannot accommodate if the criteria that the change must meet (F) are unknown. If the criteria are known, then the concept is not a higher stage concept; if they are not known, there is no way to learn them. So either there is no difference between stage one and two conceptual systems, and thus no stages, or there is no way to reach the higher stage.

Fodor's interpretation of the equilibration account is based upon his assumption that the terms *assimilation* and *accommodation* have certain meanings. First, when he states that "a necessary condition on being able to learn (x) (x is C iff x is F) is that one's conceptual system should contain F," he indicates that *assimilation* means comparing representations. Thus a representation of x is compared to a representation of criteria (F) and treated as a case of C if there are not too many discrepancies between x and F. If x meets the criteria of F, then one "learns C" by seeing that F applies to this new case that has certain features.

Second, Fodor assumes that *accommodation* refers to cases in which the features of schemata are altered (so that, e.g., F rather than F_1 is present). Given this assumption, he asserts that Piaget offers accommodated schemata as prerequisites for higher stage performance but does not explain the conditions under which the schemata are so accommodated.

Fodor (1980a) concludes that the role of learning in the equilibration account requires all cognitive structures to be innate. Why? Because they cannot be learned nor can they be acquired in any other way. Fodor draws this conclusion because he understands *assimilation* and *accommodation* as indicated above, and as shown, there is justification for so doing. But Fodor draws the conclusion that Piaget's constructivism explicitly attempts to avoid. Is Fodor's conclusion justified? Does the equilibration account fail to convince where it aims, first and foremost, to succeed? To answer this question, let us begin by examining more of Fodor's argument for his claim:

> Learning is a matter of inductive extrapolation, that is, of some form of non-demonstrative inference: It follows that a learning theory is some function that takes you from some sets of beliefs about your experiences into some sort of general beliefs; and secondly, that any such theory must acknowledge, among the processes involved in learning, hypothesis formation and confirmation. . . . The organism (child, adult, rat, or whatever) comes to develop some hypothesis as "X is *miv*, if and only if X is . . . say, red and square. . . ." [The learning theory tells us how] various choices of the attributes or various choices of the reward, or various relations between the two, affect the subject's convergence on accepting the right hypothesis. (p. 145)

According to Fodor (p. 144) the definition of learning, presupposed by everyone including Piaget, is one of hypothesis testing and confirmation. Under this definition, if one is said to learn what *miv* means, then one attributes some thing (x) with certain properties and sees if it—the meaning of *miv*—is further delineated. If it is, then a case of *miv* is at hand. The theory of learning, says Fodor, explains why the hypothesis is accepted or rejected—why the subject decides that x is a case of *miv*, and that *miv* therefore means red square, green triangle, or yellow tetrahedron. The theory, then, explains how the subjects reach their conclusions given their attributions, the subsequent reinforcements, and so forth.

Many object to the claim that the term *learning* necessarily refers to a process of forming and confirming hypotheses: Putnam (1980, p. 301) offers a kind of associationism as an alternative; Wood (Note 1) maintains that learning arises from a process of reinforcement rather than hypothesis formation and confirmation; Dennett (1978, p. 103) argues that learning may occur by disconfirming rather than confirming hypotheses; Hamlyn (1978, pp. 10-11) maintains that much learning occurs before a child can form and confirm explicit hypotheses, so not all learning occurs in that way. What sense can be made of Fodor's position? And why does this position require that concepts be innate?

When Fodor says that the term *learning* refers to a process of hypothesis formation and confirmation, he does not mean that in every case of learning, the learners think to themselves: "If I do x, then y will occur," or "(x) $(x$ is C iff x is $F)$." Fodor's claim has no implication for what thoughts occur at the level of conscious reflection. Thus, the neonate, who is presumably incapable of hypothetical reasoning, need not be incapable of learning. Furthermore, when we say that first graders learn that $2 + 2 = 4$, or I learn that my dog is in the next room, or I learn how to play chess, we need not infer that under Fodor's account, the conscious reflections of the learners have a hypothetical form.

What Fodor intends is that when learning occurs, the thinkers—by some process of reflection, reinforcement, association, and so on—reach conclusions about the applicability of their understanding. When he says that "a learning theory is some function that takes you from some sets of beliefs about your experiences into some sort of general beliefs," he means that the explanation of the learning (captured by the rule or function) tells how general beliefs are reached, given the initial beliefs. Reaching the general beliefs means, for Fodor, drawing nondemonstrative inferences. Thus, to say that first graders learn $2 + 2 = 4$ means that they combine two groups of two and form beliefs about the results of so doing. The beliefs about particular cases are subjected to testing and are confirmed in enough instances (how many is unclear) for the children to conclude that in all cases where two groups of two are added, a group of four results. The movement from the beliefs about particulars to the general beliefs is what Fodor refers to when he speaks of drawing nondemonstrative inferences.

In the same way, if I learn that my dog is in the next room, this means that a belief about my dog is—by some process—confirmed, and I conclude she is indeed in the next room. Here, I am not moving from a particular to a general belief about my dog, nor need I have hypothesized beforehand at a conscious level that the dog was next door. Nevertheless, there is a sense in which a hypothesis is formed and confirmed: When I open the door and discover the dog, I observe the dog's presence. But observing the dog only results in learning (i.e., learning the dog is there) if I hold criteria for the presence of objects and if the test (the observation) meets the criteria. The belief in the dog's presence is confirmed because the criteria for being present are met. In effect, I learn that the criteria apply in this case, as the hypothesis expressed by the belief is confirmed.

Again, if I learn to play chess, this means that I reach conclusions about the appropriateness of manipulating the chess pieces in various ways. I might hypothesize at the level of conscious reflection. I might think, "If I move my rook forward three squares, I will capture the opponent's bishop in two moves." Learning to play chess requires confirming such hypotheses and drawing inferences about the general conditions under which various moves yield success.

As Hamlyn notes, however, the latter is a very intellectual sort of learning. What of the neonate who learns to purse its lips in one way rather than another so as to suck more efficiently? Surely intellectual hypothesizing does not occur there.

True enough; to claim otherwise flies in the face of everyday observation. Still, the movement that infants make from semirandom, rather inefficient sucking to highly efficient nursing indicates that hypothesis formation and confirmation does occur. The appropriateness of some of their movements rather than others is confirmed, and those which are not confirmed are eliminated. But the means by which they make such confirmations is unclear.

One might object that what is meant by forming and confirming hypotheses in these various cases differs a great deal. Indeed, the nature of the hypothesis, and the means of confirming it, do differ widely. The essential condition of learning, which Fodor's definition captures, is that in every instance where learning occurs, behaviors of some sort are deemed applicable to given conditions. The assessment may or may not involve conscious reflection. But if the system *learns*, then in effect if concludes that *x* (e.g., *miv*) meets the prescribed criteria.

If this is what Fodor means by *learning*, why does he maintain that concepts are innate? The reason is that learning cannot explain how we come up with hypotheses, or with the concepts that are used to form these. Fodor writes:

> [According to my view of learning] it must be the case that concepts that figure in the hypotheses that you come to accept are not only *potentially* accessible to you, but are *actually exploited to mediate the learning* (that is, the confirmation of the hypothesis). The point about confirming a hypothesis like "X is *miv* if and only if it is red and square" is that it is required not only that *red* and *square* be *potentially* available to the organism, but that these notions be effectively used to mediate between the organism's experiences and its consequent beliefs about the extension of *miv*. (Fodor in Piattelli-Palmarini, 1980, p. 152)

Fodor argues that given the definition of learning, the concepts used in the hypothesis must exist in order for the learning to occur. The reason is that they mediate the learning—they make it possible to confirm the hypothesis. For what is learned—that is, the only thing that is learned—is whether the present understanding extends to the new case expressed by the hypothesis. In Fodor's example, the only thing learned is whether *miv* meets the prescribed criteria (red and square). Consequently, the concepts of red and square must be present for the learning to occur. These concepts provide the hypothetical attributes which are tested for and thus the criteria which the test must meet.

If learning has the form of inductive inference, that is, if we induce conclusions on the basis of information we get about the truth of premises which we try out, then certain conclusions follow about what must be present for learning to occur:

> I am not, of course, arguing that we should abandon the notion that a learning device is, in essence, an instantiated inductive logic. Rather, the point is that to let such a device do what it is supposed to do, you have to presuppose the field of hypothesis, the field of concepts on which the inductive logic operates. In other words, to let this theory do what it is supposed to do you have to be in effect a nativist. You have to be nativistic about the conceptual resources of the organism because the inductive theory of learning simply doesn't tell you about that—it presupposes it. (Fodor, 1980a, pp. 146-147)

Given Fodor's conception of learning, it is impossible, in principle, to maintain that concepts are the result of learning. Rather, what results from learning is information about whether the hypotheses tried out meet criteria or not. What are never learned by verifying hypotheses are the hypotheses themselves or the concepts with which they are expressed. These must be present for the learning to occur. Since the theory of learning presupposes the existence of the hypotheses and concepts, giving no account of their origins, Fodor asserts that the hypotheses and concepts must be innate.

The question here is not whether Fodor is correct in claiming that every case of learning involves hypothesis formation and confirmation. The question for us is instead: Under Piaget's equilibration account, does learning involve hypothesis formation and confirmation in the broad sense sketched above? If it does, then we may proceed to ask: Are Fodor's criticisms of Piaget justified? That is, does Piaget offer accommodated schemata as prerequisites for transition to higher stages without explaining how accommodation occurs? If so, is this because of the role which learning plays in the equilibration account? And if that is true, are we to conclude that Piaget's constructivism provides no alternative to the claim that cognitive structures are innate?

By carefully examining Piaget's use of explanatory principles, all of the above questions may be fully resolved. For when we understand what these principles are and what Piaget does with them, we can identify the role of learning in his account of cognitive change. We can also determine the extent to which he can explain how accommodation occurs and whether the role of learning limits his account of this process. Piaget's application of the explanatory principles provides a perspective for evaluating the process of his explanation of cognitive change, aside from his claims about its explanatory power. This perspective allows us to determine whether Piaget can generate an alternative to Chomsky's account of origins or not.

Let us turn, then, to an analysis of Piaget's explanatory principles. These he takes from the field of biology, and it is to this science that we must now address ourselves.

3. The Biological Model

"It's a curious sensation, isn't it? Really thrilling . . . but why? You know, I get the feeling—or rather I see it—as if the ball is made of elastic, as if it's expanding into an ellipse . . . shall we say trying to free itself?"

The clerk nodded. "That's it, without a doubt."

"And yet the ball never quite manages to free itself. Instead, at the very moment of liberation, at the very point when you feel the ball might break its bounds, when your teeth are on edge—it resumes its proper direction, its captivity." (Sansom, p. 20)

Twentieth-century psychological theory owes a great debt to principles of explanation developed in other sciences. Biology especially has been a rich source of explanatory principles for psychology. In the present chapter, I examine a biological principle that has been used by many theorists as a model for constructing psychological explanation.

The principle in question is the equilibrium principle, which may be found in a variety of formulations. I focus upon the formulation set forth by C. H. Waddington, a geneticist to whom Piaget defers on a number of occasions. I also review Piaget's own formulation of the principle, which is heavily dependent on Waddington's. By seeing how Piaget conceptualizes the equilibrium principle, one can understand why he believes his equilibration account, for which the principle functions as a model of explanation, sets forth constructivism as an alternative to nativism. One can also see whether equilibration can hope to provide such an alternative.

The chapter is divided into four sections. In the first, I define the term *model* and show how models provide the basis for formulating explanations. In the second, I explain why Waddington's version of the equilibrium principle appeals to Piaget and then describe its features. In the third section, I show how Piaget makes use of

Waddington's principle to construct his own. Finally, I examine the possibility of providing an alternative to Chomsky's nativist account using the explanatory principle Piaget derives from his biological model.

Models in Science

There is a wide range of definitions for the term *model* (see, e.g., Black, 1962; Hesse, 1974; Scheffler, 1979; Wartofsky, 1979). Yet it is frequently unclear what function scientific models are to perform. Wartofsky writes:

> In much of model-talk, models inhabit a limbo between worlds. On the one hand, they are not citizens of the blood-and-guts world or real objects and processes; or at best have only a derived citizenship by way of their reference to such a world. On the other hand, they are denied full equality in the cognitive world of purported truths, assigned only the function of instruments of such cognition: crutches, aids to the imagination, inference-machines, heuristic devices, data-ordering frameworks. (p. 3)

How are models used to develop explanations? To answer this question, Wartofsky collapses the distinction between models, theories, and ad hoc analogies, arguing that all are a species of representation. Further, it is the representative aspect of a model that permits it to aid in the formation of scientific accounts:

> [A model is] an abstractive representation of some object or state of affairs. . . . it exhibit[s] only certain properties—the ones relevant to [one's] needs and interests in using the model—of the object modelled. Thus, a model of the solar system, whether hanging from the ceiling in a Planetarium, or diagrammed two-dimensionally on a piece of paper, or described in the utterances of some speaker, represents a state of affairs in some abstractive version: *Some properties* of the model resemble, or are like, or image, or mirror, or stand in for some properties of the solar system. (p. 4)

There are three important points about models in the foregoing passage. First, a model is a representation of something else. By representation, Wartofsky does not necessarily mean a picture copy of the thing modeled. A model can "resemble" a referent in some respects only, or "stand in for" it; it need not always "image" or "mirror" the referent. Nevertheless, a model always has a referent, that is, a state of affairs which it represents in some manner.

Second, some of the properties of the model must be such that they are like, meaning the same as, features of the thing modeled. This does not mean that the model has all the properties of the referent. Indeed, there are no ping-pong balls in the real solar system, nor are there circles made from graphite. What Wartofsky means is that for one thing to model another, it must have some properties which are the same as some of the object's properties. If this were not the case, then the model could not represent the object at all.

Third, the model is an abstractive version of the thing which it represents. This means that it is not as rich as its referent, that is, it does not have all the properties of the referent. If it did have all the referent's properties and no others, then it would be the referent itself. The model might have more properties than the referent, but as it could not have all its properties, some of the model's properties would be irrelevant to those of the referent.

Because models, on this admittedly realist interpretation, refer to some state of affairs (physical or nonphysical), one may try to verify whether the referent, such as the solar system in Wartofsky's example, does have various properties of the model. In fact, the properties of the model can be a rich source of hypotheses about the properties of the referent.

For example, Boyd (1979) and Black (1962) consider how models can promote scientific explanation. Boyd talks about the case in which metaphors, functioning as models, do just that:

> Scientists use [metaphorical models] in expressing theoretical claims [when] no adequate literal paraphrase is known. Such metaphors are *constitutive* of the theories they express, rather than merely exegetical. . . . if one looks at theory construction in the relatively young sciences like cognitive psychology, one finds theory-constitutive metaphors in abundance. . . . [e.g.,] the claim that thought is a kind of "information processing," and that the brain is a sort of computer. . . . the view that learning is an adaptive response of a "self-organizing machine." (p. 360)

The theory-constitutive metaphor that Boyd speaks of is a model in the sense defined above, that is, it represents a state of affairs and asserts that there are some properties which it has in common with that given state of affairs. The theory-constitutive metaphor is used to represent the state of affairs because no more literal description of its properties can be given. The model is invoked in explanation of the referent's properties. It also suggests hypotheses about these.

For example, consider the computer model of the brain. The computer, in this case, is a metaphor used to represent some properties of the brain. Explanations of brain function frequently speak of its information processing capacity, its capacities for storage, its short- and long-term memory, all of which are properties of the computer. The computer functions as a model for the brain, and a theory-constitutive one at that, because (a) it can function as an explanation of the brain's operations and (b) it can suggest hypotheses about other properties the brain might have. The computer is selected as the model because there is no more literal description of brain operation that can be given.

Boyd explains how theory-constitutive metaphors can be a rich source of discovery in science:

> Theory-constitutive metaphors . . . display what might be called *inductive open-endedness*. Although the intelligibility of theory-constitutive metaphors rests on the reader's being able to apply to his current understanding of the primary subject some of the associated implications appropriate to his current conception of

the secondary subject, the function of the metaphor is much broader. The reader is invited to explore the similarities and analogies between features of the primary and secondary subjects, including features not yet discovered, or not yet fully understood. Thus, for example, the metaphorical claims that men are computers, and that thought is information processing, are initially intelligible because the reader knows enough about men and computers to have some idea what similarity or analogy might be suggested, but part of the function of this metaphor as a theoretical statement is to suggest strategies for future research by asserting that, as investigations of men and machines progress, additional, or, perhaps, entirely different, important respects of similarity and analogy will be discovered. (p. 363)

The theory-constitutive metaphor, then, provides what Boyd elsewhere (p. 358) calls "epistemic access" to phenomena—a source of hypotheses about the phenomena, and thus a basis for gaining deeper understanding of the phenomena's features. This additional understanding results from testing whether the new phenomena have particular properties of the metaphor. For example, an empirical investigation might be carried out to determine whether men, like computers, store facts in "bits" and "chunks." Where hypotheses are verified, the properties of the model are attributed to those of the referent as a substitute for an alternative, literal description.

In summary, I am accepting Wartofsky's assertion that a model is an abstraction which represents some of the properties of the thing to which it refers. Where a metaphor is the best characterization of the referent possible—where no more literal description of the referent is available—the metaphor may function as a theory-constitutive metaphor to provide an account of the phenomena. Such metaphors promote scientific discovery because they suggest additional features of the referent which may be investigated. The metaphors also facilitate scientific explanation because they present some features of the referent in a relation to one another which makes the referent at least partially comprehensible.

The Equilibrium Model

Piaget's Appeal to Waddington

As previously indicated, Piaget employs the equilibrium principle to explain how the ability to reason changes and improves with age. As was also noted in Chapters 1 and 2, Piaget wants to explain how the ability to reason improves over the lifetime of the individual. He believes that the biological version of the equilibrium principle proposed by Waddington can function as a theory-constitutive metaphor for cognitive change. Piaget (1967/1971) writes:

The epigenetic process which is the basis of intellectual operations is rather closely comparable to embryological epigenesis and the organic formation of phenotypes. (p. 23)

In the physiological context . . . homeorhesis makes homeostasis possible by insuring the structural composition of the organs, but homeostasis is brought about by the setting in motion of these organs under the influence of new interactions. (p. 24)

In the cognitive field, chreods can be singled out which are more or less independent, each with its own homeorhesis, and forms of final equilibrium (in the sense that they continue to exist in a stable condition while still being capable of eventual integration into wider fields of equilibrium) which might be the equivalent of homeostasis. (p. 25)

Just as artificial intelligence practitioners treat the brain as a computer and proceed to test the implications of the analogy, so Piaget treats cognitive change as "a process of intellectual epigenesis closely comparable to embryological epigenesis and the organic formation of phenotypes." The claim here is not that change in cognitive structure results from biological change in the organism (although, of course, it does). Rather, the process of cognitive change is like the process of embryological epigenesis. Furthermore, there is no more literal way to describe the process of cognitive change; the biological metaphor is the description. Hence, the process of cognitive change has its own "chreods . . . which are more or less independent, each with its own homeorhesis and forms of final equilibrium."

As will be shown, Waddington's description of embryological epigenesis is based upon the equilibrium principle. Piaget takes Waddington's model and patiently explores its features, striving to delineate as much about the process of cognitive change as possible. Consequently his use of the equilibrium principle is closely comparable to Waddington's, and the superficial structure of their accounts is very similar in certain respects.

For example, to explain the changes that compounds undergo in order to become amino acids, Waddington (1966) presents us with a stage theory:

Many of the changes required for histogenesis require an orderly sequence of steps, by which some simple compound is gradually elaborated into something more complicated. . . . In the important mold Neurospora, the important amino acid arginine is synthesized through a sequence of steps, some of which are shown in [Figure 3.1]. A number of genes, numbered 1 to 7, are known that control the formation of the enzymes that act at the successive steps in the sequence. If the mold has a mutated allele at a gene (5 or 6) controlling the step from ornithine to citrulline, this chemical reaction cannot occur, and no arginine can be produced. Growth therefore ceases, and the mold soon dies, unless arginine or citrulline is supplied to it. (p. 41)

The construction of the amino acid arginine, required for histogenesis, has the following features: First, it is described in terms of *stages* in the growth of a chemophysical structure. Thus, arginine is a structured compound which develops through the stages of ornithine and citrulline.

Second, the structures have (a) chemical elements, (b) a prescribed relation between the elements, and (c) properties which hold true for the sum of the elements. The chemical elements in arginine are related to one another in a manner which subsumes some under others and forms a compound with specific properties.

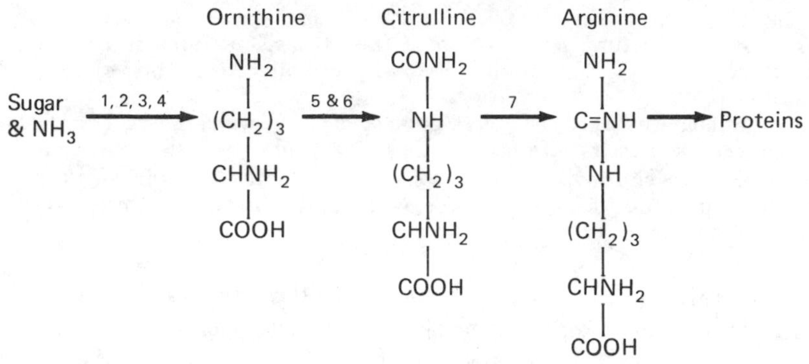

$$\begin{array}{ccccc}
 & \text{Ornithine} & \text{Citrulline} & \text{Arginine} & \\
 & \mathrm{NH_2} & \mathrm{CONH_2} & \mathrm{NH_2} & \\
 & | & | & | & \\
\text{Sugar} \xrightarrow{\text{1, 2, 3, 4}} & (\mathrm{CH_2})_3 \xrightarrow{\text{5 \& 6}} & \mathrm{NH} \xrightarrow{\text{7}} & \mathrm{C{=}NH} \longrightarrow \text{Proteins} \\
\text{\& } \mathrm{NH_3} & | & | & | & \\
 & \mathrm{CHNH_2} & (\mathrm{CH_2})_3 & \mathrm{NH} & \\
 & | & | & | & \\
 & \mathrm{COOH} & \mathrm{CHNH_2} & (\mathrm{CH_2})_3 & \\
 & & | & | & \\
 & & \mathrm{COOH} & \mathrm{CHNH_2} & \\
 & & & | & \\
 & & & \mathrm{COOH} & \\
\end{array}$$

Figure 3.1. Sequence of steps in the synthesis of amino acid arginine. (Adapted from *Principles of Development and Differentiation* by C. H. Waddington. Copyright 1966 by C. H. Waddington. Reprinted by permission.)

Third, the stages in the development of arginine occur in a fixed sequence. Ornithine must precede citrulline, and citrulline must precede arginine, because the elements of each structure are used to construct the succeeding one.

Finally, each new structure completes in some respect a construction begun at the previous level. The gene action upon a structure initiates the construction of new chemical elements, and when the next stage is reached, the construction is complete. Subsequent structures can be built from the new set of elements.

Like Waddington, Piaget describes change in terms of stages in the growth of structures. As is true in Waddington's case, the structures Piaget describes become more complex and specialized at each successive stage. Arginine is at a "higher" stage of development than citrulline because it contains additional elements and has a more complex organization and a more specialized function. Likewise, formal operational reasoning is described by a mathematical structure that incorporates more elements, has more complex relations between the elements, and narrower, more specialized application than concrete operational characterizations.

Further, the structures in both cases are described in terms of elements which stand in definite relation to each other and have certain properties. The compound arginine, as Waddington describes it, consists of the elements NH, C = NH, and so on, which stand in a very specific relation to each other (see Figure 3.1). These elements form a fixed, irreversible structure and are united by the chemical properties of arginine. Likewise, the I N R C Group structure, which Piaget uses to characterize formal stage reasoning, consists of four transformations—identity, negation, reciprocity, and correlation—that stand in reversible relation to one another (i.e., any state established by one or more transformations can be undone by another transformation in the set). Thus, each element may relate to the other in several ways. The transformations are united by the properties of closure and reciprocity.

In addition, the sequence of stages under both accounts must occur in a fixed order because the elements developed previously are needed for the new structure. Thus, citrulline must be produced before arginine. One might say that it is a pragmatic prerequisite for the construction of arginine; it must be present for construction to occur.

Finally, both Piaget and Waddington take pains to show how each state in the sequence completes (or further completes) a construction begun at earlier levels. Just as citrulline further elaborates ornithine and provides elements prerequisite for arginine, so the cognitive structures present at the concrete operational stage extend the structures of preoperational reasoning and thereby provide the elements needed to construct the formal operational structures.

We will turn shortly to Waddington's account of embryological epigenesis. To understand how Piaget uses it as a theory-constitutive metaphor to explain cognitive change, its features must be spelled out. The reader, however, may well be wondering: Why does Piaget defer to Waddington's account rather than some other? What questions does he believe it can help him resolve?

It appears that the answer to these questions are both simple and profound. Piaget seems to have believed that Waddington offered an alternative to an account of change based upon the principles of random variation and natural selection. Consequently, by using this explanation as a theory-constitutive metaphor, Piaget hopes to give an account of cognitive change that succeeds as an alternative. There are some reasons for Piaget's optimism. For one thing, Waddington shared Piaget's conviction that the principles of random variation and natural selection could not provide a complete account of change. Waddington (1960) writes:

> In conventional neo-Mendelian theory, [the] effects of the use of an organ, exerted during the organism's own lifetime, are dismissed as irrelevant to the evolutionary process. . . . We have to find the explanation for such evolutionary changes in random gene mutations, to whose occurrence the physiological processes which lead to the formation of adaptive ontogenetic changes are completely irrelevant.
>
> However, that explanation leaves us with two major points on which we may feel some lack of satisfaction. One is that we have no specific explanation for the co-ordinated nature of the changes as they affect the different bones or other subunits in the system. Can we do no better than fall back on the very general explanation in terms of the efficiency of natural selection in engendering highly improbable states? . . . Second, we are bound, both for practical reasons and on the basis of fundamental theory, to regard all forms, functions, and activities of an organism as the joint product of its hereditary constitution and its environmental circumstances; the exclusion of acquired characters from all part in the evolutionary process does less than justice to the incontrovertible fact that they exhibit some of the hereditary potentialities of the organism. All characters of all organisms are, after all, to some extent acquired characters, in the sense that the environment has played some role during their development. (p. 389)

Waddington, then, sees two limitations in accounts based solely upon random variation and natural selection principles. First, it is hard to explain why changes which occur are so well coordinated with one another if there can be no reference to the impact of the environment in the account. Why should particular well-coordinated modifications occur if the environment is not somehow the cause? Second, all characters are to some extent acquired, since the environment affects their development. A satisfactory account needs to explain the role of the environment.

Although Waddington did not feel that random variation and natural selection were sufficient to explain evolution, it is not clear that he believed he was providing an alternative to neo-Darwinian principles. It may be that he saw himself augmenting neo-Darwinian principles rather than substituting something new for them. Nonetheless, Piaget believed that Waddington's formulation did provide a basis for a viable alternative, and that his use of the equilibrium principle offered the explanatory approach he (Piaget) was seeking.

Waddington's Principle of Genetic Assimilation

Let us turn to Waddington's (1957) account of change, which is summarized in the following passage from *The Strategy of the Genes*:

> We have been led to conclude that natural selection for the ability to develop adaptively in relation to the environment will build up an epigenetic landscape which in its turn guides the phenotypic effects of mutations available. In light of this, the conventional statement that the raw materials of evolution are provided by random mutation appears hollow. The changes which occur in the nucleoproteins of the chromosomes may well be indeterminate, but the phenotypic effects of the alleles which have not yet been utilized in evolution cannot adequately be characterized as "random"; they are conditioned by the modelling of the epigenetic landscape into a form which favors those paths of development which lead to end-states adapted to the environment. (p. 188)

Waddington's account emphasizes three fundamental points. First, as is true in any evolutionary account, the goal of change is to enhance the fitness of the population so that its survival in the environment is assured. In order to enhance fitness a variety of modifications may be required. The expression of certain phenotypic features may need to be more flexible; some phenotypic possibilities may need to be eliminated from the repertoire. In any case, the changes which occur are perpetuated only if they enhance the possibility of survival.

Second, given the goal of change, it is insufficient to assert that "the raw materials of evolution are provided by random mutation." While random mutation does occur in the chromosomes, the altered alleles are selected for on the basis of their adaptive potential. Since a possibility for an alternative phenotypic character survives in ensuing generations only if it has adaptive potential, the environment contributes significantly to "the raw materials of evolution."

Third, the selection of adaptive modifications is assured by "the phenotypic effect of alleles . . . [which is] conditioned by the modelling of the epigenetic landscape into a form which favors those paths of development which lead to end-states adapted to the environment." This complex point is explored below, but the gist of it is this: The more adaptive the possible change, the more likely it is to be expressed, because the genotype that supports its expression will be selected for.

Before considering Waddington's thesis in detail, there is an important feature to emphasize. We must bear in mind that he is concerned with explaining change in the populations of species, not change in individuals. He may have believed that the same set of principles could suffice for both tasks (see Waddington, 1975). His research, however, was devoted to showing how altered phenotypic characters could be propagated through the population, so that eventually a majority exhibits traits

[1] The topic of fitness is discussed by Waddington (e.g., 1969), Dobzhansky (1970), Wilson and Bossert (1971), Wimsatt (1980).

that were found initially in only one or two members of the species. As will be seen, some serious confusions arise when Piaget modifies Waddington's thesis to explain how change occurs in individuals.

We now begin the analysis of Waddington's claim. In the interest of clarity, we must understand what he means by the term *epigenetic landscape*. Waddington (1957) writes:

> It has become commonplace that natural selection for any character will alter the general "genetic background" of the population. If the selection is for the capacity to respond adaptively to the environment, it would mold the epigenetic landscape into a new form in which this response is facilitated and perhaps adjusted so as to reach the most favorable end result. (p. 166)

The epigenetic landscape is, then, the genotype as a whole. The genotype not only specifies the possible phenotypes, but supports the development of some rather than others, given the genotype's overall characteristics. Thus, if some phenotypes prove adaptive, the genotype—the epigenetic landscape—becomes molded in such a way that these phenotypes are more likely to be expressed.

The concept of epigenetic landscape presupposes that given any genotype, a variety of phenotypic characters can be expressed. Hence, the development of an individual can go in a number of directions. The genotype which favors fitness will be selected for. Given this phenotype, the paths leading to the adaptive characters are heavily "canalized," or well-worn, meaning that expression of those characters is most likely. Once a well-canalized path is embarked upon, the terminus is likely to be reached, regardless of environmental stimuli.

The effects of natural selection can modify the epigenetic landscape, and this will occur if the external environment is drastically altered. Under this circumstance, following the well-worn path results in the expression of a phenotype that does not ensure survival. Thus, a threshold will be reached and development will follow an alternative path—one not followed frequently in the past. If the alternative phenotype promotes survival of the organism in the changed environment, it will be selected for, that is, its path will become more deeply canalized, and its expression will be more likely in the future.

We now see what Waddington means when he says that "the phenotypic effect of alleles . . . [is] conditioned by the modelling of the epigenetic landscape into a form which favors those paths of development which lead to end-states adapted to the environment." Clearly, the modeled epigenetic landscape expresses the developmental possibilities of the genotype. Further, the features of that genotype depend upon those of the environment, as the latter dictate the successful phenotypes and therefore the genes which should be selected for.

Because Waddington wishes to show that the environment makes a significant contribution to change in populations, he faces the question: By what means does the environment render change in the genotype? In response, he proposes the principle of genetic assimilation. Because it is this principle which Piaget uses as a theory-constitutive metaphor to explain cognitive change, we must be clear about its features. Waddington's principle is illustrated in Figure 3.2.

Figure 3.2 depicts four means by which an altered phenotype may appear in a

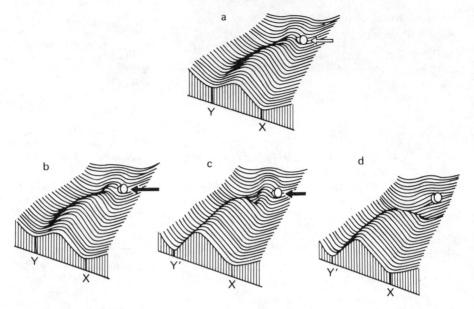

Figure 3.2. Representation of Waddington's principle of genetic assimilation. (Adapted from Waddington, 1957. Reprinted by permission.)

new generation. The wavy lines, together with the mountainous peaks and valleys, represent the epigenetic landscape or the "developmental potentialities of the genotype" (Waddington, 1960, p. 393). The deeper valleys, or paths, are the more highly canalized. These illustrate more rigid, more probable tendencies to express certain phenotypes. In Figure 3.2a, for example, the path which terminates at X is deeper than that which terminates at Y, meaning that phenotype X is more likely to be expressed.

Figure 3.2a depicts the first case in which a change in phenotype may arise: the stress from the environment (hollow arrow) may push the developing tissue (white ball) into an alternate path. In this case, no modification of the genotype occurs. Thus, the genotype must be such that the force of the environmental stimulus is sufficient to divert the course of development.

Figure 3.2b shows the second condition under which phenotypic change may occur. Waddington labels this condition organic selection, after J. M. Baldwin's concept.[2]

---

[2] The circumstance under which a gene mutation arises, favors the altered phenotype, and is selected for, was vaguely envisioned by James Mark Baldwin in the early part of the twentieth century. As Waddington's principle of change is better understood in light of Baldwin's, I will briefly review the latter.

Baldwin (1915) describes the process of organic selection in the following passage:

Assuming variations in organic forms, it is easy to see that some of them might react in a way to keep in contact with the stimulus, to lay hold on it, and so keep on reacting to it again and again—just as our rhythmic action in breathing keeps the organism in vital contact with the oxygen of the air. These organisms would get all the benefit or damage of the repetition or persistence of the stimulation and of their own reactions, again and again; and it is self-evident that the beneficial stimulations are the ones which should be maintained in this way, and that the organisms which did this would live . . . If this be true, only those organisms would survive which had the variation of retaining useful stimulations in what I have called . . . a 'circular way' of reacting. . . . We are, accordingly, left to the view that the new stimulations brought by changes in the environment, themselves modify the reactions of an organism in such a way that these modified reactions serve to hold or repeat the new stimulations as far as they are good, and further, negatively, in such a way that the former reactions become under the new condition less useful or positively damaging. (pp. 163-164; 166)

The process of organic selection is, then, one in which the adaptive behaviors of individuals in the species become characteristics displayed by the race as a whole. The process works like this: Some individuals display characters that are adaptive in a given environment, that is, that take advantage or make use of the beneficial aspects of that environment. These individuals survive and reproduce. Thus, over time, the population comes to consist of individuals that "had the variation of retaining useful stimulations"—individuals that, by their features, responded to the environment in a useful manner. Baldwin concludes that the environment effects the modifications that organisms make by rendering some useful (for survival) and others deleterious.

According to Baldwin, organic (or functional) selection is a positive force, whereas natural selection is not. In the following passage, he elaborates this point:

[Natural selection] would do no more than effect the survival of organisms which repeated or retained useful stimulations. If this worked alone, every change in the environment would wash out all life except those organisms which by accidental variation reacted already in the way demanded by the changed conditions—in every case, new organisms showing variations, not in any case new elements of life history in the old organisms. In order to do the latter [i.e., in order to show new elements in a life history], we would have to conceive one of two things: either, first, an innate capacity of the organism to anticipate and be ready for new conditions: or second, some modifications of the old reactions in an organism through the influence of new conditions, in such a way that this modified reaction serves to retain the desirable stimulations of the environment, while the old ways of reacting do not. The first of these two conceptions [i.e., the innate capacity of the organism to be ready for new conditions] might be realized in turn by either of two alternatives; first, by heredity; and second, by the special creation of each organism for its particular environment. But the first of these, besides being excluded by our hypothesis that we are at the beginning of the phylogenetic series, would leave over the question: How did the ancestors come to be adapted? And the second calls upon us to give up the conception of phylogeny altogether. (pp. 165-166)

According to Baldwin, in order to give an account which shows the life history of the species, one must (a) show an innate capacity of the organism in the species to "anticipate and be ready for new conditions," or (b) show how reaction to the environment retains desirable conditions in it. The problem with the first alternative is twofold: It can be explained either by heredity or by a theory of special creation. The heredity account is ruled out because we are trying to explain how the species is initially endowed. Clearly its initial features cannot be inherited. Nor is it clear how the ancestors become adapted. A theory which postulates that species are preadapted to a specific environment excludes the idea that a race or species has evolved. Thus, Baldwin rejects his first hypothesis and opts for the second. Waddington, following Baldwin, argues that the gene will depend, to some extent, on the features of the epigenetic landscape. The more the landscape has been canalized toward the development of particular phenotypic characters, the more likely it is that a mutation which favors development along those channels will be retained.

In Figure 3.2b a mutant allele arises by chance and replaces the original environmental stimulus. Thus, while environmental pressure initially caused the expression of an alternate phenotype, a mutation has arisen which perpetuates the expression of the alternate character, regardless of environmental conditions. In this instance, the genotype is modified, and modified solely by a chance mutation. If the mutant allele is selected for, and subsequent generations express the altered trait, it is because the mutation supports an adaptive phenotype.

Figures 3.2c and 3.2d illustrate another means by which the genotype may be modified, which Waddington calls genetic assimilation. Accordingly, there are two ways in which conditions in the environment can affect the genetic level. In the first case (Figure 3.2c), the makeup of the genome and the epigenetic landscape has shifted due to either conditions in the environment which select for fitness and/or random gene mutations. Because pressure from the environment has modified the adaptive potential of the genes, forces of natural selection have permitted effects of gene mutations which were previously impossible. Consequently, a "small gene mutation" (Waddington, 1960, p. 396) causes the development of an alternate phenotype—a switch to a new path in development. The mutation alone would have been insufficient to render the switch had the genome not been otherwise modified by environmental pressures: "the threshold protecting the wild type is lowered to some extent [and] there is an identifiable major gene which helps push the developing tissues into the Y path" (1957, p. 167). In Figure 3.2d, selection pressures have so modified the landscape that no identifiable switch gene is needed to direct development down a new path.

As Waddington stresses, modifications in the genome create a modification in the phenotype. As selection pressures alter the peaks and valleys in the landscape, the phenotypes which had certain features when initially expressed are also somewhat modified. The character Y becomes Y' because the genetic composition is no longer what it was. While the initial expression of an adaptive phenotype affects the selection (modification) of the genotype, in subsequent generations this modification effects change in the phenotypic character.

Waddington infers from an extended series of experiments with *Drosophila* (e.g., 1957, pp. 171-174) that genetic assimilation does indeed occur. He shows that when *Drosophila* pupae (aged 21-23 hours) are exposed to extremely high temperatures (40°C), some develop wing aberrations. By selective breeding of those that exhibit this trait, over many generations, he eventually produces a strain in which most of the members expressed it. When the environment is returned to normal temperatures, the offspring of this new strain, and their offspring for many generations, continue to exhibit the altered phenotype. Waddington concludes that genetic assimilation occurred. When the pressures from the environment that initially induced the appearance of the altered trait in a few individuals were eliminated, this change was not sufficient to deter expression of the trait in subsequent generations. Waddington maintains that the altered trait results because the genome has been modified.

Piaget's interest in the principle of genetic assimilation stems from his conviction that it can provide an account of origins that is not based on chance occurrence. It is interesting, therefore, to note Waddington's view of this matter. Bateman (cited by Waddington, 1957, p. 168) replicated his experiments using different and much larger populations. Her findings indicate that all the genes which enter into the genotype of the assimilated race were already present in the initial population. In reference to Bateman's data, Waddington (1957) argues:

> Is it reasonable to suppose that the observed new mutations, producing phenotypic changes of the kind for which a watch was being kept, arose by chance in that number? It is difficult to say. Personally, I should not like to take the opposite view, and claim that it was unreasonable to attribute the mutations to chance. I see in these facts no reason which compels one, or even very strongly urges one, to seek any other cause for the mutations which have occurred. (p. 180)

The use of the double negative may obscure the point, namely, that Waddington sees no connection between the selection of an alternate adaptive character and the production of a mutation that facilitated its appearance in later generations. All that can be said is that given a certain environment, a mutation which supports an adaptive phenotype is likely to be selected, should it arise. Neither the external environment, nor the appearance of an adaptive phenotype, can cause the mutation to occur in the first place.

Arguing with respect to the principle of organic selection, rather than genetic assimilation, Simpson (1953) explains why Waddington's inference is correct:

> If the Baldwin effect occurs, either there is or is not a causal connection between an individual accommodation and subsequent genetic change in a population. If there is no such connection, then the truly genetic change must occur wholly by mutation, reproduction, and natural selection, and the accommodation may be irrelevant. (p. 115)

The principles of genetic assimilation and organic selection offer no alternative to an account based on chance variation and natural selection unless it can be shown that the occurrence of a phenotypic trait causes a new possibility in the genotype to arise. Further, as Simpson argues, the Baldwin effect—the phenomenon in which adaptive modification appears to have been followed by genetic change—is completely explicable by chance variation and natural selection:

> An "acquired character" or specifically an adaptive modification (that is, an accommodation) necessarily occurs within a genetically determined reaction range. The range may be relatively broad or extremely narrow. In any case an accommodation has genetical limits and develops only in the framework of the genetical system, but in a labile reaction range the particular form taken by a developing organism depends also on interaction with the environment. The genetical system evolves and the reaction range correspondingly changes. The range may come to cover different possibilities or it may become broader or narrower. If it becomes narrower, the possibilities for individual modification of characteristics become fewer. . . . The Baldwin effect would ensue when selection for the ability to acquire an adaptive character so narrowed the developmental range that the character would usually or invariably appear. (pp. 115-116)

Simpson maintains there is a genetically determined range of acquired characters. That is, the genotype limits the characters which may possibly appear at the phenotypic level. Where a number of phenotypes may be exhibited, the one actually exhibited will be determined by interaction between the organism and the environment. As the environment changes, a new possibility—one which might have been exhibited previously but was not—is tried out so as to permit survival under the conditions. If it promotes survival, is heritable, and not positively correlated with a deleterious character, it will be selected for. If the range of possible phenotypic characters becomes so narrow that only one is possible, then this trait no longer depends on the occurrence of certain environmental conditions, and we may have a case of the Baldwin effect (organic selection).

Simpson's thesis is not that the phenomenon of organic selection fails to occur, or that the environment plays no positive role. Rather, he maintains that what appears as the Baldwin effect may be explained by chance variation and natural selection. The features of the organism, in combination with those of the environment, determine which phenotypic possibilities may remain in the repertoire. They, therefore, determine whether the adaptive capacity of the species is narrowed or broadened. But this is entirely compatible with what natural selection asserts.

The same argument can be made with respect to genetic assimilation. It is not that the phenomenon of genetic assimilation fails to occur, but rather that it can be explained by the principles of random variation and natural selection, and consequently provides no alternative to a chance account of the origin of possibilities. The argument follows.

It is true that the phenotypic possibilities which remain in the repertoire have been determined by the population in interaction with its environment, in that those members with deleterious characteristics do not reproduce. This means the features of the genotype will be influenced by the features of the environment and will be canalized accordingly. But this fact can be explained by the principle of natural selection: The forces in the environment exert selective pressures that eliminate organisms which express deleterious characters; those which reproduce are those which express adaptive characteristics; the new generation will have a range of phenotypic possibilities which is less likely to include the deleterious possibilities. The genome is modified so as to support the adaptive phenotype and is molded by environmental pressures.

Consequently, the principle of genetic assimilation, like that of organic selection, has no implications for—and is irrelevant to—the origin of the genotypic possibilities. Because genetic assimilation can be explained by random variation and natural selection, any heritable change in phenotypic character arises from change at the genotypic level. Furthermore, all the possibilities for change in the genotype arise by chance mutation. While the success of phenotypes affects the retention of the phenotypic and genotypic possibilities in the repertoire, the environment, which exerts the selection pressures, does not generate these possibilities. Rather, they arise by chance.[3] This is the crucial point to bear in mind as we consider Piaget's use of Waddington's genetic assimilation principle.

[3]One might object that under the genetic assimilation account, the environment plays a role in generating new possibilities, for by determining the fitness of certain phenotypes, it limits the range of possible changes at both the genotypic and phenotypic levels. Thus, the fact that the human brain increases the fitness of the species circumscribes the set of possible mutations that might occur.

There are two points to be made in response to this objection. First, the role of the environment in causing change here is no different than it is under the random variation/natural selec-

Piaget's Use of Genetic Assimilation

Piaget uses Waddington's principle of genetic assimilation as a theory-constitutive metaphor in constructing an explanatory principle of his own which he calls biological phenocopy. He then uses his principle of biological phenocopy to construct his principle of cognitive phenocopy. In the present section, I consider the characteristics of biological phenocopy and its use of Waddington's genetic assimilation principle. In the concluding section, I consider the account of origins that his use of this principle could permit.

Piaget takes great pains to relate Waddington's principle of genetic assimilation to his account of cognitive change (see, e.g., Piaget, 1967/1971, 1976/1978, 1974/1980a). Piaget (1974/1980a) uses genetic assimilation to construct the phenocopy principle, which functions as the basis for his account of cognitive change. He summarizes phenocopy in the following passage:

> Since every phenotype is founded on a previous genetic basis, it follows that selection may favor phenotypic flexibility or adaptability if variation occurs in the environments of successive generations. On the other hand, where the environment is constant and well-differentiated, a standard phenotype will be produced by the canalization of epigenetic processes. The same selective factors will also act upon the canalization of the mutations themselves. Because of this a new genotype imitating the earlier phenotype will be genetically fixed once a certain threshold or plane of selection has been reached. This threshold is set up because the genes become "coadapted" with correlative modifications of several distinct factors. Thus, the lowering of selective pressure (once the threshold has been attained) will not produce a reversion, whereas if the threshold is not attained, no genetic fixing will occur. (p. 56)

Piaget argues that every phenotype has its basis in the genotype. If the environment constantly changes, phenotypic flexibility will be favored, and the genome will likewise favor it. But if the environment remains constant and well differentiated, that is, contains specifically defined features that remain stable, then a standard phenotype will be produced over and over, and will become canalized by the mutations themselves. This means that mutations which favor the standard phenotype will be selected, should they arise, and these will produce a *copy* of the phenotype which was formerly under the control of the environment. Hence, a new genotype can imitate the earlier phenotype. Because the gene mutations must be coadapted with the remainder of the genome, they are selected only if a certain threshold is reached. Once selection occurs at the genetic level, the adaptive phenotype will persist, even in the face of environmental change, until a new threshold of change is again reached.

---

tion account. In both cases, the environment could be said to limit possibilities in the sense described above. Thus, genetic assimilation offers no improvement in the account of the environmental contribution.

Second, to say that selection pressures circumscribe the range of possible modifications provides no account of why one modification is made rather than another. Neo-Darwinism maintains that the modification is random—that random mutation occurs at the genetic level—and genetic assimilation does not offer a competing resolution.

It should be noted that Piaget's definition of *phenocopy* differs from the stand-ard use of the term, which Dobzhansky (1962) summarizes:

> "Phenocopies" [are] traits which resemble those produced in other conditions by abnormal genes. For example, both high and low blood pressure can be induced by certain drugs, and perhaps by some living conditions, and yet it is probable that essential hypertension and hypotension may appear in persons of certain genotypes, even if they are living under conditions in which other per-sons are free of these difficulties. The environmental hypertension is, then, a phenocopy of the genetic (idiopathic) one. (p. 112)

Here, the phenocopy is made by the environment. The elements of the environment cause effects in the organism which are otherwise under genetic control. The envi-ronment causes a copy of the response normally generated by the genes—precisely the opposite of the phenomenon Piaget describes. In the latter case, the genome causes a copy of a response which was formerly under environmental control.

Piaget reverses the standard definition of *phenocopy* because his definition is based upon the principle of genetic assimilation, which he uses as a theory-constitu-tive metaphor. As a result, he assumes the premises Waddington assumes and argues that change in phenotypic traits can result from canalization of the genome. Let us examine this point in detail.

First, Piaget's phenocopy principle, like genetic assimilation, assumes that the possibilities for phenotypic traits are specified by the genotype of the organism. This means that any phenotype expressed is but one of many possibilities under that genotype. The genotype can only *imitate* the phenotype in the sense that it can change to make the appearance of the standard phenotype more likely in future generations.

Second, the nature of the possibilities which remain in the genotypic repertoire will depend, in part, upon the nature of the successful phenotypes. If the environ-ment is stable, the genotypic possibilities may become narrower and narrower because the range of adaptive phenotypes becomes narrower. If the environment fluctuates, the genotype will permit a variety of adaptive phenotypes.

Given these two assumptions, Piaget is ready to assert the metaphor. Phenotypes, he says, become canalized. That is, the development of certain phenotypic traits will become more and more likely, given a constant environment. Selection pressures from the environment eliminate those paths of development which result in deleter-ious traits and favor those which result in adaptive ones. The genotype will be mod-ified through environmental pressures to support the adaptive phenotypes.

The principle of phenocopy is the principle of genetic assimilation. Piaget states unequivocally that the various features of phenocopy are "brought together in the process of genetic assimilation described by Waddington" (Piaget, 1974/1980a, p. 51). And yet he raises two objections to Waddington's principle:

> In the first place, a chance factor remains between the phenotypical accommo-dation and the subsequent genic development. . . . I have quoted Waddington on my *limnaea* to the effect that even before selection the earlier genotype contains "many genes tending to produce the modified phenotype under the influence of the suitable environmental stress." This is quite possible, to be sure, but to make it a necessary precondition of any convergence between the said phenotype and

the new genotype whose genesis we have to explain is to come perilously close to the neo-Darwinian idea of the selection of random mutations. The other lacuna in the approach, to my mind, has to do with the role of selection. Where survival is selection's only concern, the evocation of the initial phenotype is no doubt sufficient, but if selection is also to be made responsible for "bringing together" and "combining," to use Waddington's terms, then we must give some account of its working in the internal environment and show how this environment, as modified by the phenotype, becomes the framework destined to mold the variations which will eventually constitute the new genotype. (1976/1978, pp. 73-74)

The first point that Piaget makes is especially revealing. He objects to Waddington on grounds that the latter "comes perilously close" to a chance relation between a phenotypic adaptation and subsequent gene mutation. Of course, it is this chance relation which Piaget wishes to avoid. As I have shown, Piaget is right: Waddington offers no alternative to a random variation/natural selection account of the origin of possibility.

The second objection is to the role of selection, which, according to Waddington, is exerted only by the external environment upon the phenotype. Such pressures are supposed to explain changes at both the genotypic and phenotypic levels. If, however, one wishes to explain how selection pressures exert their influences, one needs to explain, says Piaget, how the internal environment, which itself is modified by selection pressures on the phenotype, exerts selection pressures on the genotypic variations that arise.

Shortly, we will examine Piaget's concept of internal environment. At this point, let us note that the two objections above arise from the same motivation. On the one hand, Piaget uses Waddington's principle of genetic assimilation as a theory-constitutive metaphor such that its basic assumptions are accepted and utilized in the way that Waddington uses them. On the other hand, these assumptions confront Piaget with some consequences that he is reluctant to accept; in particular, an account of change which locates the origin of new possibilities in chance occurrence. To remedy this situation, Piaget attempts to modify the principle of genetic assimilation. While accepting its basic premises, he changes some aspects of it so that the undesirable consequences can be avoided. In *Behavior and Evolution* (1976/1978), Piaget argues that the geneticist Weiss suggests appropriate modifications. Piaget writes of Weiss:

We . . . know enough by now to assert, in company with Weiss, that developmental processes occur in a system "in which the genes do not 'act' as independent autonomous dictators, but with which they simply 'interact' as cooperative parts." . . . We can thus see what Weiss understands by the origin of an innate characteristic. The genesis of a trait is not simply embodied in particular genes; it consists in a process which, though it begins with these genes, also encompasses a determinate sector of the epigenesis with which the genes interact. Its trajectory thus displays a certain unity which distinguishes it from others, with which, furthermore, it may combine. At once genic and epigenetic in character, a new variation may therefore enshrine aspects which are not preformed in the genes but which are produced by the dynamics of the genes' interactions with epigenesis. (p. 69)

According to Piaget's interpretation of Weiss, we need not locate the origin of any trait in the genes alone. The processes of development occur in a hierarchical system, and the genes interact within that system. The development of a trait is the result of a process which begins with the genes but involves, as well, epigenetic (developmental) processes. The result of the interaction is development along some trajectory, that is, the appearance of some phenotypes rather than others. The trajectory may be novel. The interaction of genetic and epigenetic processes may produce the trait which is not preformed in the genes but is, rather, produced by the dynamic of the interaction.

The salient feature of Weiss's account, as Piaget views it, is its systemic, or feedback, aspect. Piaget emphasizes the role of feedback in his phenocopy principle and argues that feedback between the genome and epigenetic processes permits an account of novel phenotypes that does not depend upon chance. (Waddington himself discusses the role of feedback in development [e.g., 1960, pp. 398-399]. Piaget's use of Weiss's work is in no way antithetical to his use of Waddington's, as will be shown.)

As demonstrated, Piaget argues that phenocopies are produced when a change occurs at the genetic level, which brings the expression of a phenotype under genetic control. He maintains that there are three moving forces, the interaction of which effect the change in the genotype. The forces are represented by the symbols $\uparrow a$, $\downarrow b$, and $\uparrow c$. The arrows beside the letters indicate that these moving forces have direction.

The first force which affects the phenocopy, $\uparrow a$, is "la construction synthetic normale, conforme a la programmation hereditiare," that is, the development of traits controlled by heredity. The information specified by the DNA directs the development of phenocopies by defining the features that the phenocopies may have. The movement of the development is "up" ($\uparrow$), "passes through the RNA into the entire system of the germ cell ... then transmitted by way of intercellular connections. ... [to] the tissues and the organs" (Piaget, 1974/1980a, p. 63).

The second force which helps generate the phenocopy, $\downarrow b$, is "l'ensemble des modifications exogenous imposées par le milieu," that is, the collections of changes imposed on the organism by the environment. The elements in the environment place demands (x, y, z) upon the organism to which it must respond with appropriate behaviors at the phenotypic level (x', y', z') if it is to survive. The information specified by $\downarrow b$ is information about whether x', y', z' meet the demands which are imposed by x, y, z. If the demands are not met, then disequilibria x'', y'', z'' are created (p. 64). The movement is down ($\downarrow$) in the sense that it brings a message back about the effectiveness of the phenotypic change.

The third force is that of $\uparrow c$, the groping trials with which the organism responds to a state of disequilibrium. The trials are trials of alternative phenotypes, which again have a basis in the DNA. The generation of the alternative, adaptive phenotypes results from the interaction of all three movements. Piaget writes:

The features [phenotypes] x', y', and z' are products of the conjunction $(\downarrow b) \times (\uparrow c)$, and in no way are products of a preformation programmed by the environment for transmission by vectors $\downarrow b$. In the case of the disequilibriums x'', y'', and z'', a fortiori, what the feedback $\downarrow b$ actually transmits will never be a message (comparable to that carried by RNA) conveying "what is happening" or "what must be done." On the contrary, the information transmitted by $\downarrow b$ vectors will be limited *exclusively* to the indication that something isn't working. Where $\uparrow c$ vectors are involved, they will comprise on every level the tentative trials or gropings instigated by conflicts between $\uparrow a$ and $\downarrow b$ vectors. These conflicts themselves (the actual result of opposition between the environment and the genetic program) will thus constitute disturbances of equilibrium or deviations from the program, and they will sooner or later be overcome (as when quickly remedied by the production of phenotypic variations x', y', or z'). Such conflicts may persist, however, in latent form, as sources of real or potential instability. This will be the case when disequilibriums x'', y'', and z'' exist, and when the phenotype is, therefore, entirely stabilized and will consequently become the source of a phenocopy. It should be added that the exploratory trials ($\uparrow c$), because of their groping nature, can only end at the solutions sought (reequilibrations to eliminate conflicts and disturbances of equilibrium) by means of an interplay of regulations and selection by both external and internal environments, primarily the latter. (p. 64)

As Piaget notes, the $\uparrow a$ vector is genetically programmed: it transmits information coded in the DNA. Its features are defined by the DNA. The $\downarrow b$ vector carries no program. Its function is to signal obstructions, or disequilibria, that arise when endogenous structures (whose features are imposed by the internal procedures of organizations, rather than the environment) come into conflict with the organism's interpretation of the environment. As a result, while $\downarrow b$ vectors influence the development of phenotypic characters, the influence is of a very different sort from that exerted by $\uparrow a$.

Piaget makes the difference in the two sources of influence very clear. He writes that $\downarrow b$ vectors "will have no more direct effect than to set in motion the gropings or exploratory trials which we will call vectors $\uparrow c$." In other words, "the features of x', y', and z' are the products of the conjunction $(\downarrow b) \times (\uparrow c)$ and in no way are products of a preformation programmed by the environment for transmission by vectors $\downarrow b$." We will examine this claim shortly.

Thus, Piaget argues that phenocopy occurs when (a) disequilibria x'', y'', z'' persist, (b) phenotypic traits exist which, if expressed, eliminate the disequilibria, and (c) the alternative phenotype becomes stabilized, as change occurs at the genetic level which supports it. The exploratory trials will persist until suitable phenotypic possibilities are identified. Further, "the exploratory trials can only end at the solutions sought . . . by means of an interplay of regulations and selection by both external and internal environments."

Note that there is a profound ambiguity here. Is Piaget describing how change occurs over a population or how it occurs in individuals? We see him vascillating between the ontogenetic and phylogenetic focus. For example, when Piaget writes that "Organic Selection thus contributes in part to a progressive reconciliation among programming ($\uparrow a$), deviations ($\downarrow b$), and attempts at their correction ($\uparrow c$)," he seems to be describing a process of change that occurs between generations of a population. Clearly, organic selection—the process by which a mutation is selected because it supports an adaptive phenotype—could only occur between generations.

In the preceding sentence, however, Piaget states that "exploratory trials, ($\uparrow c$) because of their groping nature, can only end at the solutions sought . . . by means of an interplay of regulations and selection by both external and internal environments." There are two aspects of this statement that suggest that here Piaget is trying to account for ontogenetic rather than phylogenetic change. First, "an interplay of regulations" can occur only if a regulatory or feedback apparatus is operating. The feedback that can occur between generations is very different from that which can occur within an individual. An "interplay of regulations" suggests that the kind of feedback in question is the latter variety. Second, the concept of an internal environment, as Piaget develops it, is extraneous to an account of phylogenetic change. Yet it has an important function in Piaget's account of cognitive change in individuals.

Why do we find this ambiguity in Piaget's phenocopy principle? The reason is that genetic assimilation is relevant to change across populations, while Piaget wants to account for ontogenetic change. He sees that genetic assimilation must be modified to suit his purposes. Thus, he introduces the concept of internal environment and assigns an elaborate role to feedback.

To prove my case, I will examine the roles of internal environment and feedback in Piaget's and Waddington's accounts. The differences in their use of these concepts turn on their attempts to explain different kinds of change. Let us begin with the internal environment.

Waddington (1957, pp. 132-136) identifies five factors which affect the genotypic characteristics of a population:

1. The environment ("the totality of circumstances physically exterior to the organism which affect its reproductive contribution to the next generation").
2. The direct effect of the environment on the phenotypes (these may be deleterious or advantageous).
3. The array of gene frequencies (the nature of the alleles at different loci and the frequency of their occurrence).
4. The degree and type of phenotypic canalization (this will influence the effects that genetic variation can have, and therefore, the selection value of these variations).
5. The degree of selective disadvantage associated with given divergence from the optimum phenotype (some external environments may permit considerable gene mutations, while others would select against these).

There is no mention of an internal environment in this list. Why? Because, in a population account, it is an extraneous concept. In order to explain genotypic change in the population over generations, Waddington posits a force which exerts selection pressures—the external environment—and the elements which, if selected or rejected, would influence the genotypes of future generations. Taken together, these factors are sufficient to explain population change.

According to Piaget, however, the internal environment exerts selection pressures. In describing the system's reaction to a state of disequilibrium, Piaget (1976/1978) writes:

> The genome's reaction here is to try out variations. . . . selection carried out by an environment comes into play, but . . . the environment . . . must initially, and essentially be the internal and epigenetic one. . . . [The] internal environment is endowed with homeostatic mechanisms, and inasmuch as the epigenetic system itself is specifically organized according to an "epigenetic homeostasis" (not to

mention Waddington's "homeorhesis" with its "chreods"), the disequilibrium ... is already attenuated and the conflict confined to the opposition between genic variations and internal environments ... which are now becoming re-equilibrated. ... The new genic variations can only become stabilized by submitting to the requirements of the modified internal environment. (pp. 80-81)

The internal environment of the organism includes both genetic and epigenetic processes. The latter may "conflict" with gene variations and act as a selection force upon them. This can occur, says Piaget, because the internal environment functions according to the principle of homeostasis. The homeostatic mechanisms attenuate the conflicts by favoring those genetic variations which do so. While the internal environment can be modified over generations, perhaps by the external environment, it has an explanatory role to play that is entirely missing from Waddington's account.

Why does Piaget diverge from Waddington at this point? Because it is not possible to explain ontogenetic change using genetic assimilation as a theory-constitutive metaphor if one does not so diverge. Selection pressures from the external environment may explain why genetic change occurs over generations and why given phenotypes are seen to spread through populations. But to explain the change that occurs over the individual's lifetime one must invoke an additional principle.

In Piaget's account, the internal environment is a homeostatic system that functions according to the principle of feedback. The homeostatic feedback system proposed by Cannon (1939), to which both Waddington and Piaget refer, specifies a procedure for maintaining desired chemical and physical conditions in the body. When Waddington uses the concept of homeostasis in the context of population biology (e.g., 1957, p. 41), he insists that this notion of maintaining a steady state be retained. Consequently, he does not invoke homeostasis to explain how systems develop new capacities, but rather, to introduce the concept of homeorhesis. He notes that other biologists, for example, R. Lewontin, use the concept of homeostasis to explain adaptation—to explain the case in which developmental, ontogenetic mechanisms keep the fitness of the population constant by altering gene frequencies (p. 46).

Waddington reserves the word *homeostasis* for cases in which gene frequencies are held constant:

In a relatively constant environment, which varies only over a certain limited range, natural selection ... will tend to maintain an equilibrium set of gene frequencies. This will amount to "genetic homeostasis." (p. 121)

In this context, the equilibrium set of gene frequencies is one which remains constant; the set is in equilibrium or homeostasis because it does not change over generations. Genetic homeostasis is created by selection pressures from the environment.

When Waddington speaks of developmental systems, we see that they differ from homeostatic ones in certain respects. In speaking of the operations of genes, he writes:

The catalysts' raw material may be obtained from the reactions of the lowest systems, i.e., by a feedback system. The eventual source of these is of course the material which flows into the system (of which X is an example). These materials are transformed, combined and assembled in various ways to give catalysts and substrates of diverse kinds. Some will have temporary existence, some will reach steady states or steady rates of production, some will fluctuate with the environment, some will be invariant. Although the initial substrates and catalysts will determine the early course of development, the presence of the highest class of catalysts will determine the behavior of the system more and more. As substrates for their action become available, the catalysts so produced will feed back on the system and will begin to control it. Catalysts which were not present in the beginning can thus make their appearance and open up new channels of reactions. (p. 239)

Figure 3.3 illustrates how the genes can operate to control the development of phenotypes. Thus, the new material on which the genes operate is "transformed, combined and assembled in various ways." The genes determine the behavior of the system "more and more" as the initial substrates and catalysts are transformed into more and more powerful ones, which in turn take over the control of the system.

While catalysts which were not present in the beginning can make their appearance and open up new channels of reactions, the developmental system which Waddington depicts here is closed in the sense that all the change which occurs is determined by the genes. He writes:

Neither the amount nor the nature of other catalysts is limited to that of the initial state. Both the substrate system and the catalyst system can thus expand

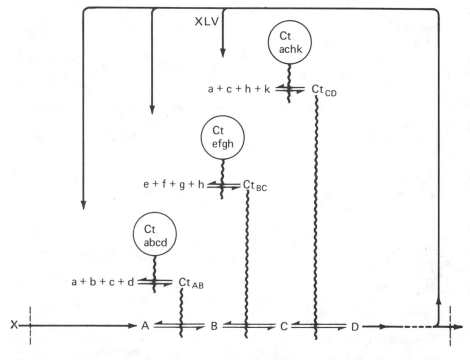

Figure 3.3. The operation of genes in the development of phenotypes. (Adapted from Waddington, 1957. Reprinted by permission.)

and change in a manner unpredictable from a knowledge of their initial quantities only. Development of the system is therefore epigenetic. The expansion is, however, controlled by the nature and quantity of the genes. Its course is determined by the interaction of the pattern of the genes with the pattern of the initial state and its subsequent changes. (p. 239)

When Waddington says that the expansion of the system is preformed, he means that the possibilities for change in the system are set by the features and quantity of the genes. While the catalytic processes and substrates "expand and change in a manner unpredictable from a knowledge of their initial quantities," the changes are the result of genetic control. Thus, if the pattern of the genes, the initial states, and the subsequent changes are known, the nature of future changes in the sequence can be anticipated.

Waddington distinguishes between nonadaptive homeostatic systems that maintain constancies or equilibrium; developmental systems, such as the epigenetic systems, that aim not to maintain constancies but to reach a predetermined end; and the evolution of a population. The feedback that can occur in each of these cases is different.

In the case of homeostatic systems, the feedback is information about the effectiveness of the system's behaviors in maintaining desired constancies. The change that occurs is a change to alternative behaviors available in the system's repertoire. The choice of behavior is determined strictly by its success in maintaining homeostasis.

In the case of the developing system, the feedback is information about the effects of gene action on the products of its action, with reference to the predetermined developmental end-state. The end-state—the adult phenotype—is coded in the genes, and the products (enzymes, amino acids) are the result of gene-specified activities. The change that occurs is a change in the products of genes—a change whose nature is defined and limited by the genes but which results from the interaction between the gene patterns and the products produced in the sequence.

In the third case—the case where gene frequencies change over generations of a population—there is no feedback system which operates in time, in contrast to the two previous cases. If there is feedback, it is not information to a system about the effects of its operations on meeting its goals. Since there is no system, strictly speaking, there are no "goals," nor is there any information received. So in what sense can there be "feedback"?

One might argue that the goal of evolutionary change is survival; that the reproduction of adaptive genotypes is the behavior directed toward meeting this goal; and that the survival of certain genotypes provides information to the genes about a genotype's adaptive value. The self-replicating capacity of genes allows them to carry information about adaptation to the new generation of survivors.

This line of argument appears contrived and one to which Waddington might well object. The evolutionary change is not change which occurs within a closed system, or indeed, in a system at all. There are accidental events of all sorts which beset both the genes and the environment in which they must survive. While survival may be the goal set by evolutionary theorists, it is hardly a goal set by a system against which it measures the effects of its behaviors. As there is no system, the feedback that might be said to occur is very different from that described in the homeostatic or developmental cases. Indeed, the term seems to be misplaced in the evolutionary context.

Let me emphasize that Waddington used his genetic assimilation principle to provide an account of the third sort—an evolutionary account. As indicated previously, he wanted to show that phenotypic change that occurs in one generation may influence the course of development in subsequent generations. Thus, he argued that change in gene frequencies over populations can occur when (a) a mutation arises which favors the expression of an adaptive phenotype (organic selection), (b) the forces of selection modify the tendency to express nonadaptive genotypes so that minor gene mutations suffice for their appearance in the new generation (genetic assimilation), and (c) the forces of selection support the tendency to express adaptive phenotypes so strongly that not even a switch gene is required for their expression.

What happens then when Piaget tries to invoke the principle of genetic assimilation to explain ontogenetic change? As shown, Waddington's principle appeals to Piaget because it appeared to offer an alternative to a chance account of origins. To use it to explain ontogenesis, Piaget elaborates the concept of the internal environment, which he depicts as operating according to feedback principles. The feedback system he uses, however, is developmental. The question is: Can this conception of a feedback operation permit Piaget to give an account of ontogenetic change which does not locate its origins in chance? We now turn to this topic.

Phenocopy and the Question of Origins

According to Piaget, Waddington's account fails to explain how the possibilities for genetic variations are released so that some, rather than others, are available to be selected. Furthermore, it cannot explain how the possibilities arise in the first place—and that this is not solely a random matter. Piaget believes that his elaboration of the internal environment renders his phenocopy principle more satisfactory than Waddington's principle of genetic assimilation on both counts.

First, he maintains that a state of profound disequilibrium existing between the organism and the external sets in motion a series of trials aimed at identifying an alternative phenotype which will eliminate the disequilibrium. Should a successful trial take place, the forces of natural selection will operate on the genotype so that the adaptive phenotype will occur more frequently in subsequent generations.

Second, because the genetic modification eliminates the state of disequilibrium by favoring the adaptive phenotype, the need created by the disequilibrium makes adaptive change in the genotype more likely. Since the occurrence of the disequilibrium sets the trials in motion, it also assures that the change to an adaptive genotype is not simply a random matter.

The process of change depicted by phenocopy is not Lamarckian. When Piaget asserts that disequilibrium makes adaptive change in the genotype more likely, he does not mean (as Lamarck thought) that the external environment species the nature of the change required. Rather, the nature of the change is determined by the success of the gene trials in resolving the disequilibrium. Further, it is the internal environment, not the external one, which registers the existence of the disequilibrium and determines the success and failure of both genotypic and phenotypic changes.

Although not Lamarckian, Piaget's principle of phenocopy is problematic—and problematic in ways Piaget did not seem to recognize. For one thing, the principle cannot explain *how* genotypic trials are set in motion. Although the internal environment registers the existence of the success and failure of each trial, it operates like a developmental feedback system which exists in time. Genotypic trials are set in motion between generations. That is, they occur when the genes line up on the chromosomes at the time of conception. Since change in the genotype occurs over generations, and occurs by chance, a developmental mechanism of operation cannot explain why given gene combinations occur. The internal environment functions as a feedback mechanism within individuals of one generation and can register disequilibrium created between the external environment and certain phenotypic trials. The effects of any genotypic change that occurs subsequently cannot be registered until the next generation.

There can be no feedback between generations, however, or at least, not of the developmental or homeostatic variety. Thus, if genotypic change occurs, it cannot be because the internal environment sets the genotypic trials in motion, as it can the phenotypic trials. Further, the consequences of the genotypic trials, that is, information about the change in phenotypic possibilities that they provide, will not be received by the system which registered the disequilibrium.

This brings us to the second and most crucial shortcoming of Piaget's phenocopy principle, at least from the point of view of his equilibration account. The phenocopy principle still locates the origins of the change in chance. Hence, it provides no alternative to the neo-Darwinian account in this fundamental respect. Let us see why.

It is clear from Piaget's account of phenocopy that the first thing necessary for change is the hereditary mechanisms that correspond to the $\uparrow a$ vectors. These mechanisms, as Piaget says, "originate in the DNA of the organism," and are realized according to epigenetic and environmental pressures. Since the mechanisms originate in the DNA, the account of change must make clear the relations between the DNA and the changes in the developmental mechanisms which are found to operate along the paths of normal hereditary development.

The second thing that must be present for change is what Piaget calls the $\uparrow c$ vectors—"the gropings or exploratory trials." If a state of disequilibrium between the organism and the external or internal environment arises, there must be a set of phenotypic possibilities to try out so that the disequilibrium can be resolved. Without these, the disequilibrium will persist.

Third, there must be some procedures for choosing one trial rather than another from the repertoire of possibilities. The procedures specify the conditions under which given possibilities will be tried out. Like the possibilities themselves, the procedures for choosing are specified by the genotype.

Finally, the fourth thing which must be present are some criteria by which to determine whether a state of disequilibrium has been resolved. The criteria are specified by the internal environment. We know this to be the case because the internal environment functions according to feedback principles—something it could not do if there were no criteria for evaluating the success of its trials.

Why must these four elements be present for change to occur? Because (a) change arises from the operation of the internal environment; (b) the internal environment functions according to feedback principles characteristic of teleological developmental systems; and (c) these four elements are necessary for such feedback mechanisms to operate. Given that these four elements are presupposed, not explained, by Piaget's phenocopy principle, what is to be made of his claim that phenocopy is "constructivist" rather than nativist or empiricist? Piaget writes (1974/1980a):

> It is worth emphasizing, finally, that this interpretation of the phenocopy is basically constructivist in nature. The new genotype constitutes the ultimate result of conflicts and interactions between organism and environment, and the environment thus necessarily intervenes as one of the transforming elements in its causality. If this is so (and here lies the constructivism), then the adaptation itself has, as its producing factor, not the environment as such, but rather, the constant action of the organism upon the environment, which is by no means the same thing. (p. 73)

The main point here is that constructivism amounts to fixation. When Piaget says "the adaptation . . . has, as its producing factor, not the environment . . . [but] the constant action of the organism upon the environment," he means that the action, together with feedback about its consequences, determines which adaptations are made. Here, "producing an adaptation" amounts to retaining a successful phenotypic possibility; it does not mean generating a new possibility. As a consequence, the new genotype, which "constitutes the ultimate result of conflicts and interactions between organism and environment," will permit the set of possible phenotypes that best resolve organism-environment conflict (disequilibrium). Again, the features of the new genotype will be fixed on the basis of their success in promoting fitness; they are not constructed in any other sense.

If constructivism amounts to fixation, then how do possibilities for changes in the genotype arise? The answer is one Piaget is loath to accept, namely, chance mutation. While the internal environment may determine whether genotypic mutations are fixed once they occur (i.e., retained in subsequent generations), it can do nothing to make these occur. Thus, by using genetic assimilation as a theory-constitutive metaphor, Piaget's phenocopy principle cannot provide an alternative to the chance origins of possibilities. The reason, as we have seen, is that the operation of a system according to the phenocopy principle, like its operation according to genetic assimilation, presupposes the existence of the possibilities rather than explaining them.

Piaget might object, saying that the concept of disequilibrium in his definition of phenocopy explains why changes in the genotype have certain features (1974/ 1980a, p. 72). This, however, can be true only in the following sense. Disequilib-

---

[4]The feedback properties of the phenocopy principle given it a teleological form. Following Woodfield's 1976 schema, we may summarize phenocopy to assert: *S* does *B* in order to do *F*, [meaning] *S* does *B* because *B* and *F* are good for *S*.

rium can explain why, if genotypic variations arise, they are fixed or rejected; it cannot explain how they arise in the first place. One consequence of Piaget's failure to realize this fact is that he fails to provide an alternative to Chomsky's nativist account. In Chapter 4 the failure is demonstrated, as I show how Piaget uses phenocopy to construct equilibration.

4. Piaget's Use of the Phenocopy Principle to Explain Cognitive Change

The boy's eyes flickered and widened. The ball had flown to hit the ceiling, had seemed to hit it, had paused like a bird fluttering above its nest, and had descended. "Did you see it? Did you?" shouted Paul. A bouyancy flooded through him. The beauty of the ball's subtle non-touch exalted him, so that now he bent down to the boy, eager that he too should understand. Yet though excited he felt shy. He alone possessed the knowledge and thus the power to expound it. He wished to tell, to make the boy understand. If the boy would only clap—or dance? Then, even if the boy had not understood he would have at least been strengthened by the boy's acceptance. Another's acceptance would help him to think. The idea would germinate more freely. Some closed door quivering in his skull would open and reveal a room filled with white revealing light.

But as he wished this, in that very instant when he was so near to grasping at this door-handle, he realized—it was a dull shock, relentless and slowly reverberating—that the boy and all other people would make every effort to remain indifferent to his explanation, they would try not to understand. Much as he wished to welcome the other[s] to look, they would refuse. It was up to him alone to open the door. (Sansom, pp. 18-19)

In the present chapter, as well as Chapter 5, we shall see how Piaget uses the phenocopy principle to construct his explanation of intellectual growth. Many features of his explanation arise from his use of phenocopy, and we shall see how this occurs.

The chapter is divided into three sections. In the first, I show that just as Waddington's genetic assimilation principle functions as a theory-constitutive metaphor for phenocopy, so too does phenocopy function in Piaget's account of cognitive change, which he calls reflective abstraction. We find that the relation between the organism and the environment depicted by phenocopy is also found in reflective abstraction. As a result, the relation between superficial and profound change (phenotypic and genotypic in the organic context) is also the same. Finally, the procedures whereby the change occurs are similar in the two contexts.

There are limitations in Piaget's reflective abstraction account which arise from the features imposed by his use of phenocopy. Some of these limitations are explored in Chapter 2. In the second section of this chapter, we see how use of phenocopy creates these problems. We find that the ambiguities about the role of necessity, the relation between cognitive structure and performance, and the meaning of assimilation and accommodation arise from Piaget's application of the phenocopy principle. Furthermore, the latter explains why Piaget can present no alternative to Chomsky's claims about what must be native. This final point is demonstrated in the third section.

The Phenocopy Principle and Equilibration

Piaget uses his formulation of biological phenocopy as a model for explaining cognitive change. It functions as an abstract representation of the process by which both superficial and more fundamental changes occur. For example, Piaget understands the relation between organism and environment set forth by biological phenocopy to be similar to the relation between the knower and the situation known. On the basis of this relation, he modifies his biological principle, which gives him the principle of *cognitive* phenocopy. The relation between organism/environment is not like the knower/known relation in every respect, and likewise, cognitive phenocopy does not have all the features of the biological phenocopy model. But as we will see, there are many commonalities. Piaget's equilibration account, which he labels *reflective abstraction*, is based upon use of cognitive phenocopy as a theory-constitutive metaphor.

In the following passage from *Adaptation and Intelligence*, Piaget (1974/1980a) indicates what he wishes to gain by using the phenocopy principle:

> If our interpretation of the phenocopy were to prove at all valid, it would allow us to furnish a common answer to the classic doctrines of both neo-Darwinism and behaviorism. This answer would be that the environment in fact plays a fundamental part at every level, but as something to be overcome, not as a causal agent of formation. Thus causal agencies would be sought at all levels of endogenous development within the organism and the subject. . . . On the one hand, this would simply mean that conquest of the environment, besides being considered an extension of the basic assimilatory tendency of life, usually begins with simple trials by phenotypic accommodation or by empirical knowledge. On the other hand it means also that, by virtue of the internal requirements of equilibration, these trials will subsequently give rise to more secure forms of assimilation. These in turn would be ranged in ascending degrees over every level of development, beginning with that of "genetic assimilation" (to retain Waddington's term for the consolidation of mutations by organic selection) or the copy of well-accommodated phenotypes (in other words the reconstruction, if our interpretation of the phenocopy is accepted), and ultimately attaining the various levels of cognitive assimilation, including those of scientific thought. (p. 79)

The essential aspect of the phenocopy principle that Piaget wants to utilize is the relation between the organism and the environment which it sets forth. According to the model, the environment does not *cause* the organism to have certain features. It does not, as the behaviorists and neo-Darwinians would have it, mold the organism to its specifications. Rather, it functions as an obstacle to be overcome by the organism. The organism responds to the environment by trying out phenotypic variations until one is found which permits adaptation (survival). The causal agents are the internal tendencies to develop in various ways. The trials, which occur when adaptation is not achieved, "subsequently give rise to more secure forms of assimilation," that is, result in the selection of different and more effective phenotypic characters, due to the tendency toward equilibration.

How does Piaget use the principle of phenocopy to explain changes in knowledge and the ability to solve problems? First, he constructs a model of the phenocopy process as it functions in the cognitive domain, using biological phenocopy as a theory-constitutive metaphor. Second, he uses the principle of cognitive phenocopy in like fashion to explain cognitive change. He calls his account reflective abstraction. Let us begin by seeing how biological phenocopy forms the basis for cognitive phenocopy. Piaget (1974/1980a) writes:

> In what follows, we shall use the phrase "phenocopy in the broad sense" for the replacement of an exogenous formation (phenotypic or cognitive, and due respectively to environmental action or experience of external objects) by an endogenous formation (due to the activities of the organism or the subject). . . . In the case of biological phenocopy, the endogenous formation which replaces the simple phenotypic adaptation consists of a new genotype, and thus of a form developed within the genome and capable of hereditary transmission. As far as intelligence is concerned, on the other hand, we understand by "endogenous" only those structures which are developed by means of the regulations and operations of the subject. . . . such constructs are not drawn from external objects, but arise from internal logico-mathematical activity engendered by the coordination of the individual's actions. . . . It is [likewise] understood that the term "exogenous," when applied to knowledge, will indicate that it is derived from physical experience. (pp. 80-81)

Piaget argues that the method of change depicted by the phenocopy principle occurs in both the cognitive and organic contexts. Broadly interpreted, phenocopy refers to situations in which a change at the surface or superficial level is replaced by a more fundamental change. In the organic context, the superficial, or *exogenous*, change results from action between the organism and the environment, while in the cognitive context it results from experience with external objects—which involves physical action upon the objects. The exogenous change, then, always results from some kind of interaction between the organism or knower and its external environment.

Likewise, there is endogenous or basic change in both the cognitive and organic contexts. In the organic context, an endogenous change involves a change in the genotypic structure of the organism. Piaget's principle of biological phenocopy asserts that a change at the phenotypic level is replaced by a subsequent change at the

[1]Waddington, too, speaks of exogenous and endogenous change (e.g., 1957, pp. 151-162).

genotypic level. In the cognitive context, however, an endogenous change is one that is "developed by means of the regulations and operations of the subject," or by what Piaget calls "the logico-mathematical operations of the subject." By these operations, cognitive schemata are related to one another so that new structures or patterns of schemes are formed. The endogenous change in the cognitive context is unlike the endogenous change in the organic context in that it does not affect the genotypic level of the organism. Thus, a change in cognitive structures is not a hereditary change. But like endogenous change in the organic context, the change in cognitive structures is not "drawn from external objects," that is, is not a response purely to the physical environment. On the contrary, the internal environment—the features of existing cognitive structures—determine the changes in structure that occur.

While there are differences between exogenous and endogenous change in the organic and cognitive contexts, there are also profound similarities. One of these is that all change results from trying out a response that exists in a repertoire of possibilities. This means that in the cognitive context, change results from selecting some response—some cognitive structure or possibility for reorganization of cognitive structures—from a set of options. Where the change is exogenous, an alternative cognitive structure is chosen from the repertoire, tried out, and tried again under similar circumstances if it proves successful. Where endogenous change occurs, two structures may be selected and related to one another on the basis of some higher order structure (or principle) that the system has. The result is an altered cognitive structure—one which permits behavior that is novel for the system. But endogenous change still results from choosing possibilities from a repertoire according to principles that the system has. Without principles or rules for selecting the trials, endogenous change in the cognitive structure could not occur. The significance of this point will become apparent in later discussions.

Let us now examine, in detail, how Piaget (1974/1980a) translates biological phenocopy into cognitive phenocopy:

> On the organic plane, vector $\uparrow a$, it will be remembered, represented the ascending progress of the synthetic processes of epigenetic development. Vector $\downarrow b$ was the downward progress of modifications imposed by the environment and of the resulting disequilibriums whose gradually progressive repercussions sometimes extended right back to sensitize the genes regulating epigenetic development. Vector $\uparrow c$, finally, represented ascending reequilibrations occurring in response to these ($\downarrow b$) disturbances—reequilibrations accomplished by semicontingent and semiexploratory trials involving selection (principally organic selection).
>
> We do find, in the cognitive domain, an analogous form of vector $\uparrow a$, one which is characteristic of successive levels in the hierarchy of cognitive structures. It thus extends through the gamut of cognitive development: beginning with the most elementary innate patterns (nervous and motor coordinations, spontaneous movements and reflexes), it extends through the simpler forms of habit (conditionings and the assimilation of new elements into reflex schemes), through the various circular reactions, the level of sensory-motor intelligence, semiotic and preoperational forms of representation, the development of constituent functions and the stage of concrete operations, up to, ultimately, the level of propositional operations. Throughout this development, except at its innate point of departure, there is constant interaction between the endogenous and exogenous processes involved. The endogenous processes will, however, be extended as a result of the constructive efforts of reflective abstraction; the exogenous processes simply

represent the utilization of experience. . . . In the case of vectors $\downarrow b$ and $\uparrow c$, however, we find a degree of difference (though only partial) between their operations in organic and cognitive epigenesis. Vector $\downarrow b$ expresses, in effect, both modifications (x', y', z') imposed by the environment and the disequilibriums (x'', y'', z'') which result from them. We have seen that in the course of organic epigenesis these disequilibriums may prove durable enough to have a sensitizing effect, by the gradual downward encroachment of their repercussions, upon the genes regulating the developmental processes. In cognitive epigenesis, we might therefore imagine a corresponding descent $(\downarrow b)$ from higher to elementary stages, ultimately reaching as far as the innate source of these latter stages. But in fact no such corresponding vector is found: on the contrary, in the case of cognitive epigenesis, b vectors follow a direction which is, on the average, horizontal $(\leftarrow)$ or only slightly inclined a little below, or even above, the horizontal. Here, in other words, the action of external objects or environmental events has a bearing only upon the endogenous processes . . . of the same level. There may be some repercussion upon the processes immediately below this level (hence the direction $\swarrow b$) or upon those which represent constructions from it (hence $\nwarrow b$), but without calling the whole previous construction into question again. Similarly, the compensatory responses $(\uparrow c)$, which in organic epigenesis consist of groping explorations coupled with action upon the environment, naturally show these characteristics reinforced in the case of cognitive development. The exploratory responses on the cognitive level lead to a partial reorganization of endogenous synthesis, and action upon the environment proceeds to the extent that there is complete assimilation and replacement of all exogenous characteristics by an endogenous reconstruction. . . . The orientation of these $\uparrow c$ vectors, however, remain symmetrical with that of the $\underleftarrow{b}$ vectors already discussed, that is, on average, it remains horizontal $(\underrightarrow{c})$. (pp. 94-96)

This long quotation provides another excellent example of how Piaget constructs psychological principles by using ones from other sciences. He asserts that the process of cognitive change *is* the process of phenocopy. Each of the three vectors ($\uparrow a$, $\downarrow b$, $\uparrow c$) that function to bring about change in the organic context has counterparts in the cognitive context. The counterpart of vector $\uparrow a$ in the cognitive context is innate processes of development (epigenesis). Among these processes are those which, in some contexts, Piaget calls *assimilation* and *accommodation*. At every level of cognitive operation, from elementary nervous and motor coordinations through sensori-motor, preoperational, concrete operational, and formal operational thinking (except at "the innate point of departure,"), "there is constant interaction between the endogenous and exogenous processes involved." There is constant interaction between the various processes of assimilation and accommodation and the subject's behaviors.

In the cognitive context, one can envision the following general pattern. First, the system (child) acts upon some aspect of its external environment using behavior patterns of which it is capable (assimilation). As a consequence of its action, it receives feedback or information about the success of its behavior for facilitating survival in the environment. If the action proves successful it may be repeated, should similar situations arise. If, however, the feedback indicates that the action was somehow unsuccessful, another mode of behavior must be selected from the repertoire. The mode of behavior tried out corresponds to what Piaget calls the *exogenous process*. It is exogenous in that it is repeated or terminated, depending upon its success or *fit* with the environment. In the feedback system, there is "constant interaction between endogenous and exogenous processes" because some endogenous procedure (some procedure of assimilation or accommodation) must respond to the success or failure of the exogenous process. The response may be to select an alternate cognitive structure on the basis of some higher order structure or principle. If that structure results in behavior which succeeds, the feedback will provide information about the applicability of the endogenous as well as the exogenous processes.

Again, a counterpart of $\downarrow b$ vectors can also be found in the cognitive context. Here, the $\underset{\leftarrow}{b}$ vectors convey the feedback from the environment about the consequences of the system's actions rather than the success of the phenotypic characters. The $\underset{\leftarrow}{b}$ vectors convey information about both the trials that have been made, in response to interaction with the environmental modifications (x', y', and z'), and the disequilibria (x'', y'', and z'') which result from these modifications.

More precisely, x', y', and z' are, in effect, trials of behaviors. Just as in the organic case, these trials are selected from a repertoire of possibilities; they are not imposed in the sense of imprinted upon the system. They correspond to x, y, z, features in the environment in that they permit success or survival with respect to x, y, z environmental conditions. Furthermore, the $\underset{\leftarrow}{b}$ vectors convey the feedback about the success of x', y', and z' trials on the environment. On the basis of this feedback, x', y', and z' are repeated under similar circumstances (i.e., selected).

However, the selection of some behaviors rather than others may create disequilibrium or conflict within the system of cognitive structures. A reorganization of the structures may be required under this circumstance. Again, the $\underset{\leftarrow}{b}$ vectors convey the information which creates the disequilibria within the system. The feedback tells whether trial x' has succeeded, and thus, whether disequilibrium x'', or some conflict within the hierarchy of structures, must result as a consequence of the trial.

Unlike the organic case, however, the $\underset{\leftarrow}{b}$ vectors do not affect the genotypic level of the organism. In the cognitive context, the feedback carried by $\underset{\leftarrow}{b}$ vectors affects subsequent cognitive operations at the same level in the hierarchy of cognitive structures and, perhaps, the levels immediately above or below. For example, a disequilibrium which arises as a consequence of functioning at the level of formal operations will not result in reorganization of the sensori-motor structures. This is why Piaget states that "the action of external objects or environmental events has a bearing only upon the endogenous processes . . . of the same level."

Finally, a counterpart of $\uparrow c$ vectors can be found in the cognitive domain ($\underset{\rightarrow}{c}$). Here, the "groping explorations" would refer to trials of—selecting or reorganizing —alternative cognitive structures. Thus, if the application of a given set of behaviors to a particular problem situation resulted in feedback which indicated that the problem had not been solved, then alternative cognitive structures would be selected from the repertoire of possibilities. The selection of alternatives might be made on a random basis, or it might be calculated on the basis of past successes in similar circumstances. In any event, it would constitute a groping in the sense of a trial attempt to generate successful behavior.

As is the case with $\underset{\leftarrow}{b}$ vectors, the effects of $\underset{\rightarrow}{c}$ vectors are likely to be felt at the same level of operation, not a much higher or lower one. Thus, a child who fails to solve the balance problem discussed in Chapter 2 may generate alternative solutions which eventually express some version of the proportional formula required. In specifying the correct solution, the subject will have a framework for viewing the facts of the problem which puts them in a new and different perspective (e.g., the correspondences between weight and distance established at the concrete operational level will be seen in a new relation to one another, due to the concept of proportion, which is applied to the problem). The proportion formula, however, will affect the understanding of the relations between weight and distance; it will not affect the child's understanding of what weight and distance are. The latter concepts were established at the concrete operational level. Relations between these concepts are the consequence of formal operational thinking, and the resolution of disequilibria felt at the formal level will tend to affect understanding at that level only.

In summary, then, the principle of phenocopy, as Piaget uses it, presents the process of cognitive change as a developmental feedback process. Change occurs by choosing alternative cognitive structures from the repertoire in the face of conflicts which arise between the subject and the environment. The feedback from the trials of various alternatives causes a change in both the exogenous and endogenous processes—the behaviors and the organization of cognitive structures. When an alternative is found to be successful, the relations between cognitive structures, as well as the subjects's behaviors, may be modified so that the successful trial will be generated again in similar situations. In this case, change in the endogenous processes will follow exogenous changes.

The principle of phenocopy provides Piaget with a model for explaining cognitive change, but it is not an explanation of cognitive change. Rather, his explanation describes a process which he calls "*reflective abstraction.*" Because the principle of phenocopy is again used as a theory-constitutive metaphor, one learns that there are exogenous and endogenous forms of knowledge. Piaget (1974/1980a) writes:

All new knowledge presupposes an abstraction, since, despite the reorganization it involves, new knowledge draws its elements from some preexisting reality, and thus never constitutes an absolute beginning. Two kinds of abstraction are distinguishable, then, according to their exogenous and endogenous sources; and it is interesting to compare the relationships between them with those existing between the phenotype and the genotype.

In the first place there is the kind of abstraction that we can refer to as empirical, because its information is drawn directly from external objects themselves. . . . This type of abstraction is exemplified in the case of a subject of any age, who, after weighing a solid object in his hand, is found to retain only his estimation of its weight: other possible results of the action (impressions of the object's color, dimensions, etc.) are disregarded. . . . A second form also exists, however, which is fundamental in that it includes all cases of logico-mathematical abstraction. We call it "reflecting abstraction," because it is drawn not from objects but from the coordinations of actions or of operations. This form is completely distinct in that it arises from the very activities of the subject: its source is therefore endogenous. . . . this type of abstraction involves "reflecting" in the sense of a physical or geometric projection. In other words, it always implies a "reflection" . . . in the sense of a mental reorganization; necessarily so, since reflection culminates on a higher level. . . . Thus the reflection of a set of successive displacements into a representation of them necessitates their reorganization into a system allowing simultaneous evocation of the different parts of the trajectory to be travelled. (pp. 89-90)

Here again, it is clear that Piaget is using the phenocopy principle as a metaphor to characterize the process of abstraction. He begins by arguing that all new knowledge, and hence, all change in knowledge, "presupposes an abstraction," in that new knowledge results from "draw[ing] its elements from some preexisting reality." Thus, by taking elements from what we already know—from some "preexisting reality"— we can make a "new reality." Piaget sometimes says that one *constructs* a new reality.

Let us remember, however, what *construction,* and hence *abstraction,* must mean in this case. By using the phenocopy principle as a model for his explanation of abstraction, the process of construction must be that of *selection,* in the sense of retaining some elements. While the elements may be used differently, that is, reorganized in new relation to one another, the construction is made up of elements which have been retained from a previous set of possibilities. The elements are not, somehow, manufactured anew.

This interpretation of construction is corroborated by Piaget's definition of the two kinds of abstraction—exogenous and endogenous. Exogenous abstraction, which has phenotypic change as its counterpart in the organic context, occurs where a possibility is selected on the basis of experience with the environment. Piaget notes the case in which one abstracts (or selects) from the object, after handling it, some notion of its weight, while the other properties are ignored. What is abstracted, namely, the notion of the object's weight, depends on how one acts upon the object. The fact that this is the consequence results from (a) the existence of the possibility for characterization in terms of weight, (b) the assimilation of the object to this mode of characterization, and (c) the fact that some other mode of assimilation was not tried out on this occasion. Again, the environment does not imprint the subject's idea of the object's weight; rather, the subject constructs the idea of the weight as a consequence of assimilating the object to weight schemata.

Likewise, endogenous or reflective abstraction, which has genotypic change as its counterpart in the organic context, occurs where a possible organization of cognitive structures is selected from the repertoire. In this case, the trial of one possible organization of assimilatory structures depends upon the rules one has for making selection and for interpreting the feedback about the success of trials. These rules are properties of the system, and they permit the knowledge gained from interaction with the environment to be reflected or abstracted to a higher level.

As an example, Piaget (1974/1980a, p. 90) notes the 3-year-old child who reflects an action in the form of a representation (what Piaget calls *interiorization of the action*). The reflected abstraction is, then, a construction which results from retaining certain of the subject's assimilatory structures. The choice of the structures is based upon higher-order rules which the subject has. The retention of certain structures requires that they be reorganized, again on the basis of other higher-order rules. The reorganization is what Piaget calls a *reflexion.*

What is the relation between exogenous and endogenous (or reflective) abstraction? On the one hand, endogenous abstractions of the past determine the kinds of exogenous abstractions that are possible. Piaget (1974/1980a) writes:

Empirical [exogenous] abstraction, whatever the level involved, never comes into operation by itself. In order to derive information from an object ... the use of an assimilatory apparatus is indispensable. This assimilatory apparatus is of a mathematical nature: it will involve the relating of one or more classes (or "schemes" of action at the sensory-motor level, but these schemes of action are already a kind of practical concept), correspondences, functions, identities, differences or equivalences, and so on. In short, a whole range of instruments is involved which is necessary to the very "reading" of experience itself. (p. 90)

According to Piaget, empirical abstraction is made possible by endogenous or reflected abstractions of the past. These reflected abstractions are an "assimilatory apparatus ... of mathematical nature [which relates] one or more classes." The reflected abstractions constitute higher-order rules or mathematical formulas for reorganizing the existing cognitive structures. Given the reorganizations that are carried out, exogenous abstractions with certain features will occur, for "experience will be read" as the cognitive structures dictate, and the higher-order endogenous structures dictate the organization of the cognitive structures that are applied to experience.

The reflected abstraction has an important property that the exogenous abstraction lacks. Piaget (1974/1980a) writes:

Its development [reflective abstraction] can finally attain a pure state. It alone supports and animates the immense ediface of logico-mathematical construction. Its growing power is particularly evident in the continual elaboration of new operations which bear upon those that have gone before (for example, proportions as relations of relations). (p. 92)

The reflected abstraction, unlike the exogenous one, may attain a pure state. The nature of an exogenous abstraction depends upon (a) the features of the object which is encountered in the environment and (b) the nature of the reflected abstractions that have occurred. For example, if a child has a concept of weight and is confronted with a physical object, he may abstract a concept of its weight from the object and ignore its other properties. He makes, then, an exogenous abstraction, which in some ways is constrained by the nature of the object encountered.

In the case of a reflected abstraction, however, the abstraction can attain a pure state in the sense that its features are not constrained by the environment, at least not in the same way. In this case, the abstraction is made by selecting certain existing cognitive structures, according to higher-order rules which the system has. The choice and organization of the existing structures depends entirely upon features of the higher-order rules. The rules themselves can change if some even higher higher-order rules are present in the system. Like all constructions that are made according to the phenocopy procedure some parts of existing elements are abstracted and reorganized with one another until the criteria for abstraction have been met. In this process, however, the demands of the external environment intrude only indirectly, as the criteria for change are specified by the system to ensure its coherence rather than its fitness. Thus, the system acquires a pure state in which its features enjoy independence from environmental pressures that is lacking in exogenous abstractions.[2]

One source of confusion in Piaget's discussions is that he uses the genotype as a model of and a basis for change in cognitive processes. The two topics are consistently run together:

> There remain two considerable differences between this cognitive activity (the endogenous source of progressively purified forms) and the formative processes of the genotype. . . . The development of these higher endogenous structures . . . does not require, in detail at least, programming from the level of the genome. Their development . . . depends rather upon self-regulating mechanisms, and though these are certainly of biological origin, they involve no direct recourse to heredity. The second and related difference is that reflective abstraction culminates by functioning in a pure state. A genotype, on the other hand, would be pure only if it were not embodied in any phenotype, and the "pure genotype" is thus only a theoretical abstraction. Even under laboratory conditions, a strain considered pure is always composed of individuals partially dependent upon the environment in which their epigenesis took place. (Piaget, 1974/1980a, p. 93)

When Piaget says that "the development of these higher endogenous structures . . . does not require, in detail at least, programming from the level of the genome," he is talking about the relation between endogenous cognitive processes and the genetic level of the organism. He argues that the features of the higher-order cognitive structures do not need to be programmed (in detail) in the genome, as they will result from the operation of self-regulating mechanisms. Now, the self-regulating mechanisms are "of biological origin," that is, they are biological mechanisms. The features of the cognitive structures that result from their operation are not inherited by the next generation, and thus are not specified in the genome.

When Piaget says "The second and related difference is that reflective abstraction culminates by functioning in a pure state [whereas] the 'pure genotype' is . . . only a theoretical abstraction," he is discussing the genotype as a model of endogenous cognitive operations. One difference between the genotype, taken as a model, and endogenous cognitive processes is that the latter can attain a pure state while the former cannot. Here, Piaget is not saying that the genotype *makes* endogenous cognitive processes achieve a pure state. In fact, the cause of this characteristic of the endogenous processes may be unrelated to the genotype of the organism, except in the sense that it defines the features of the biological processes that make cognitive operation possible. Cognitive processes can attain a pure state because they are hierarchical systems and are unconstrained by the demands of external reality. The genotype is always expressed by the phenotype and subject to selection pressures imposed by the environment.

Let us conclude this section by emphasizing the central conclusions Piaget reaches using the principle of phenocopy as a theory-constitutive metaphor, namely, that change in the deeper levels of understanding can follow superficial changes. Piaget (1974/1980a) writes:

> [In the cognitive case] . . . exogenous knowledge, because it lacks internal necessity and because the extent of its generality is unknown, will maintain a latent

---

[2]Of course, one must assume that the criterion of coherence in itself selected, as coherence ensures fitness. Hence, any change in the system is subject to the pressures of the external environment.

disequilibrium, especially when the observable facts involved have only been discovered or analyzed with difficulty because they were unforeseen. Subsequently, this disequilibrium will lead to a reequilibration by means of endogenous reconstruction. This process will proceed to the extent that the empirical findings can be assimilated to a deductive pattern of operations (sensitized by the disequilibrium those findings have produced). (p. 101)

As is the case in the organic context, the concept of disequilibrium provides the motive for change. Exogenous knowledge, which results from abstracting the properties of objects on the basis of cognitive schemata, may result in a conflict with other more general knowledge that the system has. This occurs, for example, when applying established procedures to a new problem yields unexpected results. The conflict between established understanding, as expressed by some endogenous structure in the system, and understanding of the present situation, creates a state of disequilibrium.

The disequilibrium can be eliminated by trying out alternative organizations of existing structures. That trial which permits satisfactory resolution of the conflict constitutes a new endogenous structure—new in the sense that its elements will have been abstracted from existing ones and recombined on the basis of higher-order rules. Given this reorganization, the conflict resulting from the empirical finding, or the exogenous knowledge which created the disequilibrium, is eliminated. Thus, the endogenous organization is modified so that the exogenous knowledge is entirely consistent with it. In this way, change in the endogenous structures will follow the exogenous change, much as change in the phenotype is followed by change in the genotype.

Piaget's Use of Phenocopy and Limitations in Equilibration

What are the consequences of the fact that Piaget uses explanatory principles as theory-constitutive metaphors? There are several points that could be made in response to this question, but I will consider only two of them. First, when Piaget says that the elements and relations depicted by one principle are the elements and relations which hold in a given situation, he provides the latter with features that may then be investigated and/or modified. For example, by saying that cognitive phenocopies occur, that they result from the operation of the three vectors of change, and so on, Piaget makes claims about the process of cognitive change that form a basis for further investigation. There is subsequent modification of both his explanations and his explanatory principles.

In the foregoing pages, we have seen many examples of theory modification that can arise from this strategy. Boyd (1979) is indeed correct when he says:

The use of theory-constitutive metaphors encourages the discovery of new features of the primary and secondary subjects [e.g., biological and cognitive process of change], and new understanding of theoretically relevant aspects of similarity, or analogy, between them. (p. 364)

At the same time, the use of such metaphors requires commitment to claims and assumptions that may prove deleterious. If the theorist does not recognize these commitments, and modify them, the scientific explanation may suffer significant limitations. In the present section I will show that this is what happens in Piaget's case. The limitations in equilibration identified in Chapter 2 are shown to arise from his use of genetic assimilation and phenocopy as theory-constitutive metaphors.

As has been shown, Piaget hopes that use of Waddington's genetic assimilation principle as a model of explanation can help him avoid an unacceptable appeal to principles of random variation and natural selection. In Chapter 2, I argue that Piaget fails to use these principles in a way alternative to Chomsky's. I shall now show that Piaget's failure results from constraints that necessarily arise if one uses the principle of genetic assimilation in the way that he does. Furthermore, other limitations identified in Chapter 2 also result from this use of the model, for example, the illegitimate claims about the necessity that holds between stages and the function of cognitive structures in the production of solutions.

Let us begin by recalling what genetic endowment contributes to the formation of cognitive structures. According to Chomsky:

> My guess would be that, as in the case of grammars, a fixed, genetically determined system of some sort narrowly constrains the forms that they can assume. I would also speculate that other cognitive structures developed by humans might profitably be analyzed along similar lines. (1980a, p. 35)

As shown in Chapter 2, Chomsky believes that the child is born with an innate, universal grammar which determines the features of the language he later acquires. Chomsky hypothesizes that the other cognitive structures that the child acquires are also defined at the genetic level. Piaget (1974/1980a) states clearly that this is not the case:

> The development of these higher endogenous structures . . . does not require, in detail at least, programming from the level of the genome. . . . [Their development] involves no direct recourse to heredity. (p. 93)

Without doubt, Piaget disagrees with Chomsky. The question is, does reflective abstraction explain the origins of cognitive structures if they are not innate? And if not, why not?

Putnam (1980, p. 300) observes that Piaget's *constructivism* may entail Chomsky's view of nativism. Having examined Piaget's model of explanation, we are now in a position to see that Putnam's conclusion is right, although his reasons for the conclusion are inadequate. Further, we can understand why Piaget cannot provide an alternative to Chomsky's claim about what must be innate.

In order to understand why Putnam is correct—why constructivism entails nativism—we have first to recall that under biological and cognitive phenocopy, constructivism is selection—selection meaning the retention of some possibilities rather than others. Clearly, Piaget preserves this aspect of phenocopy in his reflective abstraction account; thus, as he describes cognitive change, construction can result from no other process.

If construction is selection, then what must be present in the system for selection to occur? As argued in Chapter 3, Piaget's principle of biological phenocopy presupposes that the following are available: (a) the mechanisms for change provided by heredity; (b) the possibilities for change—the alternatives to which the system may revert; (c) the procedures for choosing alternatives for trial from the repertoire; and (d) criteria for determining whether equilibrium with the environment has been restored by the alternative selected.

By assuming three vectors of change corresponding to $\uparrow a, \downarrow b, \uparrow c$ in the organic context, Piaget's principle of cognitive phenocopy presupposes the existence of four corresponding elements in order for the system to function. These are (a) the hereditary mechanisms of operation, for example, assimilation and accommodation ($\uparrow a$); (b) the possibilities for change in behavior and organization of cognitive structure ($\uparrow c$); (c) the procedures for choosing alternative behaviors and/or cognitive structures from the repertoire, which include higher-order rules of organization; and (d) criteria for determining whether the state of disequilibrium has been eliminated by the trials and reorganization of cognitive structures.

Because these elements are presupposed by cognitive phenocopy, they are also presupposed by reflective abstraction, which uses cognitive phenocopy as a theory-constitutive metaphor. Before exploring the consequences of these presuppositions, I must first show that they are indeed presupposed.

Let us start with the first element—that which corresponds to the hereditary component. In his explanation of reflective abstraction, Piaget indicates that the reading of experience requires an assimilatory apparatus of some sort (1974/1980a, p. 90). The ability of the system to assimilate is clearly presupposed, although the nature of the assimilation changes over time. Likewise, the ability to accommodate is also presupposed, as this is how abstraction can occur. Reflective abstraction, like cognitive phenocopy, presupposes that the system can assimilate and accommodate. It therefore presupposes that processes which make assimilation and accommodation possible are present from the start. We will further explore this point below.

In the second place, abstraction—be it empirical or reflective (exogenous or endogenous)—cannot occur in the absence of elements which may be abstracted. Thus, in the first instance where abstraction occurs, there must be some preexisting reality out of which the elements are chosen. In the case of empirical or exogenous abstraction, the preexisting reality consists of cognitive structures, or substructures. One or another of these is abstracted and applied to objects in the environment so that some feature of the object is identified.

Take the case in which, after holding an object, the child retains only an impression of its weight, disregarding its shape, color, dimensions, and so forth. Here, the cognitive structure in question is that of weight. The weight schema is chosen from the repertoire and used to characterize the object. Thus, if the child had no structure of weight—no set of principles for organizing items in terms of weight—he could not retain a notion (i.e., construct an abstract notion) of the object's weight.

In the case of endogenous or reflecting abstraction, the reorganization of cognitive structures, or reflexion, could not occur unless the various cognitive structures existed to be reorganized. Thus, Piaget writes that "new knowledge . . . never constitutes an absolute beginning" (1974/1980a, p. 89). The new cognitive structure which results from abstracting some elements from existing ones and reorganizing them, thereby establishing a new relation between the elements, could not be made if the elements were not there to be reorganized.

Here we must underscore a conceptual point: Piaget's use of the phenocopy principle requires him to maintain that any element which is abstracted, at any stage or any point in time, must already exist as this element at the time it is abstracted. In other words, at any stage in the developmental sequence, be it reflex, sensori-motor, preoperational, and the like, the elements for a given abstraction must exist before the abstraction can be made. The mechanism of abstraction makes change by reorganizing existing elements; the elements must therefore exist before the abstraction occurs. Reflective abstraction asserts a temporal relation between the stages of development.

For example, take the case of empirical abstraction, where disequilibrium arises between the organism and the environment as feedback about the interaction is carried by the $\underset{\leftarrow}{b}$ vector. The $\underset{\leftarrow}{b}$ vector does not communicate the reason why disequilibrium has occurred, but simply indicates that upon trial of x', a state of disequilibrium has arisen. As a consequence of this communication, other cognitive structures must be identified and tried out.

Clearly, the schemata (y', z') must exist before the time of their trial; that is, they must exist before the trial begins. They cannot be tried out if they are not available in the repertoire. Likewise, in the case of reflecting or endogenous abstraction, where the disequilibrium arises within the system of cognitive structures itself, the higher-order rules for combining structures also must exist no later than the beginning of the trial reorganization. In this case, the $\underset{\leftarrow}{b}$ vector communicates that, for example, while cognitive structure y' eliminates disequilibrium between organism and environment, its application creates disequilibrium between other cognitive structures in the hierarchy. In order to resolve the disequilibrium, the structures must be reorganized with respect to one another. Piaget (1936/1952, 1937/1954, 1945/1962) argues that the reorganization—the reflexion—again proceeds by abstracting elements from the existing structures and relating them to one another in a new way. Any reorganization can only consist of those elements which were part of the previously existing structures. These elements must exist, as such, no later than the start of the trial. The implications of this conceptual point will be explored below.

The third thing which must be present for abstraction to occur is the set of procedures for choosing alternative trials. For example, in the case of empirical abstraction, these procedures constitute the rules for choosing given cognitive structures from the repertoire. Thus, where children abstract the weight of an object after holding it, their ability to do this depends upon not only the existence of the weight schema in the repertoire, but also the existence of a procedure for choosing it. This procedure specifies the conditions under which the schema may be tried out.

The fourth and final requirement for abstraction is criteria for determining whether the disequilibrium which motivated the change has been eliminated. In the case of empirical abstraction, the criteria provide the basis for determining whether conflict between the knower and the environment has been resolved. In the case of reflecting abstraction, the criteria are used to determine whether conflict between cognitive structures (and as Piaget says, structures at the same level in the hierarchy) has been ameliorated. In both instances, the criteria must exist before the assessment can be made.

Although the procedures for assimilation and accommodation, the possibilities for trial, the choice procedures, and the criteria for evaluating trials must be present for abstraction to occur, this does not mean they never change as the system operates. Indeed, children are not born with procedures for treating things in terms of weight, for example, nor are the criteria which behaviors must meet the same at the ages of 2 and 5. Change in all of the elements initially required for abstraction does occur.

However, the system of operation that is depicted by the reflective abstraction account presupposes that some means of assimilating and accommodating, some possibilities for trial, some choice procedures and some criteria for evaluating trials are present from the start. The existence of these initial elements is not explained by reflective abstraction. Furthermore, the system of operation requires that if change occurs in the initial elements, it is because the system has rules or procedures for making the changes. These higher-order rules are, then, also presupposed, not explained. The only alternative source of change is chance, as I demonstrate below.

If reflective abstraction presupposes the existence of these four elements, to what extent does Piaget present an alternative to Chomsky's claims about what must be present from the beginning? My response is that Piaget presents no significant alternative. Furthermore, his use of the phenocopy principle does not avoid recourse to random variation and natural selection principles in the way he hopes.

In order to compare Piaget's and Chomsky's positions, one must have a clear idea of what each is saying. Before turning to the comparison with Chomsky, I will therefore explain how problems in the relation between cognitive stages, the function of cognitive structure, and the ambiguity of assimilation and accommodation arise from Piaget's use of the phenocopy principle. It then becomes clear why Piaget can present no alternative to nativism.

Three Problems in Piaget's Account

The Relation of Necessity Between Cognitive Stages. Consider first the problem of the relation between cognitive stages. In Chapter 2, I argue that Piaget fails to distinguish between logical and pragmatic necessity and that he tries to derive the latter from the former. In other words, he argues that some cognitive structures must occur before others because characterization of one structure logically includes the characterization of another. However, pragmatic prerequisiteness cannot be derived from logical entailment.

Why is it that this fallacious reasoning occurs? To answer this question, I need not "psychologize," that is, try to guess Piaget's motives for formulating such arguments. Rather, my claim is that Piaget has tried to derive pragmatic from logical necessity because he uses the phenocopy principle as a theory-constitutive metaphor. My argument for the claim is as follows.

Piaget takes the principle of phenocopy and, in many instances, uses it as a metaphor to characterize features in his account of cognitive change. One finds, for example, that in his account of abstraction, there are the concept of empirical abstraction, which corresponds to the concept of exogenous change; the concept of reflecting abstraction, which corresponds to the concept of endogenous change; and a feedback characterization of the process of change, which corresponds to the feedback process of the model. The vectors of change ($\uparrow a$, $\downarrow b$, $\uparrow c$) characterized by the phenocopy principle, namely, the hereditary, the feedback, and the groping trials, are precisely the vectors of change found in the abstraction account.

By setting up correspondences with the phenocopy principle and thereby using it as a theory-constitutive metaphor, Piaget creates a developmental view (see Chapter 3) of cognitive change. Change is defined in relation to changes succeeding and following it. The relation between the stage descriptions is a logical one, meaning that the definition of each is logically inclusive of the one preceding it. As a consequence, the entire sequence of stage descriptions is logically related to the final one.

Now, the phenocopy principle is based on the use of genetic assimilation as a theory-constitutive metaphor. Waddington's use of genetic assimilation specifies two kinds of necessity which obtain between the stages of organic development. First, there is a logical relation which exists between the stage descriptions. For example, each stage in the synthesis of arginine is described in terms of all elements present in the preceding stages. The description of the final stage contains those elements present in the earlier stages, although the relations between the elements is not what it was at the earlier stages (see Chapter 3).

The second kind of necessity which obtains between the stages is that of pragmatic prerequisiteness. Each stage is the pragmatic prerequisite of the one which follows it because its elements are materially necessary for the formation of the next compound in the sequence. The chemical components of citrulline are used to create arginine. Consequently, each stage in the sequence of amino acid construction must occur in the order specified because no compound can be produced unless the one preceding has first been formed. The final stage, then, cannot be reached unless all the other stages have first been attained.

The fact that stages of organic development are pragmatically prerequisite for one another requires that they occur in time. The temporal relations exist because the elements created at each stage are materially necessary for the next compound in the sequence. The temporal relations do not exist because the stage descriptions are logically related to one another. Since the temporal relations between stages are present, there are good grounds for choosing a developmental principle to explain organic change.

In the case of cognitive change, we have a different situation. While the stages in the sequences of development which Piaget describes are logically related to one another, it is not at all clear that the elements of one stage are materially necessary for the next stage. In fact, it is not even clear what it would mean to make such a claim. For example, when Piaget argues that the ability to reverse combinations by the processes of negation and reciprocity is required for formal operational thinking, this does not mean that the 7-year-old child employs understanding to reach the stage of formal thinking. It is not clear what happens to cause children to reason formally at a certain point in time. There could be many causes, any of which might reorganize existing understanding in given ways. All one may infer is that *if* children reason at the formal level, then they should recognize that both modes of negation are possible.

The lack of material necessity between stages in the development of cognitive structures results in a serious consequence. There are few, if any, grounds for asserting temporal relations between cognitive stages. Although it is certainly the case that cognitive abilities can be described so that one logically entails another, this fact does not imply that the so-called prerequisite abilities must occur first in time. On the contrary, there are no implications for the temporal sequence of the cognitive structures, except that ones which are logically entailed by others must be present at the time the others are, and cannot occur later. Given his stage descriptions, Piaget has logical grounds for asserting that concrete operational schemata must exist in order for, and thus not later than, formal operational structures to exist; but he has no grounds for asserting that they must occur earlier in time.

In the balance problem example (Chapter 2), I showed how the description of formal operational thinking, which Piaget characterizes in terms of the I N R C Group, logically entails elements of grouping VII, which Piaget uses to describe concrete operational thinking. The concrete operational stage is logically prior to the formal operational stage, because all the elements of the former, for example, principles of reversing by negation and multiplying relations, are present in the formal stage description, which is based on the I N R C Group. Piaget claims that one cannot give formal operational performances if one has not acquired concrete operational schemata. But because there is no material relation between cognitive structures, there is no implication that one must acquire these schemata *before* one acquires those of formal reason.

One might object that what is meant by *abstraction* in Piaget's account, namely, reorganization of elements from an existing repertoire, implies that the repertoire of possibilities must exist prior to the abstraction. Indeed, in the present chapter, I have argued that Piaget's description of empirical and reflecting abstraction implies this point!

Piaget's use of the phenocopy principle, however, requires him to assert a relation of pragmatic prerequisiteness, and hence a temporal relation between structures and stages of cognitive development. The mechanism of abstraction cannot operate unless the structures from which the elements are abstracted are present. But as there is no material relation between cognitive structures, any grounds for asserting that one structure must exist before the next can possibly exist are lacking.

As a consequence, it is difficult to use a developmental principle like phenocopy to explain cognitive change—at least, to use it in the way Piaget does. If abilities change because they are developing in the way Piaget describes, then one must assert that each stage in the sequence causes the next in some material sense, and must be temporally prior. But because the structures at each stage are not the material causes of those at the subsequent stages, one is not justified in claiming that the structures are developing from one another.

Piaget appears to recognize that his use of the phenocopy principle constrains him to assert a temporal relation between stages. Since the pragmatic relations between cognitive stages are not material ones, and therefore are not temporal, the only grounds for asserting that pragmatic relations obtain are the formal characterizations of the stages. The formal characterizations provide a logical relation between the stages, and on the basis of this relation, Piaget asserts one of pragmatic necessity as well. His use of phenocopy explains why he does this: He wants to provide a developmental explanation of entities (viz., cognitive structures) when there are no grounds for asserting that they develop—at least in a material sense the way organic structures do. Clearly, it is Piaget's use of phenocopy which forces him into fallacious reasoning.

The Function of Cognitive Structures in the Solution of Problems. As argued in Chapter 2, Piaget appears to believe that cognitive structures are somehow used to generate solutions to problems. Thus, he argues that a subject's change in performance results from change in cognitive structure. When he describes the differences between solutions to the balance problem produced by subjects at the concrete operational and formal operational stages, he attributes these differences to the fact that cognitive structures of those subjects at the higher level have changed. We know they have changed because they can be characterized by the I N R C Group, while the structures of subjects at the lower level require grouping VII.

It was also shown (see Chapter 2) that the formal structures of the I N R C Group and grouping VII are logically related to one another. The characteristics of grouping VII are incorporated into the definition of the I N R C Group. Piaget uses this logical relationship to answer the question: In what ways do cognitive structures change so that performances of various sorts become possible? He responds by saying that the respects in which the formal structures differ from one another are precisely the respects in which the cognitive structures differ from one another. As was argued, the fact that children's solutions can be characterized in terms of a given formal structure, and the fact that the structure logically entails elements of the formalism used to characterize their previous solutions, are not grounds for asserting that the cognitive structures change in the same respects that the formal structures differ.

Why does Piaget argue so fallaciously? Again, his use of the phenocopy principle creates the problem. To begin with, the claim that cognitive structures somehow function in the production of solutions is a specious, if not a wholly unjustified claim. Since cognitive structures are not material entities, but rather patterns (procedures and rules) of reasoning, it is not clear how they function to make performance possible. This is not to say they play no role in the production of behavior, but simply that there are no grounds for specifying exactly what kind of role they do play. Certainly, it is hard to know what would be meant by saying that they cause behaviors, just as it is hard to know what is meant by saying that they cause the development of one another.

One might object that Piaget asserts no causal relation, but rather maintains that cognitive structures make solutions possible, meaning that if one does not have a given structure, performances with certain features are impossible. Thus, as suggested in Chapter 2, Piaget might argue that Mas cannot produce a formal operational solution to the balance problem because he does not have cognitive structures that permit viewing the solution in terms of ratio and proportion.

If this is Piaget's position, then he explains nothing about why children at the formal stage do produce the correct answers. Rather, he gives one reason why it is now possible for them to do so. Consequently, his account indicates nothing about how cognitive structures function in the production of solutions. To say that a new kind of solution is now possible because cognitive structures have changed, but to say nothing about how the change in structure functions in producing the new solution, is much like saying that a new level of understanding is possible because one has now reached a new level of understanding!

The fact is that it is difficult if not impossible to specify the role that cognitive structures play in generating answers. But such specification is needed, given Piaget's use of the phenocopy model, to explain change in resolution of cognitive tasks. If, like Waddington, Piaget wants to claim that change in behavior results from change in the structures of the organism, then he is obliged to show how this occurs.

Piaget does not specify the role that schemata play in the production of solutions. Yet he argues as though he has. He maintains that one may determine the features of children's cognitive structures by first characterizing their performances using a formal structure. The cognitive structures and the performances are thus described using the same characterization and appear to have the same features. He then insists that (a) performances change because the cognitive structures change, (b) new performances require new formalisms to characterize them because the cognitive structures have changed, and (c) the cognitive structures have changed in the ways the formal structures differ.

There are no grounds, however, for drawing any of these inferences unless cognitive structures are needed to produce solutions, just as the mouth is needed to eat and the stomach is needed to digest. If the cognitive structures are used in the production of solutions, then one might maintain that performances change because cognitive structures change, new formalisms are required when the cognitive structures have changed, and cognitive structures change in the respects depicted by the new formal structures. If schemata play no role in producing solutions, then neither change in performance nor the need for alternative formalisms to characterize performances can be attributed to change in the cognitive structure. Furthermore, one cannot draw inferences about the respects in which the schemata change over time. In short, unless schemata are used to produce solutions, Piaget cannot draw the inferences he draws!

Ambiguities in Piaget's Use of Assimilation and Accommodation. Now let us consider the concepts of assimilation and accommodation. Here again, the ambiguities noted in Chapter 2 arise from Piaget's use of phenocopy. I argue that when Piaget speaks of *assimilation,* it is not clear whether this term means comparing representations or converting one representation to the form of another. A resolution of this dilemma is implied by Piaget's use of phenocopy, however. This becomes clear if we consider its use in the organic context first.

The mode of interaction with the environment, as it is characterized by genetic assimilation or biological phenocopy, is as follows: The organism converts the environment to some form which it then can use to meet its own needs. The failure of a phenotype to use and thus change the environment to a form which can be utilized to meet the needs of the organism results in negative feedback, the consequence of which is to select an alternative phenotype from the repertoire. According to the principle of phenocopy, the failure of a given phenotypic character to generate behavior that converts the environment into usable form results in a state of dis-equilibrium, which arises from the feedback provided by $\downarrow b$ vectors, and which sets in motion the trial of alternative phenotypes carried by the $\uparrow c$ vectors.

While the organism converts aspects of the environment to forms which may be utilized, the model of explanation invokes the idea of comparison as a basis for evaluating the conversions. Consequently, the aim of interaction with the environment is to change it to a useful form, and when feedback (carried by the $\downarrow b$ vectors) is received about the effects of the action vis à vis the goal, the experienced out-come is compared with the expected outcome of the behavior. The subsequent action, for example, modification of the phenotype, is determined on the basis of this comparison.

Given Piaget's use of the phenocopy principle in the organic context, it seems reasonable to resolve the apparent ambiguity about the meaning of *cognitive assimilation* as follows. *Cognitive assimilation* refers to interaction between knower and environment that includes both converting the environment to a knowable form and comparing the results of the conversion to determine if the desired goals have been met. As noted in Chapter 2, converting some aspect of the environment need not mean a physical conversion of it. Rather, it involves converting ideas or conceptions of the environment to a form which can be evaluated, and thus judged useful or nonuseful for increasing one's understanding of the situation.

Piaget's use of the phenocopy principle also has implications for resolving the apparent ambiguity about the referent of *accommodation.* In Chapter 2, I argue that it is not clear whether *cognitive accommodation* means selecting alternative cognitive structures (rules for selecting structures, etc.) from a repertoire of possibilities, or modifying existing structures so that new structures become available in the repertoire.

Biological phenocopy offers two means for change, namely, (a) choice of alternatives from a repertoire of existing possibilities, as determined by a feedback operation, and (b) chance mutation of the genes. Since Piaget uses biological phenocopy as a theory-constitutive metaphor to explain cognitive change, cognitive change must originate from one of these two procedures. Piaget clearly opts for the feedback procedure. Hence, accommodation does not result in new structures, for the accommodated structures are not new in at least two senses. First, as has been shown, the elements of the accommodated structures already exist in the repertoire. Second, the procedures for reorganizing the elements also exist prior to the reorganization. The feedback operation cannot explain how new possibilities for cognitive structure enter the repertoire.

One might object that the selection procedure does generate new cognitive structures, and that the argument to the contrary is as trivial as saying that no book is ever new because the letters of the alphabet in which it is written have been used many times before. Even if it is the case that the elements of the new structure and the procedures for the reorganization are not new, a structure with properties that were totally lacking previously might be created. One might say it is a new structure in a real sense.

The problem with this objection is that the two cases are not analogous. Knowledge of the alphabet is insufficient for writing a book, although it is logically necessary. The elements of the cognitive structures and the choice procedures required for a given abstraction, however, are necessary and jointly sufficient for the new structure. This does not mean that the structure will arise if these elements are available, but only that the system has all the elements necessary for it. One cannot write a book, on the other hand, if all one knows about language is the letters of the alphabet. Thus, the book is new in a sense that cognitive structures produced by a feedback system of operation are not.

Clearly, there is only one means by which the principle of phenocopy can account for occurrence of a new structure, namely, chance. In the biological context, where change in structures occurs between generations of a population, so that offspring may have features unavailable to their progenitors, chance mutation provides a viable account. If, however, one wishes to use phenocopy as a theory-constitutive metaphor to explain cognitive change in individuals, then the fact that a chance account of origins is the only alternative to a feedback explanation becomes more problematic.

Chomsky, Piaget, and Nativism

Given the understanding of assimilation and accommodation which analysis of the phenocopy principle provides, we are now in a position to examine the nativist assumptions behind Piaget's account of cognitive change. I will argue that what can be learned under Piaget's account requires that certain things be present for learning to occur. These are much the same things Chomsky claims are native.

In Chapter 2, I argue that Piaget's conception of learning—a conception which he shares which Chomsky, Fodor, Putnam, Skinner, and others presupposes some claims about what must be present from the beginning. Fodor (1980a) writes:

> You tell me what you think is learned (when P is learned) and I'll tell you what must be innately available to the learning device. You say: "meanings are learned," and I'll show you that meanings are innate; . . . in effect, you tell me what sense of "concept" you have in mind when you speak of "concept learning," and I'll show you that you must take concepts *in that sense* to be innate. (p. 330)

Fodor defines learning as hypothesis formation and testing. If learning is verifying whether x is or is not a case of y, then one must have a concept of y to learn whether x is a case of it. Likewise, to verify whether x is a case of *miv*, one must have some concept of *miv* (e.g., red square). As Fodor notes, the concepts of red and square mediate the learning, that is, specify the criteria that the test must meet.

Where can learning enter in Piaget's account of cognitive change, given his use of the phenocopy principle? Let us recall that cognitive phenocopy stipulates three vectors through which change is affected, namely, (a) the mode of functioning, that is, assimilation and accommodation, which is stipulated by heredity, (b) feedback about the effects of behaviors, and (c) the trials of alternative behaviors or reorganizations of cognitive structures. Where can learning enter this procedure of operation —or can it?

If learning is acquiring information that the system did not have previously, then the phenocopy procedure does involve learning. First, the system acquires information about whether its behavior will permit equilibrium with the environment. Second, it learns information about whether additional trials or reorganization of cognitive structures are needed.

If these are the things a system learns, then learning occurs at only one point in the process, namely, that point at which the feedback is evaluated. At this juncture, the system learns, for example, that *x* does or does not meet the criteria of *miv*, that the goal for which the behavior was undertaken has or has not been met, that the selection of cognitive structure *x* was or was not satisfactory. In effect, evaluation of the feedback gives the system information about how the environment has responded to its behavior, and thus, whether that behavior (and the procedures which generate it) should be continued or eliminated.

It might appear that learning could occur elsewhere in the procedure, but this is not the case. First, it might seem the system can arrive at the trial by learning. This is not so. For example, in testing the hypothesis that *x* is *miv*—the guess that *x* is a red square—one must generate the trial in order to make the test. While some hypotheses may have been previously confirmed and the information used to formulate the guess that *x* is *miv*, the procedure for formulating the guess is not the procedure of learning. The system can only learn after its guess is generated; it cannot learn the trial. (This is not to say that no learning is required for the trial. In fact, the opposite is generally the case.)

Furthermore, as one cannot learn the trial, one cannot learn the terms in which the trial is expressed. If the hypothesis is that *x* is *miv*, then the meaning of *miv* must be known in order to formulate the hypothesis and thus permit testing and learning. Again, one might have learned, on a previous occasion, that *square* means *a*, and *red* means *b*. Therefore, one might infer (i.e., guess) that *miv* should be treated as meaning *red square* in the present case. But here the meaning of *red* and *square* must be available for the trial to be formed and tested.

Second, it might appear that the system can learn the rule or procedure by which to choose the trials. In other words, it might seem one can learn the procedure by which to select an alternative cognitive structure from the repertoire. Again, such is not the case. Once feedback is received about the success of a trial, the system must have a procedure for determining its next move. While subsequent feedback may indicate whether a given procedure for selecting alternatives was adequate, the procedure must be available and tried out before such information is acquired.

Third, it might appear that the system can learn the criteria its trials must meet. This again is not the case. The system must have some criteria which the evaluation of feedback must meet in order to carry out the evaluation in the first place. Learning in the past may have provided information for choosing and rejecting various criteria, but the possible criteria themselves are not learned.

To say that the system cannot learn its hypothesis, its selection procedures, or its criteria is not to say that these things cannot change in the system. On the contrary, change occurs in all these elements. The changes themselves, however, result

---

[3] For more discussion of the kinds of things that can be learned under a feedback system like phenocopy, see Haroutunian (1979, 1981).

from feedback operations which involve choosing alternatives according to higher-order procedures of the system, trying them out, and obtaining feedback about their consequences. All the possibilities for change in the trials, procedures, and criteria, then, must be available to be tried out. The changes, therefore, require learning, but are not themselves learned.

An example can demonstrate the truth of this point. Consider the case in which the solution to the balance problem given by 11-year-old children is no longer satisfactory. They give an answer with which they are dissatisfied because they know it does not explain all the facts. Piaget's use of phenocopy would require him to say that new criteria were now being applied by the children. How did the criteria change? Piaget would have to argue that the old criteria did not meet other, higher-order criteria, and that new ones had to be chosen from a repertoire of possibilities on the basis of a feedback procedure. The new ones must have existed in the repertoire in order to have been chosen. New criteria replace old ones through a process of trial and confirmation. Learning is required for the confirmation, but the new criteria are not learned.

By using the principle of phenocopy as a basis for his account of cognitive change, Piaget can present no alternative to Chomsky's claim about what must be native. Chomsky specifies a role for learning that is similar to the one defined by Piaget. And given what must be learned in the two cases, the same things are presupposed, and hence, not explained.

When Chomsky says that "In the case of grammars, a fixed, genetically determined system of some sort narrowly constrains the forms that they can assume ...." he means that the features of one's grammar are specified by the genome. The Universal Grammar, with which one is born, consists of linguistic constraints which are used to formulate hypotheses about grammatical constructions. The hypotheses get tested. Thus, one can learn, for example, whether the question "Is the woman here?" can be formed from the declarative "The woman is here." In order for the learning to occur, one must first generate the hypothesis, "The question is formed if and only if the word 'is' in the declarative is transposed to the beginning of the sentence." The hypothesis is then tested and one learns if, indeed, the question can be formed from the declarative by following the procedure indicated. The linguistic structure acquired depends upon the outcome of the test. Thus, the rules of syntax that one follows will depend on the consequences of verifying such hypotheses.

The linguistic constraints of the Universal Grammar provide more than hypotheses about grammatical constructions. In addition, they provide criteria that the syntactic trials must meet. They also indicate rules for selecting alternative syntactic structures from the repertoire if the trial fails to meet the criteria.[4]

The elements which are presupposed by Piaget's reflective abstraction account are very similar to the ones Chomsky claims are native. This is because in both cases,

[4] One might argue that under Chomsky's account, linguistic structures are *triggered* by stimuli in the environment. My understanding is that the linguistic constraints in the UG are triggered by the experience in the environment, and that hypotheses about the syntactic structure of sentences are formed on the basis of the constraints. This would explain why Chomsky speaks of "learning language" (e.g., 1980a, *passim*) and would mean that linguistic structures are acquired through a process that involves learning. Chomsky seems to say as much (1980c, pp. 54-55).

the linguistic/cognitive structures are acquired through a process of formulating and testing hypotheses. Hence, in both cases, learning intervenes at one point only—the point at which the system acquires information about whether the trials meet certain criteria. In order for this learning to take place and hypotheses to be confirmed or disconfirmed, the hypothesis, the terms in which it is expressed, the criteria for its evaluation, and the procedures for selecting alternative trials must be present.

Piaget denies that the specific linguistic constraints Chomsky speaks of are indicated by the genome. But by using the phenocopy principle as he does, and thus by giving learning its particular role, he provides no alternative to Chomsky's claim. In other words, Chomsky says that linguistic constraints must be innate. Indeed, their existence is presupposed, not explained, by his account of language acquisition. Piaget does not claim that cognitive/linguistic structures are innate, but his account of phenocopy presupposes their existence. Thus he offers no alternative to Chomsky's claim.

One might argue that although Piaget and Chomsky presuppose some of the same elements to explain the acquisition of linguistic/cognitive structures, Piaget's account differs: Unlike Chomsky, he does not conclude that because the account presupposes the existence of these elements they must be innate. Surely this is a major difference between the two positions.

Yes, there is a difference, not only in the claims about what must be native, but also in the nature of the research that has ensued. Chomsky tries to produce empirical evidence which supports his contention that the Universal Grammar is specified by the genome; Piaget tries to provide empirical evidence that shows improvements in cognitive structures at each stage in the sequence.[5]

The fact is, however, that although Piaget and Chomsky make different claims about what is innate, Piaget's account of the origin and construction of cognitive structures provides no alternative to Chomsky's nativist claim. The reason, as I have shown, is that his account is based upon a particular use of the phenocopy principle —a use that presupposes, but does not explain, the existence of the very elements (the repertoire which provides trials, the choice procedures, the criteria of evaluation) that Chomsky's account presupposes. While Piaget resists Chomsky's inference that since these elements are presupposed by the account, they must be specified by the genome, he nonetheless offers no alternative account of their origins.

But, the objection continues, Piaget's constructivist account does offer an alternative. It shows that one need not suppose that linguistic structures are specified by the genome, since reflective abstraction explains how they arise from much simpler structures, that is, from rudimentary biological structures. Thus only the latter need be specified by the genes.

The aim of the foregoing chapters has been to demonstrate that in spite of Piaget's extensive research and numerous attempts to clarify his equilibration account, he does not offer an alternative to Chomsky's claim about what must be native. The reason is not that empirical research proves Chomsky right. Rather, the reason is that Piaget's account—his reflective abstraction explanation, for example —presupposes the very elements Chomsky claims are innate. The presupposition

---

[5] In Chapter 6, I consider the question of how much evidence the empirical research actually provides for these claims.

occurs because Piaget uses phenocopy as his principle of explanation, and uses it as a theory-constitutive metaphor. Since phenocopy offers only two means of change, namely, chance variation and a developmental feedback procedure of operation, use of it as a theory-constitutive metaphor leaves Piaget with a choice between these two means. Because he rejects chance variation, his equilibration story is based upon the feedback procedure of change. I have shown how this choice leaves him with the same presuppositions Chomsky makes, and thus with no alternative account.

One may wonder why Chomsky, unlike Piaget, does not despair that his nativist claims leave too much unexplained. The reason, I think, is that Chomsky wants to give a phylogenetic account of language acquisition, not an ontogenetic one. Chomsky's program, in other words, is an evolutionary program. Thus, the role of chance as it is portrayed by neo-Darwinism, poses no problem for Chomsky. He is content to claim that changes in linguistic structures have their origins in chance mutation at the genetic level. The goal of his explanation, then, is to show how these changes spread across the population so that one can understand why, over generations, language within a community comes to have new features.

Piaget, on the other hand, wants above all to explain how change in cognitive performance occurs in individuals. His is *not* an evolutionary program and the role of chance as specified by neo-Darwinism is unsatisfactory. If the change in possibilities for cognitive structures can only occur between generations, then all possibilities are specified at the beginning of each generation. Piaget tries to modify the other means of change offered by phenocopy, namely, the feedback procedure, so as to have a principle that can explain the origin of new possibilities without recourse to chance variation. As we have seen, this attempt fails.

All this is not to say that Piaget's account is not illuminating or that he has failed to discover a great deal about patterns of human reasoning. Indeed, there is no question that the contrary is the case. Nevertheless, it is important to be clear about what his equilibration account explains and what it presupposes and thus *does not* explain. Given our analysis of phenocopy, we are now in a position to identify a number of other limitations in Piaget's account of cognitive change and to show how these arise.

5. Additional Limitations in the Equilibration Account

"But do you really understand? I mean do you see that . . . "

The clerk interrupted, nodding more vigorously. "A most excellent throw, sir. Indeed, indeed—I'd like to take the liberty of offering my congratulations." He wagged his head and now smiled like an old man over some past and always pleasing reminiscence.

Paul frowned, and felt a premonition of monotony begin to sap the exuberence from him. He said slowly, in doubt: "Then have you nothing to say? No questions? Nothing to add?"

The clerk answered quickly: "Well, sir—I did think—shouldn't we perhaps send this young fellow off to play downstairs?" He took a step forward, in the same breath putting his suggestion into practice, as if it had been agreed upon instantly, adding: "Come on, young fellow, take that ball of yours off downstairs." (Sansom, pp. 20-21)

In Chapters 2-4, I argue that Piaget's use of the phenocopy priniciple does not permit him to provide an alternative to nativism. The question is: How significant are the limitations which arise from using phenocopy, and more generally, using equilibrium as a theory-constitutive metaphor to explain cognitive change? This is tantamount to asking: Should theorists stop trying to account for growth in reasoning ability using a developmental feedback procedure? I urge no resolution to the question. But I will reflect on the matter by reviewing some additional limitations that arise from Piaget's application of the phenocopy principle.

The chapter is divided into five sections. In the first section, I specify the criteria that Piaget's account of cognitive change must meet, given his use of phenocopy. After reviewing suggestions by Peters (1972, 1974) and Hamlyn (1975), I argue that in order for Piaget's account to be successful, it must meet the developmental criteria Hamlyn proposes. In the second and third sections, I evaluate the roles of decentration and contradiction in reflective abstraction. Again, I consider the contributions of these concepts with respect to the developmental criteria. In the fourth section, I explore the features of the interaction between the organism and the environment under phenocopy. In the final section of the chapter, I summarize the problems that have been discussed in Chapters 2-5.

Criteria of Developmental Explanations

As has been shown, Piaget explains cognitive change as the consequence of *cognitive development*. That he does so is a direct consequence of using the phenocopy principle as a theory-constitutive metaphor. Does equilibration fulfill the criteria that an account of development must meet? Many of the conceptual criticisms leveled at Piaget challenge this possibility. Before we can evaluate the adequacy of equilibration as a developmental explanation, we must be clear about the criteria it must meet. Then we may proceed to ask: Does Piaget's account fail to meet the criteria in the ways the critics charge? If so, can his account be changed to eliminate the problems, or does his use of phenocopy render such modification impossible?

The first task, then, is to consider the criteria Piaget's developmental explanation must satisfy. Peters (1972, 1974) argues that if the ability to reason and solve problems is said to develop, then the account of its development must explain three things:

> Ernest Nagel [1957] gives . . . criteria for use of "development" which are taken from a range of cases in which what is potential becomes actual—e.g. cases such as the development of a photograph or oak tree. He therefore suggests the criteria of 1. some pre-existing structure, 2. processes which either "unfold" or are more actively assisted by outside agencies and which are irreversible, and 3. some end-state which is the culmination of the process. . . . There is little difficulty using these tight criteria when applying the concept to human beings at the physical level. . . . The question is, however, whether this concept can be applied with these criteria at the mental level. (1972, p. 502)

Thus, Peters agrees with Nagel that, at least in the physiological context, x is said to develop when three conditions obtain. The first is that x is some structure which exists before its development begins. Second, its development is the result of processes which unfold, so that the structure is seen to mature. This maturation is assisted by environmental conditions, such as food, water, and air, which permit the potential for change to actualize itself. Once the change has occurred, the processes which caused it cannot undo or reverse it. Finally, the development of the structure is seen to reach an end-state which is clearly definable. This end-state is the culmination of the process—the goal toward which the process of change has been moving.

Peters argues that each of Nagel's criteria must be redefined in order to fit the case of mental development. With regard to the first criterion—that a case of development of x involves change in a preexistent structure—Peters (1972, p. 502) makes two fundamental points, namely, that there are *mental* structures, but they do not preexist.

Peters defines a mental structure as a *mode of consciousness*, an awareness of the world that results from organizing it according to certain rules. Understanding involves organizing the world in some way. To understand *x* as a cake, for example, is to classify it as such, and in order to make such a classification, *x* must seem to conform to certain criteria specified by the rule. The rule for classifying *x*, and for organizing experience, constitutes the mental structure. As such it relates to other mental structures. If we want *x*, it means we impose a rule which relates *x* to some end we desire. In wanting something, we impose a means-end structure on the environment.

Mental structures are subject to change, but they do not preexist (Peters, 1972, p. 503). When Peters says that mental structures do not preexist, he seems to mean that they are neither specified by the genome nor present at the time the organism first begins to develop (e.g., conception). This would explain why he says structures can preexist in biology and botany, for these structures meet both these conditions. To argue that mental structures preexist would seem to mean that there is innate knowledge—an innate set of means-ends relations that are specified by the genes and present from the start. Peters is reluctant to argue such a claim and instead mantains that mental structures do not preexist.

We must assume, however, that mental structures do preexist in the sense that they appear no later than the point at which they begin to develop. Therefore, they precede development. Even in the case of industrial development, where a structure is set up out of diverse elements and subsequently modified, it is clear the changes in it could not occur unless the structures existed before the modification began. It is not clear that Peters recognizes this point, however.

Nagel's second criterion is that processes of development unfold or mature. Peters, on the other hand, maintains that the development of mental structures is not the consequence of unfolding processes—or at least, not these alone—because interaction with the social environment in part determines the content of one's mental structures. Therefore, the content of mental structures is not simply the consequence of some innate structures unfolding. If the sequence of cognitive structures is invariant, it cannot be because one change is somehow used and is pragmatically prerequisite for constructing the next.

Nagel's third criterion of development is that the process tends toward a clearly definable end-state. What is the end-state toward which cognitive development moves—or is there one? Peters (1972, p. 511) argues that some desirable end-states, such as autonomy, critical thinking, and creativity, could be seen as "natural" ends rather than normative in that their development is not imposed by society and required of all human beings. Rather, these ends are the perfection of natural tendencies in the organism. Since not all persons must achieve this state of perfection, the achievement in some evokes admiration by others, rather than approval.

In summary, all three criteria of development set forth by Nagel must be reinterpreted to make sense in the cognitive context, says Peters. First, in the cognitive domain, one cannot hold that an adequate account of development will explain how one structure develops out of a preexisting structure because there is no such preexisting structure. Second, while the processes of cognitive development are occurring in a fixed sequence, it is not because they unfold. In the terms of the Feldman and Toulmin distinction, no stage of cognitive development is the universal means for bringing about the next (instrumental necessity), the way watering a plant brings about the growth of a plant. Third, the goals of cognitive development may be viewed as natural only in cases where they embody the perfection of natural tendencies. Thus, critical thinking may be said to develop while specific moral values may not.

In spite of the fact that all of Nagel's criteria must be redefined to fit the cognitive context, Peters still maintains that cognitive abilities develop. Hamlyn (1975), however, squarely rejects the possibility of redefining Nagel's criteria as Peters proposes. Hamlyn writes:

> It is the interrelationship between pre-existing conditions, necessary sequence and end-states within a pattern which we see as natural to a given kind of thing that is important for an understanding of the notion of development. Within this pattern it is quite feasible for us to view the fact that something is a necessary condition for some later state as a sufficient condition of its occurrence, and this enables us to bring the explanation of events which constitute stages of a developmental process under the general heading of functional or teleological explanation. (pp. 33-34)

If x is said to develop, then there must be a functional relation between the initial (preexisting) state of x, the sequence of stages, and the end-state. This means that the achievement of the end-state must be seen to be the natural function of the stages. If the stages do have this natural, functional relation to the end-state, then each is, in the terms given by Feldman and Toulmin, instrumentally necessary for the occurrence of the next stage and the end-state. The fact that each stage is necessary for the end is sufficient condition for its occurrence. Unlike Peters, Hamlyn claims that functional necessity must obtain between the stages in the sequence and the end-state. The acorn, then, can be seen as a stage in the development of an oak tree, and can in fact be said to develop because it has a functional connection to the mature state. Its function is to make possible the oak tree. This function is the rationale for the acorn's existence. Given the fulfillment of certain environmental conditions (soil, water, temperature, etc.), the natural or essential function of the acorn is to become an oak tree (Hamlyn, 1975, p. 33).[1]

In Hamlyn's account, the crucial factor in determining whether x is a case of development is "the interrelationship between pre-existing conditions, necessary sequence and end-states within a pattern which we see as natural to a given kind of thing" (p. 33). The end of the sequence of development can be described in such a way that certain elements are functionally required for its occurrence. The entire sequence can be described so as to indicate the function of each stage. When this is done, it is clear how the initial event is transformed into the final one and how the potential for the transformation was, in some clearly specifiable way, present at the start of the developmental sequence.

---

[1] In making this comment, Hamlyn explicitly refers to Charles Taylor, *The Explanation of Behavior*, (1964). His consideration of Taylor's position is further elaborated in his review of *The Explanation of Behavior* (1967).

Let us note that while there are differences, there are also criteria upon which Hamlyn and Peters agree. In the first place, Hamlyn acknowledges that in any case of development, there is something which develops. Hamlyn puts it by saying that there must be a "principle of identity for the series of events" (Hamlyn, 1975, p. 31). The "principle of identity" may be a mathematical rule, a person, or even general understanding.[2] Second, Hamlyn agrees with Peters that development must proceed toward a clearly definable end-state. In other words, an adequate account of development must show how an initial condition is changed so that a clearly described final point is reached. Third, Hamlyn would agree with Peters that the process of development is cumulative and unidirectional. When Hamlyn says that the "interrelationship between pre-existing conditions, necessary sequence and end-states within a pattern" is most important, this is because the process of development must be shown to move toward the goal.

These points of similarity between Hamlyn and Peters should not blind us to the significant differences in the criteria for development that each sets forth, however. The first point of difference is that according to Hamlyn, in any case of development, there must be some preexistent state or structure. An adequate account of the development of this state will explain how its features are transformed so that the end-state in question is reached. By preexistent, Hamlyn does not necessarily mean specified by the genome, although this may be the case. But since the principle of identity must exist before the development begins, some state which is transformed by that principle of identity must also preexist. Hamlyn clearly recognizes this point, and argues for the necessity of a preexistent structure.

Second, Hamlyn, unlike Peters, maintains that in any case of development, the relation between the stages cannot be purely logical; that is, the necessary sequence of stages cannot be necessary simply because the definition of each stage is included in that of the next. Rather, each state is instrumentally necessary, in the Feldman and Toulmin sense, for the subsequent ones and for the end. There is, then, a functional relation between the initial state, the stages, and the end, as the function of the stages is to bring about the end, given the initial states. An adequate explanation of development will explain how the stages function.

Since in any case of development there must be a preexistent structure, and the relation of that structure to its stages of development is a functional one, Hamlyn would also maintain that development occurs by the unfolding of inner potential. Hence, we have a third difference between Hamlyn and Peters, who argues that mental development does not result from the mere unfolding of such potential.

The issue is not whether Hamlyn or Peters is correct about the criteria that an account of development must meet. The issue is rather: Which criteria must be met by Piaget's account of cognitive change? My claim is that Piaget's explanation of development must meet the functional criteria set forth by Hamlyn. That is, it must explain how some initial state naturally unfolds so that the end-state identified by Piaget is acheived. It must also explain why each stage in the sequence has as its natural function the realization of the next state and ultimately the final goal. Piaget's account must meet the functional criteria because he uses the phenocopy

[2] Specific categories for understanding—the understanding that is expressed by specific concepts—do *not* develop, however. See Hamlyn (1975, p. 38).

prinicple as a theory-constitutive metaphor. By using the principle as he does, he sets up certain criteria that reflective abstraction must satisfy, including the functional criteria that Hamlyn identifies.

To see why this is the case, recall that Piaget uses phenocopy so that each feature of reflective abstraction has a corresponding feature in the phenocopy principle. The concept of empirical abstraction corresponds to the concept of exogenous change; the concept of reflecting abstraction corresponds to the concept of endogenous change; the feedback characterization of change is present in both cases; the three vectors of change in reflective abstraction (heredity, feedback, and groping trials) are precisely the vectors of change presented by the phenocopy principle; and the role that each vector has in the process is also similar. The principle of phenocopy asserts that the process of development occurs when the system generates and evaluates trials from a repertoire of possibilities according to certain procedures that it has. What must be explained, then, is how the feedback operations of the developmental processes bring about the expression of given phenotypic/cognitive possibilities.

Because Piaget uses phenocopy as a theory-constitutive metaphor, reflective abstraction asserts a "preexisting reality"—a preexisting repertoire of structures. It maintains that change in these structures occurs by generating and evaluating trials according to the system's procedures. What must be explained is how the feedback brings about the end-state—the formal operational structures—given the initial ones.

The phenocopy principle, if used as a theory-constitutive metaphor to construct an explanation, requires that the explanation meet the functional criteria Hamlyn describes. The explanation should make clear why certain changes are made in the structures which preexist in the repertoire—why the stages of development unfold from one another in the way they do. Further, it should explain why each stage is necessary for the subsequent ones and for the end-state. Therefore, the explanation should make clear why each stage has, as its natural function, the achievement of the goal.

The demand to meet the functional criteria comes from the features of phenocopy and from the way Piaget uses it to explain cognitive change in individuals. Reflective abstraction, which is based upon the phenocopy principle, holds that the change which occurs in cognitive performance results from change in the cognitive structures of the organism. Furthermore, there is a goal of cognitive development, namely, the ability to solve certain logico-mathematical problems, that is achieved by transforming the initial structures into ones which permit logico-mathematical reasoning. The transformation occurs through a feedback process that involves $\uparrow a$, $\underleftarrow{b}$, and $\underrightarrow{c}$ vectors of change. Clearly, reflective abstraction seeks to explain change in cognitive performance by asserting that feedback transforms the initial structure into the end-state. By invoking this procedure of change, Piaget commits the reflective abstraction account to meeting the functional criteria Hamlyn identifies.

There are, then, several things that reflective abstraction must make clear. First, it must specify what the initial structures are, that is, what features the initial possibilities in the repertoire have. Second, it must make clear why feedback ($\underleftarrow{b}$) about the consequences of trying out these initial structures results in one kind of change (exogenous or endogenous) rather than another. This involves specifying the procedures for choosing and organizing possibilities from the repertoire and explaining where the criteria that the change must meet come from. Third, it must describe what the criteria are. If reflective abstraction can meet Hamlyn's functional criteria, then it will show why each transformation in structure follows from the previous ones, and has as its natural function the achievement of formal operational reasoning.

Decentration

Piaget appears to be well aware that reflective abstraction needs to meet functional criteria. Indeed, there are a number of carefully elaborated concepts, or subaccounts, in reflective abstraction which aim to explain how each stage in the sequence unfolds from the previous one and why each stage has as its natural function the realization of the subsequent stage and the final goal. One of these subaccounts is decentration. To what extent does decentration help reflective abstraction meet the functional criteria?

First, let us review the concept of decentration. Piaget maintains that in order for children's solutions to become progressively more correct, their views of situations must become decentered. In effect, Piaget (1970/1972) argues that the process of decentration permits the child to move from one stage of performance to the next. He writes:

> The young infant relates everything to his body, as if it were the centre of the universe—but a centre that is unaware of itself. In other words, primitive action exhibits both a complete indifferentiation between the subjective and the objective, and a fundamental centring which, however, is basically unconscious because connected with this lack of differentiation. . . . To understand the lack of differentiation and the centring of primitive actions, we need to take account of the fact that actions are not yet co-ordinated together; each constitutes a small isolable whole which directly relates the body itself to the object, as, for example, in sucking, looking, grasping, etc. From this there follows a lack of differentiation, for the subject only affirms himself at a later stage by freely co-ordinating his actions, and the object will only be constituted as it complies with or resists the co-ordinations of movements or of positions in a coherent system. (p. 21)

According to Piaget, neonates do not distinguish between their bodies and items external to them. The primitive actions or reflex behaviors of which they are capable permit relations with things. The nipple may be sucked; the finger may be grasped. However, the infant centers upon the primitive actions, meaning that the nipple and the finger are part of their sucking and grasping behaviors. No distinction is made between the behavior and its object.

Once primitive actions become coordinated, for example, once sucking becomes linked with extending and grasping in an action pattern, the effects on the items change. As a result, items will become *seen as* suckable, graspable, and so on, depending on the effects of various treatments. The rattle, for example, will be seen as suckable and graspable but not edible, given the consequences of action upon it. As actions are coordinated, items are treated in various ways and gradually become differentiated from the actions.

The process of coordinating actions involves decentration. It requires that the infant cease to be fixated upon one view of the item. How does decentration occur? As the rattle is shaken, rather than sucked or grasped, the effects fixate the children's attention on a different aspect of the toy, and an additional feature is gradually attributed to it. In effect, new ways of viewing the item result from treating it in different ways (Piaget, 1970/1972, p. 22).

The process of decentration—of coordinating actions and thereby changing one's view of objects—is a feedback process of the second sort described in Chapter 3 and is based on use of phenocopy as a theory-constitutive metaphor. The infant, portrayed as such a feedback system, acts on items using available reflex behaviors (e.g., sucking and grasping) and acquires feedback about the success of behaviors. Primitive actions are coordinated with one another on a random or semirandom trial basis when the criteria for coordinating behaviors have not been reached. If the trials modify the item in such a way that the organism's needs are met, they will be seen as having features (effects) that result from that treatment (Piaget, 1970/1972, pp. 24-25, 35-36).

According to Piaget, the views of an item established through the decentration procedure will be consistent with one another. The features which are attributed to things (and eventually to ideas) as the result of various actions will be viewed in relation to one another. Further, the relations will be irreversible, or fixed, where things are perceived. For example, when a rattle becomes seen as shakable, graspable, and suckable, it is seen as an object with certain characteristics whose interrelation is fixed and irreversible.

To what extent does the concept of decentration help to explain why each transformation in structure follows from the previous one and has as its natural function the achievement of the goal? Let us begin by recognizing what this question means in the present context. The process of decentering is the process of ceasing to be fixed on one aspect of an object to the exclusion of the others so that an objective view of the item is possible. Infants, for example, have decentered when they can view the various aspects of the rattle in relation to one another, but also when their view of it is not distorted by a subjective, idiosyncratic perspective. If decentration is to answer the above questions and help reflective abstraction satisfy the functional criteria, then it must explain why the understanding at each stage becomes progressively more objective. In what follows, I shall explain more about what objectivity of thought involves.

An objective view (or thought or statement) is not necessarily a true view. It is a view in which subjective performances or prejudices have not been allowed to influence the recognition of conditions which normally obtain. Concern for objectivity is therefore a concern for "normal conditions of the attainment of truth, not with the attainment of truth as such" (Hamlyn, 1972, p. 247).[3]

[3] I have selected Hamlyn's conception of objectivity as a basis for the ensuing discussion for the following reasons. First, it falls within the Kantian tradition which undergirds Piaget's conception of mind and thus his account of how the mind functions and changes. Second, it draws out some implications of Kant's concept of mind and clarifies commitments which those, like Piaget, who accept a Kantian view of the mind must make. Therefore, it provides a basis for understanding why, given Piaget's use of phenocopy, decentration fails to help reflective abstraction meet the functional criteria. A brief explanation of these points is needed.

If one argues that objective views as defined above are possible, then one may assume that there is something which we call reality and that it is possible to be more or less correct about its description. Thus, one may make lawlike or objective statements about the relations between certain conditions and events. One may say:

There is objectivity in this sphere, there are criteria of truth, and it is not the case that it is all a matter of convention (as for example instrumentalists like Duhem have supposed). What this in turn may suggest is that there is, so to speak, a realm of scientific fact, the ascertainment of which is our aim. (Hamlyn, Note 2, pp. 27-28)

The "realm of scientific fact," needs careful definition. Hamlyn (1970) states that a fact is not necessarily something concrete in the world, although it may be. Objectivity requires something

that is involved in one particular word-world relationship. . . . [Facts] relate to what is in the world. But they do not constitute a state of affairs that is in any sense concrete or even empirical. (p. 139)

As noted in Chapters 2 and 6, Piaget like Kant argues that experience of the world is not direct but results from applying one's schemata to items encountered and interpreting these according to criteria that one has (assimilation). The nature of one's experience depends on the features of the schemata that are used to assimilate reality. Both Kant and Piaget have the following problem: If the nature of experience depends upon the features of one's schemata, then how can there be common experience? And if there is no common experience, then how can there be a correct understanding of the world? (See Broughton, 1981b, p. 266.) Clearly, we interact with one another under the assumption that some understandings are correct while others are not. What makes correct understanding possible?

As Strawson (1966) notes:

A necessary condition, then, of admitting spatially independent worlds of experience is that the members of a cultural community should be able to claim a shared membership [in a world which is] supposed to adhere to its own and unsympathetically exclusive standard of objectivity. (p. 152)

Where does the "unsympathetically exclusive standard of objectivity" come from? For Kant, it is connected to the unified conception provided by the categories of pure intuitions of space and time. Wittgenstein's answer, however, contributes additional elements to the Kantian perspective. Again, as Strawson notes:

We should remember that all Kant's treatment of objectivity is managed under considerable limitation, almost, it might be said, a handicap. He nowhere depends upon, or even refers to, the factor on which Wittgenstein, for example, insists so strongly: the *social* character of our concepts, the links between thought and speech, speech and communication, communication and social communities. (p. 151)

Dummett (1978) agrees that Wittgenstein is right to stress that the social character of thought makes objectivity and hence correct understanding possible (p. 424). He applauds Quine (1961) for guiding philosophers back to a theory of meaning that reflects Wittgenstein's insight (Dummett, p. 412), and criticizes Frege (1949) and Kripke (1972) for failing to recognize its importance (Dummett, pp. 429-430).

Hamlyn, in his discussion of objectivity (e.g., 1970, 1972, 1978), preserves and elaborates Wittgenstein's insight. He explains how the social aspect of concepts, that is, their intersubjectivity, makes objectivity of understanding possible. Because his analysis extends the Kantian perspective, it permits us to understand why Piaget, who holds the Kantian view, wants to explain objective understanding and why he fails to do so.

For example, $2 + 2 = 4$ is a fact, that is, the statement $2 + 2 = 4$ refers to something in a world. It does not refer to a physical object. Rather, it refers to a nonmaterial state of affairs which necessarily exists if the base 10 number system is assumed and if the quantities of 2 and 2 are added together under that system. The notion of objectivity assumes only that there are *facts*—that material and nonmaterial states of affairs which can be picked out by statements necessarily exist in the sense indicated, given the occurrence of certain normal conditions. In short, there must be a world which exists independently of ourselves if there is to be objective understanding, but this world is not necessarily one of physical objects.

While the physical objects are optional in Hamlyn's picture, the existence of an intersubjective system of concepts is not. He writes:

> Thus there would be no room for objectivity if there were not intersubjectivity. . . .
> What we can state about the world depends on this agreed, intersubjective system of concepts. These bring with them criteria of truth, so that there must be points of agreement concerning the applicability of these criteria of truth. Hence there must also be points of agreement on what is to count as fact and what is not. That there must be facts, therefore, that make certain statements true is a precondition of any view about the world. (1970, pp. 140-141)

The notion of intersubjective agreement is one which Hamlyn takes from Wittgenstein. There is intersubjective agreement when people share a set of concepts with one another. They can be said to share a set of concepts when (a) they understand and agree upon certain criteria of truth, (b) they agree upon the conditions under which the criteria of truth apply, and (c) they agree on the results of applying these criteria. Facts can only be picked out and described given the set of shared concepts. Further, the view of these facts, and hence what is taken to be the objective view of these facts, will be defined by the shared concepts.

An intersubjective set of concepts permits one to make objective statements. An objective statement is one which takes the form "If a, b, and c conditions obtain, then x will occur," and one in which a, b, c, and x are expressed by shared concepts —concepts about which there is intersubjective agreement. The statement is one with which others could agree, provided they shared the concepts of a, b, c, and x, and provided they agreed upon the relation between a, b, c, and x asserted by the statement. The statement would be true, however, only if it picked out a fact—only if something referred to as x did occur when a, b, and c did obtain. The objective statement specifies the conditions under which truth holds. The fact that a statement is objective is not sufficient to make it true, however.

I have thus far distinguished between objectivity—a concern for the conditions under which a state of affairs usually holds—and objective statements—statements consisting of a shared set of concepts that assert relations with which others may agree. Those statements which we say constitute our body of knowledge are objective in the sense Hamlyn indicates. They are also ones with which many have, in fact, agreed.

For us to say that the statement "If a, b, and c obtain, then x will occur" is knowledge, it must be the case that the relation expressed by the statement is one to which people can agree, which presupposes that they agree on the meaning of the concepts in terms of which the relation is stated and accept the relation between the concepts that the principle sets forth. In addition, some must also agree that the statement correctly picks out "facts," that is, that the concepts do indeed refer to things in some world, and that the relation the statement sets forth between these things appears to obtain in that world. What is not assumed is that the statement is indeed true—that things are as it says they are. Rather, it must be the case that given the means of investigation available, some appropriately designated persons agree that the statement picks out events and relations which appear to obtain in some world.

There seems little doubt that Piaget is trying to explain how children become capable of objectivity and of making objective statements. Notice I did not say true statements.[4] Piaget is concerned with explaining how children acquire our body of knowledge, and the statements which make up that body of knowledge are taken to be true but may or may not be true. They are, however, objective. The understanding that the child has at the formal operational stage is objective. Given this fact, the task for Piaget is to explain why the thinking at each stage becomes more objective and how objective thought finally becomes possible.

Does decentration help Piaget meet his goal? Hamlyn argues that it does not. In Hamlyn's view (1978), decentration provides the motivation for change by saying that sense experience requires alteration in perceptual and cognitive structures. Sense experience is distorting, and perceptual structures must change in order to eliminate the distorted perceptions. When one decenters, one ceases to "fixate upon what is immediately presented . . . in perception" (p. 53).

In the case of perceptual decentration (there are other types of decentration as well), the problem Hamlyn sees is this. In order to decenter, the perceptual structures must somehow be modified so that sensation does not result in distorted perception. The elimination of distortion requires the structures to accommodate, as Piaget puts it. How does one recognize that accommodation should cease and that the perception permitted is objective rather than subjective and distorted? Since sense experience is distorting, sense experience cannot provide the criteria. Hamlyn argues that under the decentration account, the subject cannot acquire criteria for judging whether perception (and, by implication, all understanding) is objective (Hamlyn, 1978, p. 56). One cannot judge, then, whether one's accommodation of structures permits an objective understanding.

The objection Hamlyn raises is crucial. If he is right, then decentration has failed to help explain things which must be accounted for if decentration is to help meet the functional criteria. If it does not explain how one can determine that one's criteria for evaluating trials permit objective understanding, then it fails to meet criterion 2 discussed previously, that is, it fails to explain why modification in cognitive structure will terminate only when the final stage (i.e., objective understanding) is reached.

My view is that Hamlyn is right. Decentration does not help Piaget meet the functional criteria. It does not explain why the understanding at each stage of cog-

---

[4] Broughton (1981b) discusses the necessity for Piaget to explain objectivity.

nitive development becomes more objective and why subjects at the formal operational stage are capable of objectivity. Further, decentration fails because it is based upon use of the phenocopy principle as a theory-constitutive metaphor. It is Piaget's use of phenocopy which prevents decentration from explaining how subjects become capable of judging whether their understanding is objective or not. My argument is as follows.

I have shown that the process of decentration is a developmental feedback process which has the features of phenocopy's feedback procedure. As noted in Chapter 4, learning has a specific role in this process. It provides information about whether particular rules meet certain specified criteria. Such learning results from treating some particular object, say x, as a case of y. The system learns not only whether treating x as y meets the criteria, but also whether selection and metaselection rules involved in the trial have succeeded. Where the trial fails, alternate procedures are selected from the system's repertoire.

Given the role of learning under phenocopy, behavior patterns that are established must satisfy criteria for assessment which the system has. The criteria are used to determine whether the trials meet the goals for which they are executed, and consequently whether the accommodation of the cognitive structures has been adequate. Should the criteria for evaluating trials and accommodations change, it is only because the system has procedures for changing them; it is not because new criteria are somehow introduced by an agent external to the system.

Since there is no means by which criteria for assessing results can be introduced by an agent external to the system, there can be no principled account of how agreement between persons can be reached. This means that the distinction between right and wrong cannot even be introduced. The system simply has no basis for determining whether meeting its criteria does or does not permit objective understanding.

To understand why an adequate account of objectivity requires that one explain how people reach agreement about the criteria of evaluation, consider the following statement that Wittgenstein (1958) makes:

> Let us imagine a table (something like a dictionary) that exists only in our imagination. A dictionary can be used to justify the translation of a word X by a word Y. But are we also to call it a justification if such a table is to be looked up only in the imagination?—"Well, yes; then it is subjective justification."—But justification consists in appealing to something independent.—"But surely I can appeal from one memory to another. For example, I don't know if I have remembered the time of departure of a train right and to check it I call to mind how a page of the time-table looked. Isn't it the same here?"—No; for this process has got to produce a memory which is actually *correct*. If the mental image of the time-table could not itself be *tested* for correctness, how could it confirm the correctness of the first memory? (As if someone were to buy several copies of the morning paper to assure himself that what it said was true.)
>
> Looking up a table in the imagination is no more looking up a table than the image of the result of an imagined experiment is the result of the experiment. (pp. 93e-94e)

Wittgenstein's analysis shows what is required for the possibility of agreement about criteria, namely, the introduction of an independent criterion that can be used for justification. In his example, in order to agree (with one's self or another) that the train does leave at 4:00 PM, one must justify one's belief on the basis of some criterion which is independent of one's beliefs and is taken as correct. Given the independent criterion, the belief can be evaluated and judged true or false.

Likewise, for agreement to be reached about which criterion a trial must meet, an independent criterion must be introduced against which the competitors may be evaluated. This independent criterion must be taken as correct—as the standard. Just as the actual timetable was accepted as the independent criterion against which memories could be evaluated, so some independent criterion must be accepted as the standard. By accepting this independent criterion, the possibility of right and wrong is introduced, and this permits agreement about criteria to be reached.

The consequence of Wittgenstein's argument is that unless some independent criterion can be appealed to, objectivity is impossible and a process of agreement cannot take place. Unless, that is, a system can evaluate its conclusions against not only its own criteria but also criteria independent of itself, it cannot reach agreement proper. Somehow, the independent criterion must be introduced—interjected perhaps—and the system must evaluate its conclusion with respect to it. (See also Wittgenstein's private language arguments, 1958, e.g. sections 246-258.)

Piaget's use of the phenocopy principle describes a feedback procedure which cannot refer to an independent criterion of evaluation. Every evaluation the system makes is based solely upon its own criteria. It cannot reach agreement with others about which criteria to satisfy. Therefore, the system can learn whether the outcome of its behavior, as it interprets this, meets its criteria, but it cannot arrive at criteria through a process of justifying them against an independent criterion. In other words, it cannot evaluate whether its conclusions are objective.

Let us be clear about the problem here. It is not that it is impossible for individuals to hold the same criteria and to apply concepts in similar ways. Indeed, if one possesses the right criteria, one might be reinforced for applying them, provided they are tried out. Should reinforcement occur, the "right" criteria might be tried again under similar circumstances. The problem is, however, that one has no basis for judging whether the understanding afforded by meeting such criteria is objective. Indeed, there is no basis for distinguishing between objective and subjective understanding because all understanding is the result of the same process. Another way of putting this point is to say that whether one is reinforced for subjective or objective understanding the same process occurs, namely, one makes an interpretation of the feedback from one's trial and selects behavior to try out. One has no basis for determining whether the criteria one applies in making the evaluation are objective or not.

Since Piaget uses the phenocopy principle as a basis for decentraton, decentration cannot explain how one becomes capable of objective thought—why each stage of understanding becomes progressively more objective. We must conclude, then, that decentration does not help reflective abstraction to meet the functional criteria.

Contradiction

Contradiction is another subaccount of reflective abstraction which aims to help it meet the functional criteria. Piaget's elaboration of contradiction and its role in the process of cognitive change may be his most significant attempt to meet the explanatory goal. The transition to a new developmental stage is motivated by some conflict which arises between the organism and the environment. The environment is "something to be overcome"—a barrier which forces one to change one's behavior. What creates the barrier between the organism and the environment? And why does the presence of this barrier motivate change in one's level of understanding? Piaget (1974/1980a, p. 101) tells us that a barrier between the organism and the environment can arise where exogenous knowledge—knowledge about the properties of objects—is used to interpret (assimilate) new objects that are encountered in the environment. Because the exogenous knowledge lacks internal necessity, that is, its implications are not yet understood, a contradiction can arise when some new observable facts are encountered. If these facts have been discovered or analyzed only with difficulty, it is because they meet some the assimilatory criteria but not others—a fact which raises questions about the implications of the criteria. Thus, a partial but incomplete overlap between what is expected and what is experienced creates a contradiction for the organism. It is the contradiction that leads to the reequilibration.

Contradiction can also arise when endogenous abstraction occurs (Piaget, 1974/ 1980a, pp. 89-90). In this case, a contradiction between schemata occurs because modification (accommodation) is required to assimilate a new element in the environment and the modified schema conflicts with other schemata. Reflection then occurs so that the schemata are reorganized with one another in such a way that the contradiction between them is eliminated. The result is a higher level structure— higher in the sense that the contradiction has been eliminated.

In the case of both exogenous and endogenous abstraction, conflict between the organism and the environment is seen to motivate change. It motivates change by creating contradiction, and the presence of contradiction requires that one's level of understanding move to a higher stage if continued functioning in the environment is to occur.

To what extent does Piaget's use of contradiction help reflective abstraction to meet the functional criteria? More precisely, to what extent does contradiction provide sufficient motivation for the transition to objective thought?

The first point to recognize is that there is much ambiguity about how the concept of contradiction functions in the reflective abstraction account. For example, Mischel (1971, p. 332) believes that Piaget offers *felt* contradiction as a motive for transition to higher stages.

According to Mischel, the felt lacunae or the recognition of contradictions motivates transition because they provide goals for reconstructing the schemata. Without these felt needs, there would be no necessity for modifying schemata and moving to higher stage performances.

Given this reading of Piaget, Mischel might say that transition is prompted by the conscious recognition that a perturbation exists—conscious recognition of conflict between one's present experience and prior understanding. Once the contradiction is felt, a desire to change behavior in order to resolve the conflict is forthcoming.

Wohlwill (1966, p. 73), on the other hand, maintains that Piaget does not offer felt contradiction as the motive for stage transition. According to Wohlwill's reading of Piaget, transitions to higher stages are motivated by an imbalance of pressures on the child. The goal of the transition is therefore to relieve excessive demands rather than eliminate felt conflicts. For example, in a case of perceptual change, a demand could arise from visual features of a situation. If these distract the children from considering other important factors, their solutions to the task could be inappropriate. A change in focus on the elements in the situation is required to avoid error.

Wohlwill might argue that the processes of assimilation and accommodation do not depend on a person's feelings about situations. Although conflicts are felt, these are irrelevant to and happen independently of the change in understanding that is made. Rather, assimilation occurs until the interpretations permitted by existing schemata do not represent the factors in a situation appropriately. In this circumstance accommodation may occur whether or not a discrepancy is felt. Thus, Wohlwill notes that expressions of conflict are often observed where accommodation is or has been made, while sometimes no conflict is observed when the demands on the child are not in proper relation to one another.

Rotman (1977, p. 79) sees the role of contradiction in still a third way. He agrees with Wohlwill that the disequilibrium or contradiction, which results from conflict between the organism and the environment, provides a nonaffective motivation for change. Thus, it is the cognitive malfunctioning—the inadequacy of the cognitive structures—which creates the contradiction and motivates the change, whether the contradiction is felt or not. At the same time, Rotman understands Piaget to mean that feelings are a source of energy, and he cites the following passage from Piaget in support of his position:

> Of course, affectivity is always the incentive for the actions that ensue at each new stage of this progressive ascent, since affectivity assigns value to activities and distributes energy to them. But affectivity is nothing without intelligence. Intelligence furnishes affectivity with its means and clarifies its ends. (Piaget, 1964/1968, p. 69)

Rotman interprets Piaget to mean that affectivity motivates actions, but intelligence assigns certain values to various goals and behaviors, and thereby directs the energy of the organism. The assumption is that feelings will energize the actions that will eliminate the contradictions by motivating change in cognitive structure. Thus, while Rotman does not understand Piaget to mean that the contradictions are felt conflicts, as does Mischel, he does not take Piaget to mean that nonaffective contradiction alone could motivate the transition to higher stages of understanding. Rather, these contradictions, which arise from conflicts between organism and environment, motivate transition if there are feelings that energize certain actions to resolve the contradictions.

As Rotman recognizes, his interpretation of Piaget raises a fundamental problem: "How does a subject *know* which encounters with his environment are disequilibrating?" (p. 100). In other words, on what basis does one identify the barriers in the environment and relegate one's energy to certain actions rather than others to eliminate these barriers? If there is no means by which feelings are linked to the actions that overcome these barriers and resolve the contradictions that have arisen, then Piaget cannot argue that transitions to higher stages, each of which permits more objective thought, are motivated by conflict between organism and environment.

Priogine (Inhelder et al., 1977) has identified a related problem. At a conference that took place in 1976, equilibration was the primary topic of discussion, and Priogine made the following comment to Piaget:

> I do not clearly understand the mechanism by which, under [your] model, one cognitive form follows another cognitive form. M. Piaget speaks to us on the subject of positive feedback, of amplification, which very much interests us. But he states that such amplifications can have no place in a strategy of equilibrating compensation. As he says in *L'equilibration des structures cognitives,* 'A lacuna does not constitute a perturbation drawing forth a compensating reaction except to the extent that it corresponds to an already activated schema.' The amplification is, from the start, a function of a 'goal directed' behavior which responds to a difficulty, and which permits reinforcement of finalized and centralized operations which constitute the action of the subject or organism. Lacuna or perturbation, the macroscopic event which throws into gear the compensatory process of transition between cognitive forms, ought for Piaget to be significant at the global semantic level of the system: it cannot lead the latter to change if there is no contradiction. (p. 26; my translation)

When Priogine says that there must be some "macroscopic event" which "throws into gear the compensatory process of transition," he means that the existence of a lacuna or inadequacy is not sufficient to bring about change. Rather, the inadequacy must somehow be recognized—it must be "significant at the global semantic level of the system." Thus, if there is a lacuna which exists because of inadequacies in the cognitive structures, the state of affairs must be taken as a contradiction by the system if it is to motivate change. It is this recognition of contradiction which motivates compensation. An adequate account will explain, then, how the recognition occurs—how the compensatory mechanism in the system is set in motion.

Priogine does not argue that the contradiction must be felt at an affective level. He maintains that it must somehow be recognized or identified *as* a contradiction in order for it to motivate change in cognitive structure. Rotman would agree, but would add that this recognition motivates because it calls for certain actions by relating them to the resolution. Furthermore, if the source of the contradiction is not identified, then the change in understanding which ensues may not permit more objective thought.

Piaget (Inhelder et al., 1977) recognizes that he must address Priogine's question if his account of change and the role of contradiction in it are to be sufficient. He acknowledges that change in cognitive structure occurs *only if* a contradiction has been identified by the subject. But what he goes on to say (p. 32) does *not* explain how the subject comes to recognize that a contradiction exists. Specifically, he does not explain how the system recognizes (a) the aspects of the environment which create the conflicts with the organism and (b) the contradiction that arises from the conflict. Instead, he reiterates the point that when a contradiction is identified, the compensatory process is thrown into gear. He does not indicate how the existence of a contradiction arising from actual conflict between organism and environment, is ascertained.

It is clear that Rotman's and Priogine's criticisms of Piaget's account are sound. Piaget does not explain how conflict between organism and environment, and contradiction arising from this conflict, are identified. Consequently, his account of contradiction cannot explain why thought at each stage becomes more objective. It cannot, therefore, help the reflective abstraction account to meet the functional criteria.

The failure of contradiction arises from Piaget's use of phenocopy. By using this principle as he does, Piaget cannot provide an account of contradiction which meets the criteria he establishes. According to his explanation, the recognition of a contradiction (state of disequilibrium) depends entirely upon the organism's interpretation of the feedback that it receives about its interaction with the environment. If it does not find the feedback conflicting with its criteria, then the series of trials is not set in motion. What this means is that in Piaget's account there is no way to explain how an *actual* conflict with the environment is identified. Hence, he cannot describe the conditions under which the series of trials is set in motion to eliminate contradictions arising from actual conflicts.

One might object that, on the contrary, the feedback character of the system does explain how all contradictions are recognized—including those which arise from actual conflict between organism and environment. As shown in Chapters 3 and 4, the system's interpretation of feedback is made on the basis of whether certain criteria are met by a given trial. Thus, the conditions under which a contradiction will be identified are those under which certain specified criteria are not met. Further, the mechanism by which the contradiction is identified is a mechanism of matching. The feedback about consequences of actions is matched with the desired conditions or consequences.

It is true that Piaget's use of the phenocopy principle explains why a system asserts the existence of contradictions under some circumstances, namely, those where interpretation of the environment does not match criteria of evaluation. It cannot explain, however, how the system can distinguish actual conflicts from pseudoconflicts. In Piaget's use of phenocopy, the environment does not function as a barrier to be overcome (in spite of claims to the contrary!). The barrier is rather the organism's interpretation of the environment. The conflict is generated by discrepancies between what it perceives and what it expects to perceive. The contradiction which arises under this model has its source not in the conflict between organism and environment but in the organism's conflicting interpretations of the environment.

Since the organism cannot distinguish actual conflicts from pseudoconflicts with the environment, contradiction cannot explain how thought becomes more objective. In this account, the organism could be wrong. Its actions may, in fact, be meeting the appropriate criteria, but it may not realize this. Likewise, its behaviors may not be meeting these criteria and it may fail to perceive this point. One problem with Piaget's use of the phenocopy principle, then, is that it assumes that what the organism sees or takes as correct is correct, whereas in fact, the organism has no basis for distinguishing correct from incorrect. There are no means by which the interpretations that the system makes are linked to the actual state of affairs—linked to conditions in the environment that are genuinely perturbing. Indeed, if actual conflicts are identified, this occurs by chance!

One must conclude, then, that Piaget's account of contradiction, which is based upon his use of phenocopy, cannot provide motive for change to a higher level of understanding—one where increased objectivity is possible. It cannot, therefore, help reflective abstraction to meet the functional criteria.

Interaction

The foregoing analysis of contradiction has focused on the source of many limitations in reflective abstraction, namely, the interaction between the organism and the environment that Piaget's use of phenocopy entails. In what follows, I explore the features of this interaction more fully and identify an additional limitation that arises from it. The focus is now upon Piaget's use of cognitive phenocopy. As we shall see, the relation between the organism and the environment that it establishes provides yet another reason why reflective abstraction cannot meet the functional criteria.

In order for the feedback process of cognitive phenocopy to operate, there must be (a) the innate processes of assimilation and accommodation ($\uparrow a$ vectors); (b) the feedback from the environment about the effects of the system's actions and the organization of the cognitive structures ($\underset{\leftarrow}{b}$ vectors); and (c) trials aimed at resolving disequilibria between the organism and the environment ($\underset{\rightarrow}{c}$ vectors). There is interaction between these three, but our concern here is with the nature of the interaction between the subject and the environment. Given the principle of cognitive phenocopy, the features of this interaction are as follows.

First, the behavior of the environment is viewed as a response to the activity of the subject. In other words, whatever the environment does in interacting with the subject depends upon how the subject has treated it. Given this assumption, subjects may infer the results of their actions by examining the behavior of the environment once they have acted. The environmental response provides subjects with feedback about the effects of their behavior.

One might imagine that the reverse is true—that in Piaget's account, the behavior of the organism depends on the response of the environment. Indeed, it seems that if alternative behaviors are selected on the basis of their success in resolving disequilibrium, then the behavior of the organism does depend on that of the environment.

This position is untenable, however, given the feedback procedure specified by cognitive phenocopy. While it appears that the environment determines whether a given behavior is tried and selected, this is not really so. On the contrary, according to cognitive phenocopy, what is tried depends on how the organism interprets the consequences of its behaviors on the external environment. Given its interpretation of these consequences, it makes a choice from the repertoire of possibilities. Its choice of a trial is therefore determined by its interpretation of the success of previous trials and its rules for selecting alternatives.

We have here, then, a second and related feature of the interaction that occurs between organism and environment under cognitive phenocopy, namely, that the environment does not impinge on the subject directly. The environment exerts no effect except as the subject interprets the environment's behavior. The feedback (b) about the effects of the subject's actions is not raw data which the environment provides, but rather the subject's view of the consequences of its actions.

This second point means that in cognitive phenocopy there is no direct interaction between the organism and the environment. While the organism does act on the environment, it reacts to what it perceives to be the effects of its acts, not to the effects per se. It cannot learn from these effects if it does not make an interpretation of them. While the organism acts directly on the environment, the environment cannot act directly on the organism, nor can it convey effects of the organsim's actions except as the organism interprets them. Hence, the organism may act on the environment, but it *interacts* with the environment only insofar as it acquires information about the actual effects of its actions upon the environment.

In the previous section on contradiction, I showed that given the nature of the interaction between organism and environment, Piaget cannot explain how contradictions arising from actual conflicts between them are distinguished from those which result from pseudoconflicts. Consequently, postulating contradiction does not help reflective abstraction meet the functional criteria. Now we shall consider another reason why Piaget's concept of interaction fails.

Many, including Toulmin (1971, p. 57) and Hamlyn (1978, p. 45), have expressed concern over Piaget's inability to explain how the interaction between organism and environment permits acquisition of cultural values. Toulmin (1971, pp. 31-32) raises the question: What kind of relation can the developing organism have to its culture such that "the patterns and structures of public socio-cultural demands" have an impact on what is learned? Clearly, enculturation does occur, and any account of cognitive change needs to make clear how this happens. He further argues (p. 58) that Piaget's account of cognitive development cannot provide a satisfactory account of how people become enculturated. Piaget assumes, says Toulmin, that children's capacities are preadapted so that every child "reinvents" the same conventions. Toulmin believes a satisfactory account will explain how the conventions that are acquired result from life in a cultural context, not simply the maturation of preadapted abilities.

Both Hamlyn (1978, p. 51) and Toulmin object to the fact that Piaget explains the acquisition of conventional understandings—for example, concepts like conservation and classification—using biological prinicples. They believe that Piaget does not put great weight on social and cultural influences because he uses these principles. It is not exactly clear what Hamlyn means by biological principles. Our analysis of the phenocopy principle, however, indicates why he and Toulmin are quite correct when they object to Piaget's account on these grounds. The problem is that the kind of interaction possible between children and the environment in cognitive phenocopy cannot permit a satisfactory explanation of how conventions and mores are acquired.

I have shown that in cognitive phenocopy (a) the behavior of the environment is viewed as a result of the organism's activity and (b) the environment does not act directly on the organism. If we define the socio-cultural environment as social/ cultural values and conventions, then according to Piaget's conception these values and conventions are part of one's total environment. Like the other parts they must be understood to have certain features because of the action upon them, that is, because society has defined them in certain ways. Furthermore, the effects of conventions and values upon individuals depend on the interpretation that each person makes of them. They can have no direct impact.

Consequently, if phenocopy is used as a theory-constitutive metaphor to explain the acquisition of social values and conventions, they are acquired only if they are available in the individual to be tried out. Just as a behavior can be acquired only if it is first generated by structures chosen from the repertoire, so a cultural value or a conventional understanding can be acquired only if its meaning can first be generated from a repertoire of possibilities by the individual. Once that occurs the conventional understanding can be selected if its application meets certain of the individual's criteria. In short, others in the environment cannot introduce a value or a conventional meaning to the subject if the subject does not first identify that value.

Let us consider the case in which children acquire the conventional understanding of conservation. Given Piaget's use of the phenocopy principle, we would understand that the children (a) formulate the possibility that changing the shape of an item does not alter its amount, (b) modify the shape of the item, and (c) evaluate the consequences of so doing against some criteria they hold. If the criteria are met, in the children's judgment, they conclude that changing the shape has not altered the quantity.

Now, if the children treat some object as though changing its shape will not affect its quantity, someone in the environment may respond in a way which the child interprets to mean "I may repeat this behavior." The teacher's behavior provides evidence that the children use to evaluate the veracity of their hypotheses. However, a teacher's behavior must be interpreted by the children if the behavior is to have this consequence. The way the teacher's behavior is interpreted—the message the children receive about the effects of their actions—depends entirely on the features of the children's assimilatory structures. Thus, the teacher cannot *introduce* the children to some interpretation which makes them recognize new grounds for interpreting the consequences. The teacher can affirm or deny the children's interpretation, but the children must accept the teacher's response as one which meets their own criteria.

One might object that this is an outrageous conclusion. Clearly, teachers introduce possibilities to children and thereby teach them. If children had to come up with the right answers all on their own, they would probably never come up with them. (This objection is raised in Hamlyn, 1981, and implied by Wilden, 1975, p. 112.) Outrageous as it may seem, however, Piaget's use of the phenocopy principle forces him to argue precisely as I have indicated. In other words, Piaget must maintain that while it appears that teachers introduce possibilities to children, in fact the teacher teaches by confirming the right possibilities (of values, meanings, behaviors, etc.) once the children generate them. If they are never generated by the children, the children will never acquire them.[5]

If a possible value (meaning, etc.) is selected, it is because the possibility meets the child's individual and perhaps idiosyncratic criteria, not because it meets some independent objective criteria. If the child's criteria are not objective, then such criteria cannot be introduced unless the child comes up with them. Again, those in the socio-cultural environment can provide evidence that meeting objective criteria is appropriate, but these criteria must be invoked by the children before the evidence can be taken as such. Even if the proper criteria are invoked there is no guarantee that evidence about their appropriateness will be correctly interpreted.

Children in a society may acquire values and mores that do in fact agree with objective, socially acceptable ones. But if this occurs (as it often appears to), Piaget can only explain it by saying that the children have somehow generated the appropriate values and conventional meanings and that the environment has provided evidence that the children take to mean, "I can try these values and meanings in the future."

Again, one might reverse the objection and argue that this is precisely what happens when teachers try to teach, that is, they can only confirm appropriate behaviors if they are generated, they cannot introduce them. The problem is that if this is the process by which instruction occurs, then one must ask: How do social values and conventions become established in the first place? There is no account of this process here. As Wittgenstein maintains, values and meanings are a matter of convention. To establish these conventions requires that people reach agreement about the criteria that behaviors must meet. This requires that individuals invoke independent criteria against which competing criteria are evaluated. Piaget, given his use of the phenocopy principle, can explain the process by which individuals select behaviors which meet their own criteria. He can also explain how some criteria change so that others are met. One cannot use cognitive phenocopy, however, as a theory-constitutive metaphor to explain the process by which people arrive at a decision about which criteria are objective. It cannot help to account for how conventions are established.

According to Piaget's use of cognitive phenocopy, the "patterns and structures of socio-cultural demands" have an impact on what is learned only if (a) behavior trials happen to fit those patterns or meet the social/cultural demands, (b) meeting those patterns/demands satisfies the criteria an individual holds, and (c) the individual is correct when judging that trials meet the criteria. These conditions are jointly sufficient to ensure that one's behavior will be conventional.

[5] This point is somewhat different from the one Brainerd (1978) makes when he writes: [According to Piaget] unless the structures appropriate to a given concept are already present, learning cannot operate to induce the concept. If a child's current stage is several steps below the one at which a given concept spontaneously emerges, then training the concept is "completely useless" because the relevant structures are absent. (p. 94)

My point is not simply that the appropriate cognitive structure must be available but that in addition the child must bring it to bear in the appropriate situation *if* the proper lesson is to be imparted. Should children not take the instruction as the teachers intend—even if they have the appropriate structures—the teachers could not teach what they intend to teach.

We can now see another reason why reflective abstraction does not meet functional criteria. It cannot explain how conventional meanings are reached because the role of the environment is too narrowly defined. Consequently, the environment provides evidence for use in determining the modifications needed in cognitive structures, but it cannot introduce a modification that the subject does not first generate, introduce the criteria that must be met by the behaviors tried out, or influence the judgment about whether the criteria have been met. The problem is that the interaction possible under cognitive phenocopy cannot help to explain how conventional understandings unfold from one another because it does not permit an account of how conventional understanding is possible in the first place.

There is a final concern which the criticisms of Hamlyn and Toulmin raise. While Piaget's use of the phenocopy principle requires reflective abstraction to explain how each stage of understanding develops from the stage previous to it and has as its natural end the achievement of the final stage, the question is: Should an account of cognitive change meet these criteria? In other words, should one assume that objective understanding develops through a sequence of stages, each of which unfolds from the previous one and has as its goal the achievement of fully objective thought? And do the conceptual limitations of reflective abstraction justify Piaget's use of phenocopy as a theory-constitutive metaphor?

To help the reader ponder these matters and thus to determine whether the advantages of using the equilibrium principle as Piaget does outweigh the disadvantages, I will summarize the conceptual limitations that my analysis of phenocopy has revealed. In Chapter 6 I examine Piaget's conception of mind in order to understand why he employs the phenocopy principle as he does, given the difficulties that arise from so doing. The analysis in the final chapter provides a perspective from which to evaluate the use of the equilibrium principle in psychological explanation.

Summary

The conceptual problems in Piaget's equilibration account may be sorted into three categories, and the problems in each are related to the problems in the others. The first category includes problems that equilibration has in meeting developmental criteria. The second category consists of limitations in the phenomena that equilibration can explain. The third category includes the failure of reflective abstraction to improve upon other accounts of cognitive change—ones which it aims to better.

With respect to the first category I have advanced four claims. First, I have maintained that in order to explain cognitive change using phenocopy as a theory-constitutive metaphor, the reflective abstraction account must meet functional criteria specified by Hamlyn (1975). It must show how each stage in the sequence of developmental stages has as its natural function the achievement of the subsequent stage and the final goal of development. It must make clear why one change rather than another occurs at each stage in the sequence. A description of change in biological structures can meet these criteria, as there is a material relation between the structures. Consequently, temporal relations exist between them, and the claim that one structure has as its goal the achievement of other structures and the final goal is a meaningful claim. However, there are no grounds for asserting that either material or temporal relations hold between the stages in the developmental sequence of cognitive structures. Furthermore, Piaget's decentration, contradiction, and interaction concepts do not help him meet the functional criteria and thereby resolve the problem.

This brings us to the second claim, namely, that Piaget confounds logical and pragmatic necessity. Because descriptions of cognitive structures are logically inclusive of one another, Piaget contends that each is prerequisite (in the Feldman and Toulmin sense) for the succeeding one and for achievement of the goal. Clearly this confounding results from Piaget's attempt to meet the functional criteria that his use of phenocopy imposes. Given this fallacious reasoning, Piaget fails to explain how increasing necessity arises—why each stage is likely to be more logically coherent than the previous one.

The lack of material and temporal relations between cognitive stages has another consequence—and here we come to a third claim. It is not clear what role cognitive structures play in producing solutions. That is, the relation between cognitive structures and performance is ambiguous. Nevertheless, Piaget argues that performances change because cognitive structures change, that new performances require new formalisms to characterize them because cognitive structures have changed, and that the cognitive structures have changed in the ways the formal structures differ. None of these inferences is justified unless schemata function in the production of solutions. If they have a function, the function must be explained. If it is not explained but is merely asserted then the grounds for drawing the above inferences are still lacking. Piaget's fallacious reasoning again arises from his attempt to meet the functional criteria imposed by his use of phenocopy.

Fourth and finally, the ambiguities in Piaget's use of assimilation and accommodation arise from his application of phenocopy. Thus, while assimilation appears to mean either comparing or converting representations, the perspective afforded by phenocopy suggests that it refers to a process of converting representations that involves comparing them. Likewise, while accommodation could mean either modifying schemata or selecting alternatives from a repertoire, the phenocopy perspective suggests that the process is one of modifying cognitive structures through a feedback procedure that involves reorganizing existing elements. The feedback conception of change results in a further limitation, however. Piaget maintains that transition to higher stages occurs because schemata are accommodated; he does not explain why one accommodation rather than another occurs. Hence, accommodation cannot explain why stages with given features arise.

Let us turn now to the second category of limitations—the phenomena equilibration cannot address. Because Piaget uses phenocopy as a theory-constitutive metaphor, he generates many hypotheses about children's understanding at given points in time. The insights that have been gained as a result of this research are enormous. At the same time, his use of phenocopy does not enable him to address three things which he needs to explain.

First, Piaget does not explain how objectivity is possible. While his subaccounts of decentration and contradiction aim to explain how objective understanding of situations becomes possible, each fails. The problem is that under Piaget's use of phenocopy, change occurs by selecting options from a repertoire, trying them out, and judging whether they meet specified criteria. In this procedure there can be no account of how people reach agreement about criteria that the trials must meet. Because the processes of decentration and contradiction are based on this use of phenocopy, they contribute nothing toward the goal of explaining objectivity.

Second, given Piaget's use of phenocopy, there is no basis for explaining how conventional understanding is possible. Conventional understanding can be acquired if the organism makes appropriate trials and judges the trials to meet its criteria. However, there is no account here of how some meanings rather than others become conventional, as there can be no account of how agreements between persons that are needed to establish such conventions are reached.

A third limitation, closely related to the first two, is that equilibration inadequately explains how people teach one another. Given Piaget's use of phenocopy, teaching is defined as providing evidence that may or may not be used to affirm trials. There are at least two problems with this conception of teaching. First, the learned behaviors are modified only if the student generates an alternative behavior. This means the teacher cannot introduce a new alternative to the student. Consequently, correct behaviors can never be learned if they are not present in the student's repertoire and tried out. Second, even if the correct behavior is generated and affirmed by the teacher, it will be selected only if the feedback about its consequences meet the student's criteria for success. These criteria may or may not be correct, and if they are not there is no way to introduce the correct ones. All that can be learned from a teacher is information about the effects of one's actions. The behavior which is tried out, the rules for selecting alternatives, the criteria the behavior must meet, and whether the criteria have indeed been met—none of these things can be learned, nor can they be taught by one person to another.

With respect to the third category, I have argued that there are three ways in which Piaget aims to overcome limitations in other accounts and yet fails to do so. First, as argued in Chapters 2 and 4, he hopes to provide an alternative to Chomsky's explanation of the origins of cognitive/linguistic structures. He rejects Chomsky's claim that constraints on the linguistic structures are specified by the genome. Yet his use of the phenocopy principle prevents him from otherwise accounting for their origins.

Second, Piaget hopes to modify Waddington's principle of genetic assimilation to avoid the claim that cognitive structures arise by chance. He introduces the concepts of disequilibrium and internal environment into his version of phenocopy and argues that the nature of endogenous abstractions (modifications in cognitive structures) depends on the success of exogenous abstractions. Hence, those changes in the schemata which resolve disequilibria created by responses to the external environment will be selected. As argued in Chapter 3, Piaget's adaptation of genetic assimilation does not avoid recourse to an account of origins based upon the principles of chance variation and natural selection.

Finally, Piaget hopes to use the prinicple of genetic assimilation to explain onto-genetic change. Again, he modifies the principle by elaborating its process of developmental feedback. He then argues that cognitive change in individuals occurs through a process of development. Piaget's account fails to meet the criteria that a developmental account must meet, namely, functional criteria; he fails to demonstrate that cognitive structures *develop.*

Given these limitations one might well wonder why Piaget elaborates and applies the phenocopy principle in this way. In Chapter 6, I present a perspective on this matter which helps to resolve the question: Should psychology abandon use of the equilibrium principle to explain cognitive change?

6. The Representational Theory of Mind: Philosophical Implications

"I, too, have something to say to you, Ada. Just as you wish to impress me I wish to instil something into you. I don't expect you'll understand. I don't really hope. My feeling is that you never could have understood what I am going to say —never would have wanted to, and almost certainly you won't in your present condition. But I can't help hoping. At least you are another person. I can't help giving this other person in front of me—even though it's you, Ada—at least a chance to understand. You're a fool—but there's still an itch to instruct a fool." (Sansom, p. 42)

My aim thus far has been to describe the phenocopy principle and to show how Piaget's use of it places certain limitations on his account of cognitive change. Two final questions will be addressed in this concluding chapter. First, why does Piaget use the equilibrium principle as he does, given the problems which arise from so doing? Second, how useful is the equilibrium principle for generating adequate psychological explanations?

The chapter is divided into four sections. In the first I argue that Piaget's use of phenocopy results from assuming what Fodor (1975, 1981) calls a representational theory of mind (RTM). After characterizing RTM and indicating why I think Piaget assumes it, I argue that Chomsky too holds this theory of mind, and that similarities between Chomsky's and Piaget's accounts, particularly with regard to the nativism controversy, arise from this fact.

In the second section of the chapter, I examine some possible objections to my claim that the similarities in Chomsky's and Piaget's nativist commitments result from assuming RTM. I first argue that Piaget's appeal to the concept of steady state does not alter his nativist assumptions. I then try to show why empirical research has failed to resolve the fundamental questions raised by assuming RTM, these being: What is the nature of the mind's initial representations? Where do they come from? I maintain that both Chomsky and Piaget leave these questions unanswered.

In the third section, I consider three attempts to resolve a related problem that is created by assuming RTM, namely, intentionality: If the mind cannot operate unless it can represent things and attach meaning to them, how does it become capable of so doing? I first examine Dennett's (1978) claim that Fodor raises the problem unnecessarily. I then show how neither Dennett's appeal to artificial intelligence nor Hamlyn's distinction between learning and coming to know resolve the matter.

In the fourth and final section of the chapter, I return to the question of why Piaget uses the phenocopy principle as he does. I argue that because he assumes RTM his account of cognitive change needs to explain a number of things for which phenocopy, applied as a theory-constitutive metaphor, seems appropriate. While it does permit an account of some vital matters, it leaves other significant ones unexplained. I conclude the chapter by considering whether, on balance, the equilibrium principle serves the aims and needs of psychological explanation.

The Representational Theory of Mind

Definition

In Chapter 2, I present Fodor's (1975, 1980a) criticisms of Piaget's equilibration account. Fodor argues that Piaget does not explain how the mind changes so that over time its concepts become more powerful and children become able to solve certain kinds of problems they could not solve previously. Fodor's point is based upon the assumption that Piaget holds what Fodor (1980a, 1981) calls a representational theory of mind (RTM). Fodor (1981) characterizes RTM as follows. First, it assumes that the mind represents things (situations) in the world. Second, the organism can be in a mental state, the nature of which is defined by its representations and the relation the mind bears to these. The relation is expressed in terms of propositional attitudes (e.g., the belief that Marvin is melancholy). Third, the mind functions by manipulating the representations according to rules it has for so doing. The rules permit one to have mental states with a variety of contents (I can believe in $a, b, c, f \ldots$) and experience a variety of mental states (I can think x, believe that x, hope that x, etc.).[1]

Fodor claims (1981, p. 259) that all classical theories of concept acquisition—in effect, all theories of concept acquisition—hold some version of RTM. This seems to me a plausible claim although Fodor does not provide a definitive defense for it. For example, RTM is quite in keeping with the Kantian tradition (Kant, 1929, p. 105). In Kant's conception knowledge is acquired via concepts. Concepts specify rules which relate representations to one another. Thus, representations constitute the

---

[1] Fodor (1980b, pp. 63-64) distinguishes between RTM and CTM—the computational theory of mind. In my view, the latter may be a species of the former and may not differ on the grounds that Fodor specifies. In fact, CTM may have the properties attributed here to RTM.

mental objects on which the mind operates using the rules provided by the concepts. The results of manipulating representations on the basis of rules are judgments that may be expressed by mental states inducing beliefs, desires, hopes, and the like. Judgment, therefore, requires a representation of objects in the world and constitutes what Fodor calls a "propositional attitude."

If Piaget's account presumes RTM, what does this mean? In Piaget's case, the mental representations which are manipulated are both the products of using cognitive structures to organize experience and the cognitive structures themselves. For example, the structures of classification, conservation, and so on, could be said to provide the subject with rules for organizing situations. The organization or assimilation of situations which results from applying these rules is represented. The representations are manipulated according to principles including those of feedback. At the same time, we have seen that in the case of endogenous abstraction, the schemata, like those of conservation or classification, are themselves manipulated according to higher-order rules so that new ways of representing phenomena become possible.

What could it mean to say that cognitive structures provide rules for manipulating representations? Here, the manipulation involves (a) generating a representation of the environment on the basis of some cognitive structure which is selected from a repertoire, (b) evaluating the representation and hence the cognitive structure to see if certain criteria are met, and (c) selecting alternative structures until an adequate relation between organism and environment is generated. Both the cognitive structures and the representations of the environment can be combined or built up, provided the organism has rules for so doing.

According to Fodor's conception of RTM, the principles with which the mind makes what Kant calls *judgments* are principles of induction—rules for drawing nondemonstrative inferences. In Chapters 2 and 4, I show how cognitive structures such as those represented by grouping VII constitute rules for drawing inductive inferences. I also show how they function and I explain how the procedure for modifying them was itself based upon principles of induction. This is why any change in structure that occurs results from forming and confirming hypotheses.

It appears to me that Piaget's definition and application of the phenocopy principle assumes a form of RTM. In fact, one could go so far as to say that Piaget might not have used the phenocopy principle in this way had he not assumed RTM. Given that he does assume it, his application of phenocopy provides the content for his particular version of RTM.

If Fodor is right that Piaget is not alone in assuming RTM (but instead is in company with Hume, Locke, Descartes, Kant, and many contemporary philosophers and psychologists), the ensuing analysis may provide a basis for identifying features and limitations in other accounts. Indeed, it may help us to understand why certain issues in the philosophy of mind and the philosophy of psychology are present and the extent to which we can hope to resolve these issues and produce more satisfactory psychological explanations. Further, it will give us insight into why Piaget uses the equilibrium principle as he does—in spite of the drawbacks.

RTM's Assumptions About What Must Be Innate

In what follows, I argue that by assuming RTM one lays constraints on one's psychological explanations. The model of explanation one invokes must acknowledge these constraints. The explanation that results will, then, have certain characteristics arising from the restrictions imposed by RTM and the explanatory model.

To defend this claim, I return to an issue that has preoccupied me throughout this book, namely: What must be innate in a system where change is explained by using the equilibrium principle as Piaget does? I have answered this question in the foregoing chapters. I will now argue that Piaget's assumptions about what must be innate, and Chomsky's as well, can be understood to arise from assuming RTM.

Stich (1975, p. 8) argues that there are two different views of what is meant by saying that "x is innate." The first, the Cartesian, takes the dispositional view that a characteristic need not be manifest at birth in order to be innate. Nonetheless it must be the case, if it is said to be innate, that it has appeared at some point (t) from birth to t, or that it will appear at the appropriate stage, given the normal course of events. We see that x is, then, a disposition present from birth to manifest a given characteristic under certain circumstances.

The second view of what must be innate, drawn from the Platonic tradition, maintains that the innate characteristic is made manifest by something which triggers its appearance. (Stich notes that it is not certain whether Plato would have subscribed to this conception of innateness. It is, however, consistent with his views.) In this conception, the innate characteristic x has specific content and is present from birth. It must, as Plato puts it, be recollected. What is innate, then, can be manifested if a triggering device somehow releases it. The triggering device does not supply or affect the content of x. Thus, what is innate is not a disposition to develop x but a particular characteristic which presumably exists in the repertoire of possible behaviors and needs only to be expressed (Stich, p. 14).

In foregoing chapters, I argued that Piaget, in spite of claims to the contrary, offers no alternative to what Chomsky maintains must be innate. The reason is that Piaget's account is based upon the use of explanatory principles that prevent his providing an alternative. We are now in a position to understand why their views are so similar. The basic reason is that both Chomsky and Piaget assume RTM. Their use of explanatory principles and hence their fundamental nativist assumptions also result from this fact. Furthermore, while it appears that Chomsky's and Piaget's accounts might be viewed as examples of the two nativist traditions sketched above, the similarities about what must be innate in the two cases show there is but one tradition, which they share. I shall consider some objections to my arguments at the conclusion of this section.

Chomsky Assumes RTM. Like Piaget, Chomsky assumes RTM. This is clear from the summary of his position given in Chapter 2. The representations in Chomsky's account of language acquisition are grammatical rules that specify the phonetic, syntactic, and semantic characteristics of the sentences that the child comes to produce. Acquiring a language involves acquiring not only a competence for producing correct sentences, but also strategies "for putting this knowledge to use," that is, performance and production strategies. How are the grammar of a language and performance systems acquired? Chomsky argues that, at least in the case of the grammar, "a fixed, genetically determined system ... narrowly constrains the form [it] can assume" (1980a, p. 35). This fixed, genetically constrained system is the Universal Grammar (UG). In effect, the UG provides a representation of the features the acquired grammar may have.

In terms of Fodor's characterization of RTM, we can say that in Chomsky's account the representations are the constraints provided by UG, which are used as a basis for manipulating grammatical rules, and the representations of the linguistic data that result from applying grammatical rules to them. The grammar one acquires depends upon the features of the UG and the judgments that are made about the candidates for grammatical rules. Thus, the constraints specified by the UG constitute, for Chomsky, a set of primitive representations which provide a basis for constructing the grammar.

What process does Chomsky envision for the acquisition of syntax? He writes (1965) that a child who is capable of learning a first language must have:

i) a technique for representing input signals
ii) a way of representing structural information about these signals
iii) some initial delimitation of a class of possible hypotheses about language structure
iv) a method for determining what each such hypothesis implies with respect to each sentence
v) a method for selecting one of the (presumably, infinitely many) hypotheses that are allowed (iii) and are compatible with the given primary linguistic data. (p. 30)

Given the above, a feedback system that is based upon the representations provided by the UG can operate. For the UG to function there must be a technique for representing input signals and a way of representing structural information about those signals. The UG provides the initial delimitation of the class of possible hypotheses about language structure. Given a means of representing input and the structural information about these signals, the UG provides criteria that restrict the range of candidates for syntactic rules. The criteria provided by UG are used to determine which candidate is tried out. Because the system has a method for determining what each hypothesis implies it can use feedback from the trial to evaluate its appropriateness. In cases where the criteria specified by UG are met, a hypothesis is confirmed, that is, the syntactic rule is tried under similar conditions in the future.

The Source of Some Commonalities in Chomsky's and Piaget's Accounts. There are several striking points of similarity between the Chomsky and Piaget explanations. One is that the mind functions by manipulating representations using criteria and procedures specified by the system. The procedure of operation in both cases is one of drawing nondemonstrative inferences based upon criteria the system has—a feedback procedure. The inferences are determined by the system's procedures and criteria.

Is this feedback procedure of operation a necessary element of RTM? My answer is yes. If one assumes that the mind operates by manipulating representations, then there must be rules for manipulating those representations. And if the system acts with reference to rules, it must get information about the consequences of its manipulation. Some form of feedback procedure is required to provide the system with this information. Only a feedback procedure can provide a means for translating the consequences into a form that determines whether the rules followed on one occasion should be followed again. Without this information, a system which functions by manipulating representations with reference to rules would cease to operate.

If a feedback system of some sort is required for RTM, then RTM is committed to at least three points about what must be initially available for the system to operate. The first is that some representations must be present. Second, these representations must have meaning to the system. In other words, the system must be able to interpret and respond to the consequences of manipulating them. Third, there must be procedures for formulating alternative trials and criteria for evaluating them.

As shown in Chapter 4, Chomsky's and Piaget's accounts both assume the availability of procedures for selecting alternative trials and criteria that the trials must meet. If these things must be available from the start, then there must be an initial set of representations which is used to formulate the trials (hypotheses). Further, the representations must have meaning for the system if the system is to evaluate the consequences of manipulating them. The fact that Chomsky and Piaget assume RTM allows us to understand why their accounts share these premises.

But the commitments to what must be present initially do not stop here. Given the nature of feedback systems, any changes that can occur in the representations at some point in the future must also be somehow represented at the start. If the account asserts that the primitive or initial representations get built up, or modified in some way, there must be systemic rules for making these modifications. The rules for modification must exist in the system from the beginning and indicate the probabilities that change of one sort rather than another will occur. They may be very complex rules, specifying all kinds of conditional possibilities. They may also specify circumstances under which new modification rules will be formulated. Nevertheless, any change that does occur in the representations and in the rules for changing them, no matter how far in the future, must be circumscribed from the start. This means that the complex, structured representations that eventually result are initially represented somehow in the system. By assuming RTM, both Chomsky and Piaget are committed to this position.

One might object that the procedures for change in representations (in rules for manipulating representations, etc.) could be specified initially without being represented. That is, one could maintain that the feedback operation of RTM is carried out by the *hardware* of the mind (e.g., physiological processes). Changes in representations might, then, be determined at this level without being represented by, say, rules of induction.

It is true that procedures for change in representations must be specified at the hardware level—the machine level of the system. If there is to be a change in the rules of induction that the system follows, such that it is now following rules it could not have followed before, then the machine has to operate differently at the hardware level. If it continues to operate as it has in the past, then no new possibilities for induction are made available.

If, however, change in representations (or in rules for representing) is made possible by change at the hardware level, then we must ask: How does that change occur? Either the system is provided with new procedures of operation that permit new representations (new induction rules, etc.) *or* there are alternative procedures of operation which already exist at the hardware level and which are applied for the first time. If the latter is the case, then the following questions arise: Under what conditions are alternative procedures for operation at the hardware level chosen? Under what conditions will these procedures be repeated in the future? In other words, the same questions which confront us at the level of representation now confront us at the hardware level. The answer to such questions is that there are rules that the system has for resolving theses matters and the rules are somehow represented in the system. Pushing the problems to the hardware level solves nothing.[2]

Of course, it is possible that through some means the system is provided with new procedures of operation. For example, one might also argue as Chomsky does (1980a, p. 75) that there is "successive-maturation of specialized hardware" that makes some procedures for change available later in time. In this case, the gradual maturation of, for example, the physiological level, could be said to open up possibilities for representation (or change in representations) that were not available initially, and thus alter the probability functions.

If, however, maturation of the hardware occurs, this requires rather than eschews the possibility that the changes in representation (rules for representing) that appear in the future be specified from the start. If additional mechanisms come into operation later in time, it is because the system was built to make them available under certain conditions which did not obtain initially. Even if the system is very complex and new possibilities for representation are specified as each phase of the maturation occurs, the system must be built so that the range of possible changes that may arise is constrained initially. In other words, the range of features that may mature must be established initially if maturation is to occur. The information which established the range of features is represented in the genes.

In summary, then, RTM assumes rather than explains that the possibilities for representation and for change in the rules of representation must be specified from the beginning. Further, these possibilities are represented somehow in the system. To argue that the changes can be specified at the hardware rather than the program level of the system, or that they arise from maturation, cannot neutralize either claim. Finally, procedures for manipulating representations and for evaluating the manipulations must also be present for the system to function.

One Nativist Tradition, Not Two. The constraints imposed by assuming RTM result in some profound similarities between Chomsky's and Piaget's accounts. Thus, while Piaget appears to exemplify the Cartesian tradition and Chomsky the Platonic, as defined above, a closer look reveals that the main distinction between these traditions collapses.

The difference between the two positions, says Stich (1975), is that in the Cartesian case, dispositions to develop are innate, while in the Platonic case, preformed

---

[2] Dennett (1978, pp. 84-85) makes a similar point when he argues that where change by self-design occurs, the same things must be present and the same issues are raised.

entities, whose expression need only be triggered by something in the individual's experience, are innate. The fact is that the expression of characteristics occurs in precisely the same way in the two cases. That is, the process of triggering and the process of development are fundamentally the same process.

This claim may appear mistaken, because in Chomsky's account the linguistic data which the child receives releases the application of certain already present constraints (e.g., structure-dependence rules), whereas in Piaget's account experience releases the development of the structures. The difference between the two is that in the latter case the structures that are expressed do not appear to exist fully formed from the beginning.

But to distinguish Chomsky's from Piaget's account on these grounds is to overstate both positions and polarize them inappropriately. As we have seen, Chomsky speaks of the "successive maturation of specialized hardware," and such hardware surely includes physiological capacities for language acquisition. The neonate cannot and does not acquire language. Instead, the various physical and cognitive systems must mature until it becomes possible to acquire a first language. One might say that the child is born with the disposition to mature so that language learning eventually becomes possible. Only after maturation has occurred will experience with linguistic data trigger the application of the UG and the acquisition of language.

On the other hand, it is quite clear that in Piaget's account the development of cognitive structures cannot occur unless maturation has occurred, thereby making available new structures of a physical sort. Given the maturation changes in cognitive structure can occur. Piaget (1964/1968, p. 103) acknowledges this point. In both Chomsky's and Piaget's accounts, the child is born with the disposition to mature physically so that the potential for acquiring complex cognitive structures may be actualized.

Thus, both Chomsky and Piaget are Cartesians in the sense that they attribute to the organism innate dispositions to develop physical capacities. In addition, the disposition to acquire cognitive/linguistic structures, given the prerequisite physiological maturation, is also present in both accounts. I show how Piaget assumes a feedback procedure for constructing cognitive structures (Chapter 4); I also show how Chomsky assumes a feedback procedure for acquiring linguistic structures (Chapter 6). The tendency to follow the procedures indicated, and thus to acquire the mental structures, is present in the system, given both accounts.

At the same time, both Chomsky and Piaget are Platonists (i.e., what Stich calls "Platonists") insofar as both must maintain, given RTM, that the cognitive capacities that may develop are constrained from the start. This means that the probabilities that certain characteristics will arise given the fulfillment of certain conditions are initially established. Although Piaget denies that the constraints on linguistic structures are specified by the genome, I argue that he provides no alternative account of their origin. By assuming RTM, he commits himself to somehow explaining where cognitive structures come from, since they are initially available in the sense defined above.

---

[3] Interestingly enough, it is precisely this difference which Fodor (1981, pp. 278-279) claims distinguishes the rationalists from the empiricists. My suspicion is that the distinction is bogus in this case as well.

Possible Objections to the Claim

The Concept of Steady State

In editing the debate between Piaget and Chomsky, Piattelli-Palmarini (1980) raises the possibility that the concept of steady state, particularly as depicted by Von Foerster (e.g., 1960), affords Piaget a principle that can permit an alternative to Chomsky's claims about what must be present for the mind to function and cognitive development to occur. The implication of my analysis is that by invoking the concept of steady state, or the noise-to-order principle, Piaget does not purchase an alternative to these claims. In his last writings on equilibration (1975/1977, 1974/1980a) he tries, but to no avail. For example, he states (1974/1980a):

> In a study of the relations between information theory and biology, the biophysicist H. Atlan . . . summarizes his thesis as follows: "The self-organizing systems are not only resistant to noise (collectively, the random hostilities of the environment), but actually make use of it to the extent that they transform it into an organizational factor." . . . [t] his inversion of meaning corresponds quite strikingly to that by which external perturbations . . . become variations within the system . . . in the cognitive process. . . . And this of course has been summed up already, by H. V. Foerster, in the well-known phrase "from noise to order." (p. 110)

Piaget seems to believe that when Atlan describes self-organizing systems as making use of noise—random hostilities of the environment—he gives an account which does not require that the change which occurs in the system be defined from the start in the form of probability functions. When Piaget says that "This inversion of meaning corresponds quite strikingly to that by which external perturbations become variations within the system in the cognitive process," he seems to believe that a self-organizing system uses the *noise* provided by the environment in such a way that modifications in procedures for operation are defined (or determined).

The self-regulating system is, however, a closed system. This means that any change in structure, or procedure, occurs only if conditions already specified by the probability functions with which the system begins have been met. Although Von Foerster (1960) argues that some changes in structure permit more than one possibility for behavior, and that thereby the probabilities for change in structure are not fully determined initially, this point is irrelevant. Even where change in structure permits several possible behaviors, the probable structural changes given the execution of one behavior or another are determined initially. Furthermore, one can predict which of the probable configurations of structure are likely to be acquired provided one knows the features of the environment and the system's rules for responding to it.

Again, one might object that this is quite different from the picture Chomsky presents, according to which one can predict the linguistic structures that will be acquired with much less information about the environment than is needed in Piaget's case. As explained above, however, only a simplistic and misleading interpretation of Chomsky's position can lead to such an objection. In order to predict the grammar and the language that will be learned, one must know the constraints on responses to linguistic data, that is, the constraints specified by the UG. These constraints will permit the acquisition of more than one type of linguistic structure, and hence the acquisition of more than one language. Thus, to predict the linguistic structures most likely to be acquired one must also have extensive information about the environment, that is, the linguistic data that the system encounters. Just as is true in Piaget's case, the likelihood of selecting one grammatical structure rather than another from the range of possibilities can be predicted only if the features of the environment, the rules for responding to it, and the constraints upon the application of the rules are known.

In short, Chomsky, Piaget, Atlan, and Von Foerster presume a closed system of operation that requires that the probabilities for change be defined initially. Dennett (1978) sums up the point with respect to closed, self-regulating systems like the ones these theorists propose. He argues (pp. 84-85) that in a closed system the only source of novelty is chance. If the system is such that all information on which change is based comes from within, no novelty occurs. If the system is such that some or all of the contribution which changes it comes from without, then the contribution must be arbitrary, or undesigned. In short, there is no way a closed, self-regulating system can acquire a new capacity for changing its operation unless it is altered by some force other than that of its own design.

Empirical Research

Again, one may object that while both Piaget and Chomsky assume RTM and provide accounts that presuppose a closed system of operation, there is still an important respect in which their explanations differ. Chomsky insists (e.g., 1980a) that the existence of UG is an empirical matter, and that there is empirical evidence that it does exist. Here Chomsky's position seems to entail predetermination at the genetic level, whereas Piaget claims that the features of cognitive structures, linguistic or otherwise, are not specified by the genome.

Do genes specify constraints on the linguistic structures that may be acquired? This is an empirical question. An answer to it requires empirical data that provide evidence about the information carried by the genome. The problem has been to define appropriate empirical tests which give viable evidence on the matter. Many argue that this simply has not been done by either Chomsky or Piaget.[4]

My claim is that the research thus far undertaken fails to permit the identification of primitive structures. Consequently there has been no basis for drawing inferences about what is or is not specified by the genes. Thus, while Fodor is right that the issue is empirical, he fails to recognize why research has not yielded appropriate evidence.

Fodor (1981) argues that some concepts are innate and specified by the genome. The release of these basic primitive concepts into the conceptual repertoire is triggered by the environment. Once we can determine which concepts are so triggered

[4] See, e.g., Searle (1980b, p. 37) and Dennett (1980b, p. 19) who argue that Chomsky provides no adequate empirical evidence for his claims; Chomsky (1980a, pp. 36-37) argues Piaget has not provided it. The question is, if not, why not?

we may draw inferences about the information given by the genome. Fodor's conception (p. 313) is that once the basic concepts have been released and exist as part of the conceptual repertoire, they can release others, provided certain experience in the environment occurs, and provided they are linked to these nonbasic concepts. Complex, phrasal concepts—ones which do not have one-word predicate terms—are constructed according to principles of induction that are based on the semantic relations between the component concepts.

What does Fodor mean by *triggering*? He tells us that triggering is a "relation between *stimuli* and concepts" (p. 307). In the case of the basic primitives the stimuli are not related to the concepts through the mediation of other concepts. Rather, "certain inputs trigger the availability of certain concepts" (p. 273). In the cases where basic concepts trigger nonbasic ones, the former do mediate the latter. Triggering, therefore, refers to the release of conceptual properties or potentials that already exist. There is, says Fodor, reason to think that there may be "a hierarchy of triggers" (p. 308). This seems to mean that the mechanism of concept release has a network structure such that the release of some concepts is required before others can be released.

It might seem that the mechanism of triggering is merely another label for induction. Fodor claims this is not the case because in the case of induction concepts are *learned* from their instances, whereas in the case of triggering they are "triggered by their instances."

According to Fodor (p. 310), the difference between acquiring a concept through triggering, as opposed to induction, is that in the former case exposure to the object referred to by the concept releases that concept so it becomes part of the conceptual repertoire. In the case of triggering, then, there appears to be a direct relation between the stimuli and the basic primitive concepts.

Using the concept of triggering, Fodor proposes to investigate whether some concepts are acquired through mere exposure to their referents. If there are such concepts, they are basic primitive concepts. And if these basic concepts are structured from a semantic point of view, that is, involve other concepts, then one will be able to draw inferences about the nature of the information specified by the genes vis à vis primitive linguistic structures.

The problem with Fodor's proposal is that the data collected under it do not identify basic primitive concepts. He says that certain stimuli in the environment provide inputs into the system and automatically release the basic primitive concepts that exist. Thus, when the child acquires the concept dog, which Fodor claims is a primitive concept (p. 311), we are to imagine a situation in which the referent (dog) appears frequently in the environment, and when it appears, appears in relation to the word (sound) *dog*. The concept of dog is thereby released by the process of ostension. The child is exposed to the referent (a dog) which is identified as such, and seeing the referent releases the concept dog into the conceptual repertoire. In other words, the presence of the dog causes the child to relate a collection of properties represented by the innate concept dog to a stimulus in the environment.

Fodor's process of triggering shares some features with the innate releasing mechanism described by ethologists such as Konrad Lorenz. Lorenz argues (1965, p. 34) that structures which are elaborately adapted to aspects of the environment faced only later in life must be blueprinted in the genome. The structures which permit the adapted behaviors are released under certain situations. Lorenz (1970) writes:

> The receptor correlate corresponding to an elicitory stimulus combination (i.e., the basis of the specific tendency to respond to a specific key combination and consequently to spark off a certain chain of behavior patterns) has been termed the *releasing schema*. . . . The instinctive, *innate* releasing schemata play a particular role in the behavior of birds. If the releasing schema of a response is innately determined, it always corresponds to a relatively *simple* combination of individual stimuli, which as a unitary whole represent a key to a specific instinctive response. The innate releasing schema of an instinctive behavior pattern is based on a restricted selection from the wealth of available stimuli, and the schema responds selectively to these stimuli in setting the behavior pattern in operation. (pp. 243-244)

According to Lorenz, there is a physiological process (often a visual one) that takes place in the organism when it encounters certain stimuli in the environment. These stimuli elicit from the organism a highly specific response which occurs when the receptor correlate or the releasing schema is stimulated. Where the releasing schema is innate, the stimuli that cause its release, says Lorenz, are a relatively simple combination that together unlock it. No other responses are needed to mediate the effect of the stimulus.

The process which Lorenz describes here is a causal process, not a learning process. In fact, Lorenz distinguishes sharply between these two (e.g., 1965, pp. 117-120) on the grounds that causal processes, such as those invoked in the release of innate schemata, make learning possible. In addition, innate "released" behaviors achieve an "instantaneous adaptation" to the environment. Finally, the behavior results from a "highly differentiated, phylogenetically adapted mechanism" (1965, p. 9).

Fodor urges that the process of triggering basic primitive concepts which he describes is also a causal process—that the concepts are specified by the genome, as is Lorenz's innate releasing mechanism, and that the basic concepts are released into the repertoire by the occurrence of certain stimuli in the environment, much as the key stimuli release certain behaviors in animals. The process of releasing primitive concepts in the repertoire is like the following case:

> In the greylag [goose], the innate mechanism releasing the escape response to the one flying predator endangering this species (the white-tailed eagle) is comparatively simple and unselective. The response is released . . . by any object silhouetted against the sky and gliding along slowly—as measured in multiples of its own length—and smoothly without any additional quick fluttering movements. (Lorenz, 1965, p. 50)

But the question immediately arises: Is the process by which the collection of properties is released (the concept related to the environmental stimulus and thus released into the repertoire) a causal process or one which involves learning? Let us begin by considering the question in light of the distinctions between the two processes which Lorenz offers.

First, is it the case that the release of triggered concepts makes it possible to learn other concepts? Fodor tells us this is the case (1981, p. 313) and I see no grounds for denying the truth of this claim.

Second, does the application of triggered concepts to the environment achieve "instantaneous adaptation" to it? In other words, is the first application of a triggered concept such as house or dog correct? Is it properly applied to only houses or dogs? Fodor gives no evidence that this is the case. Furthermore, studies in developmental linguistics would suggest that it is not what occurs. Indeed, language acquisition data indicate that proper application of all words and concepts is not immediate but becomes perfected over time. It would seem plausible that the initial connection between the environmental stimulus and the supposedly *triggered* concept may be a consequence of learning, and that the connection between the meaning and stimulus is not perfectly preadapted.

Third, is there evidence that the so-called basic primitive concepts are available because they are released into the repertoire by a "highly differentiated, phylogenetically adapted mechanism"? Or could one just as easily infer that the concepts so identified result from learning? Fodor claims that basic primitives will meet two criteria, namely, ontogenetic availability and ostensive definability (p. 312). The mechanism for releasing the primitives into the repertoire is adapted to the features of the primitives and the external environment; it will release those concepts which meet these criteria if certain conditions obtain.

However, there is no evidence for inferring that those concepts that are found to be present and that meet the criteria are present because they meet the criteria and have therefore been released by the preadapted mechanism. The fact that existing concepts meet the criteria is insufficient for inferring *how* they entered into the repertoire. Because concepts are related to one another in terms of semantic hierarchies, it is always possible that any given concept is *not* primitive but is available because it was learned on the basis of other concepts already present in the repertoire. One cannot tell whether the concept was triggered by a "highly differentiated, phylogenetically adapted mechanism" or not.

One might wonder what sort of evidence would be needed to prove that *x* was a basic primitive and thus resulted from the triggering of an adaptive mechanism. Lorenz (1965) describes what he calls *deprivation experiments*. He argues that if a behavior is innate rather than learned, then depriving the organism of the information it would need in order to learn the behavior should prove the case. As will be seen presently, deprivation experiments are not ones to which Fodor defers.

In short, Fodor provides us with little reason to conclude that some concepts are released into the repertoire via the causal process of triggering. Furthermore, there is little empirical evidence for denying the opposite conclusion that so-called basic primitives are the consequence of learning. If this is so, does identifying the triggered concepts following Fodor's procedure help to determine what the genome must specify about linguistic/cognitive structures? The answer is no. The reason is that if the so-called triggered concepts are really present because they were learned, then these triggered concepts are not basic primitive concepts. Unless basic primitives can be identified as such there are no grounds for drawing inferences about the kind of information provided by the genome.

A brief examination of one triggered concept proves the point. According to Fodor (1981, p. 311), the data collected by Brown (1958) and Rosch, Mervis, Gray, Johnson, and Boyes-Braem (1976) indicate that concepts like car, table, dog, and house are basic primitive concepts because they are acquired before others in a given heirarchy. The data, says Fodor, show that children acquire the concept house before building or bungalow. This may be true. But are we to infer that house is a basic primitive concept—that its acquisition does not depend on the acquisition of still other concepts acquired previously? The data reveal whether the concept of house is available to the child at a given point in time. They also show that the concept x is available to the child before concepts y or z. But the data cannot demonstrate whether the concept of house is acquired independently of others, that is, without their mediation. Such must be the case if house is in fact basic primitive concept.

Because the concepts Fodor identifies as *basic* primitives could be either triggered or mediated, there is no assurance that these are ones with which the mind begins. Consequently, even though we can enter the hierarchies at given points and determine that concept x appears in the repertoire before concept y, it is still the case that x may depend on the existence of other still unidentified concepts (semantic hierarchies of concepts).

One might respond that all this is trivial. While Fodor's data may not identify basic primitives, one can impose arbitrary stopping points. If one finds that house is acquired before bungalow or building, one can say "Look, this is good enough. Let's see what criteria house meets because it is more primitive than bungalow or building, and besides, we can't identify any concept *more* primitive than house in this hierarchy—at least, not yet!"

We can pursue this strategy—as Fodor might suggest. But have we made any progress in gathering empirical data that will help us resolve the question of whether primitive concepts are structured or unstructured, or whether some concepts are specified by the genome, or whether Chomsky is right and Piaget wrong? Of course not, for we have not identified, or made any progress toward identifying, the basic primitive concepts. Clearly, Fodor's proposal is meaningless unless we can specify these, and as I have shown, his research strategy fails here.

In summary, then, we have the following predicament. By assuming RTM, as do Chomsky and Piaget, one assumes that representations must be present for the system to function and that these must have meaning to the system. But what is the nature of these primitive representations and how did they get there? Chomsky responds by saying that the primitive representations that make language acquisition possible are linguistic constraints specified at the level of the genome—the UG. This is an empirical claim. To test it, an observation-inference method like the one sketched above (which Fodor describes) has been pursued:

1. One observes behavior that seems to provide evidence about the nature of the primitive representations (e.g., one generates certain data).
2. On the basis of the data, one draws inferences about the nature of these primitive representations (e.g., that the concept house is a primitive concept).
3. On the basis of these inferences, one draws further inferences about what, if anything, must be specified at the level of the genome *if* these are the representations with which the mind begins.

The problem with the research thus far, however, is that it fails to demonstrate that the so-called primitive representations are, in fact, primitive and unmediated. As long as their presence in the repertoire could result from mediation by other concepts, the nature of primitive concepts remains unknown. While Piaget and Chomsky make opposing claims about genetic constraints, research has yet to verify either position.

Intentionality

The Origin of Meaning

The problem of designing appropriate empirical research is not the only problem that proponents of RTM have had to face. There is a related conceptual dilemma that many have struggled with, which is this: If the mind cannot operate unless it can represent things, this means it cannot operate unless it can attach meaning to its representations. How does it become capable of meaning? As philosophers (e.g., Searle, 1981) put the question: How does the mind become capable of intentionality?

Fodor has undertaken the herculean task of drawing out the implications of assuming a representational theory of mind. For example, in *The Language of Thought* (1975), he argues that if the mind functions by manipulating representations, then these representations must have meaning, that is, some translation in the language of thought. Assuming RTM presupposes that some representations, and thus their translations in mentalese, are available to be manipulated according to rules for so doing, that is, they are innate (pp. 79-83).

Dennett (1978, p. 107) finds Fodor's position highly debatable. He recognizes that assuming RTM requires that the representations have meaning, but he refuses to hold a position which asserts that meanings need to be explicit and that they are acquired in the way Fodor describes (1978, p. 107). Dennett takes an "intentional stance" and asks: Under what conditions do we *attribute* intelligence (and hence, intentionality) to a system? He assumes no model of the mind but instead concerns himself with specifying the above conditions. This involves reinterpreting the evidence for RTM. He argues that one need not maintain that thinking is a process of hypothesis formation and confirmation, and consequently one need not conclude that meanings are explicitly represented or that one must assume RTM.

Why does Dennett object so to Fodor's view and opt for the intentional stance? Dennett advances several claims against Fodor, two of which I will discuss. First, he maintains that Fodor's argument is incomplete, as one may disconfirm as well as confirm hypotheses (1978, p. 103). The procedure of disconfirmation, Dennett maintains, would allow a child to eliminate false hypotheses; the true ones would remain, not because they conform to specified criteria but because they do not violate any criteria. Since one could learn without forming and confirming hypotheses, the latter need not be taken as the mechanism of learning.

Second, Dennett argues that the beliefs we hold are far more numerous than the hypotheses we entertain (1978, p. 104). We believe that zebras do not wear overcoats, but we believe without trying out some hypothesis to this effect and determining whether results of the trial meet certain criteria. Consequently, there is much mental functioning which takes place without hypothesis formation and confirmation.

My analysis of RTM provides a basis for evaluating Dennett's arguments that learning need not be a matter of hypothesis formation and confirmation. The first point to underscore is that *if* learning is a consequence of hypothesis formation and confirmation, then the meanings of representations must be explicitly represented to the extent that they meet four criteria. First, the translations of the representations must identify the other representations (the other concepts) that are involved, such that, for example, *snow* means x and *white* means y. The translation of *snow* must be related to the concepts of wet, cold, crystalline, and the like; the translation of *white* must relate to the concepts of color, absence of color, and so on. As meanings are defined by relating concepts to one another in this way, translations must specify these relations.

Second, the translation of *snow is white* must specify the meaning which occurs if one relates the concept of snow to the concept of white using the predicate *is*. If these two concepts are so related, then a claim, say c, is asserted about conditions in the environment. The translation must specify the meaning of this claim. Furthermore, the meaning is derived from the meaning of the component concepts.

Third, the translation must specify the conditions in the environment under which one is justified in trying out the belief that snow is white. It might indicate, for example, that one can believe snow is white when one observes a, evaluates a to have the characteristics specified by the translation of mentalese x (meaning *snow*), and observes that a also has the characteristics specified by the translation of mentalese y (meaning *white*).

Fourth, the translation specifies the criteria that must be met if the belief that snow is white is a justified belief. Thus in addition to indicating when experience with the environment permits us to try out the hypothesis, the translation also indicates the conditions that have to be satisfied if that hypothesis is verified. These criteria allow the thinker to judge, "Yes, a has the characteristics specified by mentalese x and may be taken to be snow; yes, a also has the characteristics specified by mentalese y; therefore, the assertion that 'snow is white' is justified—I can believe it to be true."

It may not be apparent why, in Fodor's account, the mentalese translation of *snow is white* must have these four characteristics. The reason is that if learning occurs through a process of hypothesis formation and confirmation, then the mind must function by manipulating representations that have meaning. The mind must therefore possess the language of thought (which Fodor describes) because this provides the representations with meaning. How can hypotheses be formulated if the terms of a hypothesis do not correspond to some mentalese translation that specifies the features of the terms by linking them to certain concepts (point one above)? And how can the terms in the hypothesis be related to one another in such a way as to form the hypothesis if the meaning of so doing is not specified (point two above)? And how can the hypothesis be verified if the environmental conditions necessary for its verification are not specified (point three above)? And how can the hypothesis be verified unless there are criteria for its evaluation (point four above)? If learning is a consequence of hypothesis formation and confirmation, then the language of thought must be present, and a translation of the language must be explicit enough to specify these four things.

Now let us return to Dennett's objections—that in some cases one learns things without forming and confirming hypotheses, and that we know more than we can possibly confirm. Recall that if the process of learning is not fundamentally a process of hypothesis formation and confirmation, then there would seem to be no need for claiming that the meanings of representations must be explicitly represented or for assuming RTM in the first place.

Consider the first claim—that one can learn without forming and confirming hypotheses. Dennett (1978, p. 103) asserts that a child could learn something that determined the extension *is a chair* by disconfirming such hypotheses as "*x* is a chair is true iff (if and only if) *x* is red." Dennett guesses that Fodor would respond to this example by saying that if children did disconfirm this hypothesis, and hence learned that chair did not have to meet the specified criterion, they would eventually arrive at the proper criteria—the criteria that any *x* called a chair must meet—through conjunction of the disconfirmed hypotheses.

I believe Fodor would respond as Dennett suggests and that explicit representation is still required. If the conjunction of disconfirmed hypotheses does generate the appropriate criteria, there must be criteria to which the set of disconfirmed hypotheses would conform. The criteria would be specified by the system. The process of disconfirmation as Dennett describes it provides no alternative to the problematic aspect of forming and confirming hypotheses. In either case, if learning occurs—for example, if the child arrives at the understanding that the concept chair applies under conditions *a*, *b*, and *c*—there must be certain criteria, specified by the truth rules, that the trials must meet (point four above). As shown, the truth rules are set forth by the language of thought and are present in the system. If there were no truth rules—no criteria for trials to meet—neither confirmation nor disconfirmation of hypotheses could occur.

But, Dennett continues (1978, p. 104), Fodor's account is unsatisfactory from an empirical point of view. It is highly unlikely that animals or even people actually engage in a process of hypothesis confirmation and/or disconfirmation in order to learn. Furthermore, can one ever test the claim that the mind functions by forming and confirming hypotheses?

Both these complaints are weak. First, even if it is the case that we cannot prove, using empirical evidence, that the process of learning involves hypothesis formation and confirmation, we cannot disprove it either. The claim is accepted by Fodor because it allows him to explain certain phenomena. Dennett argues much more persuasively when he shows how Fodor's assumptions confront him with conceptual limitations he cannot overcome (see below). The fact that Fodor's position cannot be empirically verified is not the most telling blow against it. The claim that processes of hypothesis formation and confirmation and/or disconfirmation are unrealistic or implausible procedures for learning is again a weak objection because its grounds are speculative. Implausible or not, it may still be correct.

Perhaps it is now apparent how Fodor would answer Dennett's other objection— that we know more than we can possibly have hypothesized. The cases in which we appear to know without the benefit of such procedures can occur because we have already confirmed and/or disconfirmed many other hypotheses, and their conjunction permits us to draw inferences that turn out to be correct. We believe zebras do not wear overcoats (when someone asks us to think about it) because we have tried out and confirmed many other hypotheses about zebras and overcoats, the conjunction of which implies the truth of this proposition. Further, the system has a rule which specifies the criteria that the conjunction must meet. Of course, to know if the conjunction were true, one would have to take a trip to West Bengal to be certain a new Macy's has not been recently erected near the zebra feeding grounds!

In summary, then, I have shown that while Dennett objects to Fodor's approach, his arguments do not undercut Fodor's claims that learning is a consequence of forming and confirming hypotheses, that representations must be explicit, and that the mind functions by manipulating representations. Furthermore, in Fodor's account, the meanings of the representations must be explicit enough to specify the information described in points one through four.

Fodor's position requires that some representations and their meanings must be available initially, explicit in the senses indicated, and he claims that some meanings are innate. If one argues that meanings are not innate, as Dennett does, then where does meaning come from? This brings us to Dennett's own resolution of the intentionality dilemma.

Can Artificial Intelligence Stop the Regress?

Dennett (1978) states that traditionally, the intentionality dilemma has been posed in the following way:

> The only psychology that could possibly succeed in explaining the complexities of human activity must posit internal representations. . . . But . . . nothing is intrinsically a representation of anything; something is a representation only *for* or *to* someone; any representation or system of representations thus requires at least one user or interpreter of the representation who is external to it. Any such interpreter must have a variety of psychological or intentional traits: it must be capable of a variety of *comprehension*, and must have beliefs and goals (so it can *use* the representation to *inform* itself and thus assist it in achieving its goals). Such an interpreter is then a sort of homunculus. . . . psychology *without* homunculi is impossible. But psychology *with* homunculi is doomed to circularity or infinite regress, so psychology is impossible. (pp. 119-122)

The issue here is the issue of reduction: If psychology must assume that the mind functions by manipulating representations, then it must assume that the mind has some means for interpreting the representations—for giving them meaning. One alternative to claiming meanings are innate is to provide an interpreter for the representations, namely, the homunculus—a quasi-humanoid creature who stands external to the representations and reads them. The homunculus has beliefs and goals and is capable of comprehending, that is, attributing meaning. In short, it is capable of intentionality.

The problem with the homunculus proposal—apart from its obvious implausibility—is that the question now arises: Who tells the homunculus that x is to mean a? The possible responses are (a) nobody, which means that we explain nothing by positing the homunculus because we still do not know where meanings come from, and (b) another homunculus, which means we have an infinite regress because the question above must again be asked of it. There are only these two answers, each unsatisfactory. In neither case have we explained where the meanings of the representations—especially the initial representations—come from.

Dennett (1978) says that the science of artificial intelligence (AI) promises to provide us with a resolution of this age-old dilemma. It permits us to view *apparently* intentional behavior as the work of a rule-governed "army of idiots":

> One starts, in AI, with a specification of a whole person or cognitive organism—what I call, more neutrally, an intentional system . . . and then breaks that largest intentional system into an organization of subsystems, each of which could itself be viewed as an intentional system (with its own specialized beliefs and desires) and hence as formally a homunculus. . . . If one can get a team or committee of *relatively* ignorant, narrow-minded, blind homunculi to produce the intelligent behavior of the whole, this is progress. A flow chart is typically the organizational chart of a committee of homunculi (investigators, librarians, accountants, executives); each box specifies a homunculus by prescribing a function *without saying how it is to be accomplished*. . . . If we then look closer at the individual boxes we see that the function of each is accomplished by subdividing it via another flow chart into still smaller, more stupid homunculi. Eventually, this nesting of boxes within boxes lands you with homunculi so stupid (all they have to do is remember whether to say yes or no when asked) that they can be, as one says, "replaced by a machine". One *discharges* fancy homunculi from one's scheme by organizing armies of such idiots to do the work. (pp. 123-124)

Dennett says AI solves the regress problem by showing that *apparently* intentional behavior can be viewed as the result of a system of nonintentional operations. Behavior which appears to be the result of "understanding" or attributing meaning is instead the consequence of following certain rules which have been programmed in and specify the conditions under which behaviors of various sorts are to occur. At the higher levels of the flow-chart, the behaviors of the (apparently) more intelligent homunculi are in fact ones which may be followed by a number of other behaviors, thanks to the complexity of the rule structure.

It seems to me that there are two ways to view Dennett's use of AI here, neither of which solves the regress problem.[5] The first is to understand the "committee of homunculi" as precisely that—a hierarchically organized work force, the members of which are capable of attributing meaning to behavior. From this perspective, Dennett can be seen as attacking the regress problem head on, for he is speaking to the traditional formulation, that is, how the representations get "read." The answer he gets from AI is that the reading of representations can be broken down into subtasks, each of which requires a less intelligent reader. Here "one discharges fancy homunculi" by showing that an army of progressively more "stupid" ones—ones who "read" by responding yes or no under very narrow conditions—together generate a complex meaning.

Does this committee of readers help to explain how the system becomes capable of reading the representations in the first place? More precisely, does it explain who tells the homunculus at the top that x is to mean a? If by this second question we mean: How does the homunculus at the top come up with the interpretation that

---

[5] I am indebted to Denis Phillips and John Searle for helping me to calrify Dennett's position.

x means a? then AI gives an answer: The members of the committee tell the homunculus at the top that x means a when certain conditions of various sorts are fulfilled. To put it precisely, committee members "tell" the homunculus at the top when those conditions have been met in particular cases.

If, however, the second question means (as I think it does): How must the homunculus at the top come to recognize that the "reading" it makes must depend on the fulfillment of certain conditions? and: How are the conditions arrived at?, then the AI perspective tells us nothing. Here is the argument. The operations of every homunculus in the hierarchy are based upon manipulating representations and attaching meanings to the consequences of the manipulations. While the homunculi of a given level may not understand how their operations relate to those of the other homunculi in the system, they do understand the meaning of their maneuvers in terms of one another. We may envision each homunculus functioning as a feedback system—trying out behaviors, evaluating consequences, and selecting alternatives on the basis of these evaluations. Each of these steps requires that the homunculus attach meaning, that is, understand what it does. Intentionality is thus present at every level of the hierarchy.

The consequence of this fact is that according to the present view of Dennett's position there are no stupid homunculi and no intelligent ones, only more or less intelligent ones. That is, the ones at the lowest level operate with a very narrow repertoire of possible meanings to attach to their behaviors. But they still attribute meanings. The homunculi which need only respond yes or no under simple conditions must still represent the conditions under which yes is an appropriate response and assess the situation accordingly. While they may understand nothing about the significance of their responses, they still must understand in order to respond.

The fact that the homunculi on the bottom of the hierarchy are only less intelligent than those above them, rather than stupid, means that replacing one homunculus with a committee fails to explain how the system reaches the conditions for or the necessity of attributing meaning. For the homunculi at the lowest level still know when to attribute some meanings rather than others. And if they have knowledge—even very limited knowledge—then they have all the other characteristics of a system that can attribute meanings. Replacing one homunculus with a committee fails to explain how the system comes to attribute meaning to its behaviors. Instead, the hierarchy of homunculi proposed by Dennett presupposes that the system can attribute meanings to its behaviors from the start—that it is an intentional system from the start. It seems to me that the question is: How does the system become capable of attributing meaning?, not How does the system carry out its rules-following procedures? Given the present interpretation, Dennett's position and his use of AI has little consequence for an adequate resolution of the intentionality dilemma.

There is, however, another perspective from which to view Dennett's text. Instead of seeing the committee as an intentional work force of readers, one might understand the hierarchy to depict as unintentional the committee's *apparently* intentional behavior. Dennett's conception is diagrammed in Figure 6.1. Here, behaviors which occur depend on the responses given to previously executed behaviors (those at higher levels of the hierarchy). The dependence is entirely rule governed so that the machine does x if and only if certain conditions are fulfilled.

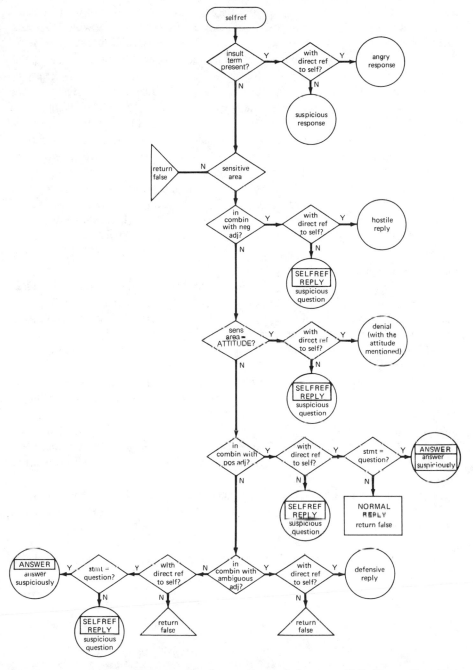

Figure 6.1. Diagram of Dennett's "committee of homunculi." (From Dennett, 1979. Reprinted by permission of Humanities Press Inc., Atlantic Highlands, N.J.)

A "higher level" behavior, which might appear to require a "more intelligent" homunculus in order to carry it out, can instead be seen as one for which there are several possibilities for subsequent action, given the operational rules in the system. The realization of the subsequent behaviors requires no "intelligent" being but simply the fulfillment of certain conditions.

Does either interpretation of Dennett's position help to stop the regress? Does either explain how the system becomes capable of attributing meaning? Unfortunately, the answer to both questions is no. In the first interpretation, Dennett's view fails because intentionality is present at every level. In the present interpretation it fails because intentionality is completely absent from the picture. When the various contingencies for behavior are pursued, it may appear that the machine is attributing meaning and making choices—more complex choices at the higher levels. In fact, the "choice" is no choice because the behaviors at every level are always necessary given the fulfillment of specified conditions. Since there is no intentionality anywhere in the system, it can only "explain" intentional behavior by identifying the conditions under which the behaviors *look* intentional, that is, when a variety of subsequent behaviors is possible.

The problem with this view of the intentional stance is that it dodges the issue. It defines meaning as rule following and gives up trying to explain how the system comes to follow rules or how it arrives at the rules it follows. Since the focus is on the conditions under which intentionality is *attributed* to a system, the intentional stance once again tells nothing about how meaning or understanding is possible for that system.[6]

Fodor is not content with the intentional stance. Instead, he tries to face the issue and answer the following questions. What is the source of meaning? How do meanings become available to the system? The source of meaning, he says, is the language of thought—the set of primitive representations and meanings with which the mind begins. The meanings become available when the representations are released into the repertoire via triggering. Furthermore, they are innate in the sense that they are specified by the genome.

As I have shown, however, Fodor's triggering account is problematic. Thus, his claim that (some) meanings are innate is not substantiated on empirical grounds. The problem is that if one assumes RTM, one needs to provide an account of how the representations with which the mind begins acquire their meaning. To say that some meanings are innate is fine if one can provide empirical evidence for this claim. Both Fodor and Chomsky fail here.

Learning and Coming to Know

Hamlyn suggests an alternative resolution to the dilemma. He argues that the first knowledge a child acquires cannot be learned because the process of learning requires the existence of knowledge already (1978, p. 94). Thus, to answer the question of how first knowledge, and hence the attribution of meaning, becomes possible, he introduces a distinction between learning and coming to know.

---

[6] For further discussion of the intentional stance vis à vis intentionality, see Searle (1980a, 1983) Dennett (1980a).

Any acquisition of knowledge involves the connecting of items. . . . In learning
. . . the connection is between what one comes to know and what one knows
already, so that it is right to say . . . that learning implies knowledge that is
pre-existent in time . . . Even if coming to know involves connecting things . . .
there are no *temporal* implications about the connecting. (p. 92)

The solution of the problem, then, is that while the acquisition of knowledge or
understanding through learning implies the existence of preexisting knowledge,
coming to know is a means of acquiring knowledge other than learning and one
which does not require preexisting knowledge.

Can it be that knowledge may be acquired through a process that does not require
preexisting knowledge? Hamlyn (1978, p. 91) says that if children are in a position
to have knowledge, and they distinguish between x and y where the distinguishing
does not appear to be chance behavior and there is an actual difference between x
and y, then we might say that they have come to know a difference between x and
y. We would not say the children have learned, says Hamlyn, because they could
have come to this knowledge without any prior knowledge.

Hamlyn is careful to point out (pp. 93-94) that in the above example, the children might be wrong about the difference between x and y, yet we would still
attribute knowledge to them. Even if they do not know what distinguishes x from
y, they do know that x and y differ in some way. This, says Hamlyn, may be very
minimal knowledge, but it is knowledge, provided x and y do actually differ. If the
children have some knowledge of x and y, then we can attribute meaning of some
sort to them.

Does the distinction between learning and coming to know stop the regress? My
position is that it does not. We still have the problem of explaining how the child
becomes capable of attaching meanings. My argument is this:

Hamlyn's claim that learning requires preexisting knowledge while coming to
know does not rests on the assumption that coming to know is possible without
preexisting knowledge—that one can come to know something without that knowledge depending on previously existing knowledge. Let us take the case where children come to know that there is some difference between x and y. What they come
to know is that two objects, x and y, differ. The knowledge acquired—what the
child comes to know—is knowledge about the two objects x and y, namely, that
they differ.

By what means can children possibly come to this knowledge? The procedure
may work like this. The children already have some concept of difference, encounter
objects x and y, and evaluate them according to the criteria of that concept. When
it is said that children come to know that objects x and y differ, one may mean that
they know what it is for two things to differ—that they have some concept of difference and that the features of that concept have some features in common with
those of its public version. The children, then, come to know whether the two
objects in question meet the criteria set forth by the public concept of difference.

If this is the procedure for coming to know, then it involves (a) attributing the
concept of difference to two objects x and y, (b) coming to know that they meet
the criteria specified by the concept of difference, and (c) arriving at the same conclusion that others who share the concept of difference would also reach should

they apply it to x and y. If others sharing the concept of difference agree that x and y differ, then one may conclude that the children know x and y differ.

One might object that coming to know need not involve the process described here—that some alternative process is possible. Perhaps the brain is injected with the information that x differs from y, in which case one would know it after the injection had occurred. Even in this case, however, to say that one comes to know that x and y differ means that one is given the information (via injection) that x and y meet the criteria specified by the concept of difference. Thus one must already have the concept of difference in order to know, after the injection, that x differs from y.

Again, one might also object that even though the process of coming to know something requires the existence of some concept, for example, the concept of difference, that concept need not preexist. Indeed, Hamlyn (1978, p. 94) claims that to come to know anything one must come to know a variety of things all at once. He argues that coming to know x and y differ requires that one contrast them to one another, which yields knowledge about each—at the very least, the knowledge that they differ. This contrasting yields both the information that they do differ and information about the differences between them.

Hamlyn is quite right that coming to know one thing involves coming to know others. But the point is that in order to come to know either that x and y differ or the ways in which they differ, one must already have some concept of difference that shares features with the public version of that concept. Another way of making this same point is to say that to come to know that x and y differ, the children must be in a position to have knowledge, as Hamlyn says. That is, they must be in a position to recognize truth as truth and take correction as correction. But what can it mean to be able to recognize truth as truth except that one already *has* a concept of truth, and thus can recognize a case of the truth when one comes across it! Given this, one may recognize that x differs from y. The question now is: Where does one get that concept of truth? Isn't its acquisition that which needs to be explained if one is to account for the possibility of attributing meaning?

Hamlyn might respond by saying that one comes to know what truth is (one acquires a concept of truth) at the same time one comes to know that x and y differ. Alternatively, one comes to have a concept of difference at the same time one comes to know that x and y differ and what the difference is. All this may be, but the fact is we have yet to explain why children come to know any of these things. A satisfactory answer will involve some description of the factors which bring this about, and their relation to a functioning mind. While Hamlyn discusses some of the relevant factors and their roles (e.g., 1978, 1981), he does not explain how the mind functions such that a concept of truth is acquired. His distinction between learning and coming to know does not, therefore, terminate the regress.

RTM and the Equilibrium Principle

Piaget's Use of Equilibrium

Dennett (1978) states that traditionally philosophers have assumed that "the only psychology that could possibly . . . explain the complexities of human activity must posit internal representations" (p. 119). While Hamlyn (Note 3) maintains he does not hold RTM, he nowhere denies the existence of mental representations. The tradition of representing reality and manipulating the representations according to rules is fundamentally the Kantian tradition. It is a tradition shared by Piaget, Fodor, Chomsky, and many others. All of these theorists subscribe to the following Kantian claim:

> The knowledge yielded by understanding, or at least by the human understanding, must therefore be by means of concepts, and so is not intuitive but discursive . . . concepts rest on functions. By "function" I mean the unity of the act of bringing various representations under one common representation. . . . Now the only use which the understanding can make of these concepts is to judge by means of them. . . . Judgement is therefore the mediate knowledge of an object, that is, the representation of a representation of it. (Kant, 1929, p. 105)

The seeds of the representational theory of mind are all to be found in this quotation. Kant maintains that the mind can understand things only as it represents them and represents its representations. The representations which provide understanding are made in terms of concepts. If concepts are to provide understanding of the world, then they must be manipulated. This is what Kant means when he says "concepts rest on functions." The functions are rules for manipulating the concepts —for bringing "various representations under one common representation." They are higher-order concepts, and Kant envisions a hierarchical system of concepts by which the mind judges its treatment of the world. Kantian knowledge is, then, a "representation of a representation" of objects. It is the judgment of whether one's representation of the world meets certain criteria.

Toulmin (see reference note 4) distinguishes five ways in which some things can represent others. For example, the representation may be a kind of proxy or intermediary which stands between the perceiver and the perceived and brings knowledge of the latter to the former. When concepts, mental pictures, or propositions are said to represent objects, however, the representation may stand for the object. Here, the mind "holds or grasps" its objects in the world by means of these representations. Where brain states represent those elements in the world to which they are responses, the representation "carries" knowledge in the sense of giving direction for physiological response rather than standing for an object or mediating between the knower and the known. The fourth notion of representation applies to maps, mathematical equations, and computer programs, that is, cases in which the representation brings together, represents, or sets forth (*stellen . . . dar*) aspects of the world, and thus makes them "intelligible." Finally, individual experience may be "internalized" and expressed in the form of pictures or images "in the head." In this case, the representation is not taken as setting forth the object. Rather, it is the object that can be manipulated without reference to the world.

Given Toulmin's classification scheme, the Kantian notion of representation falls into the fourth category. According to Kant, the mind operates by manipulating representations which set forth (*stellen . . . dar*) things in the world by putting them into forms and making them knowable. The main task of the mind, then, is to represent things and evaluate the adequacy of the representation, that is, determine how well the representation actually sets forth what is in the world.

Given Kant's conception, the mind needs an initial set of representations (concepts) which can be applied to things encountered, and functions, or higher-order concepts, for manipulating the representations and evaluating their fit with the world. Furthermore, given the hierarchical organization of these functions, the possibilities for change in either the representations or the functions themselves need to be indicated initially.

My point is that we can thank Kant for the contemporary representational theory of mind. His legacy has brought with it certain questions, some of which Kant himself tried to address (e.g., the nature of the categories and primitive concepts; see Strawson, 1966). Among these questions are:

1. What is the nature of the initial representations with which the mind begins?
2. Where do these representations come from?
3. How does one explain the possibility of objective understanding if the mind is a hierarchical system which operates according to the principles of feedback?
4. How does one explain the possibility of conventional understanding?
5. How does one explain intentionality (the possibility of attributing meaning)?

It seemed to Piaget that by using the equilibrium principle he could resolve the above questions. In the preceding chapters, I show that this is not the case. The question is: Why did Piaget believe that use of Waddington's genetic assimilation principle as a theory-constitutive metaphor would permit him to be successful?

The answer appears to be quite simple. While Piaget's use of the equilibrium principle cannot resolve the above questions, it does provide a basis for explaining how the mind, viewed under Kant's representational conception, can operate in the first place. By using genetic assimilation as a theory-constitutive metaphor, Piaget provides himself with a motive both for why things are represented as they are and why representations (and rules for manipulating representations) change. The motive is to maintain equilibrium with the environment. Consequently, we find Piaget arguing that representations of certain sorts persist under certain circumstances (i.e., there is assimilation) when the representations permit one to interact with the world in ways which meet one's needs and thereby maintain equilibrium. Furthermore, representations and functions for manipulating representations change when a state of disequilibrium with the environment is created.

There is no question that assuming RTM constrains one to explain why things are represented in some ways rather than others and why representations change. Piaget's use of the equilibrium principle permits him to answer these questions, and this is no small point in its favor. However, it does not allow him to address other questions that are also raised if one assumes RTM and tries at the same time to explain the acquisition of reasoning ability.

The State of Psychological Theorizing

What conclusions can be drawn from the foregoing analysis about theorizing in psychology? I have argued that Piaget's use of the equilibrium principle, in spite of its appeal and appropriateness in some respects, leaves his account of cognitive change with severe inadequacies. One wonders whether some other use of the equi-

librium principle might prove more satisfactory or whether, on balance, the principle is simply inappropriate for explaining why reasoning improves. My analysis
implies three conclusions in answer to this question.

First, I have argued that one biological version of the equilibrium principle,
namely, genetic assimilation, if used in a certain way, creates serious limitations in
an account of cognitive change. There are two properties of genetic assimilation
that are problematic. In the first place, it sets forth a developmental process of
change. The process is defined in terms of the feedback principle and its attendant
features, including assumptions about what must be available for the system to
operate. The developmental process assumes that there is something which develops
(e.g., structures of some sort) and that these develop toward predetermined ends.
The second problematic property of genetic assimilation relates directly to the first,
namely, its theory of origins is based, fundamentally, upon principles of random
variation and natural selection. Piaget, as I have shown, fails to recognize that these
characteristics are intrinsic to the principle of genetic assimilation and cannot be
eradicated from it.

Genetic assimilation is a version of the equilibrium principle, and the latter is
fundamentally a principle of conservation. This means it provides a motive for
explaining why, in the face of environmental change, the system reverts to an alternative behavior in its repertoire. The equilibrium concept is modified by Waddington (genetic assimilation) and Piaget (phenocopy) so it can have relevance to cases
where one wishes to explain how the operations of the system improve. Indeed, the
genetic assimilation and phenocopy versions of equilibrium are more appropriate
for explaining cognitive change than is, say, homeostasis. Still, these developmental
versions are inadequate, and the features which render them so, including the feedback process of operation that they set forth, are intrinsic to the equilibrium concept. I conclude that the fundamental features of the equilibrium principle are
inimical to the goal of explaining cognitive change.

Second, I have maintained all along that it is not simply the properties of genetic
assimilation which prove disadvantageous. Equally important is Piaget's use of it as
a theory-constitutive metaphor. It is this application of genetic assimilation which
requires Piaget to explain cognitive change as a consequence of developing cognitive
structures whose features are either predetermined at the outset or arise by chance.
It also constrains him to give a functional account of cognitive development—an
objective which he cannot fulfill. As I have argued, his use of genetic assimilation
cannot explain the possibility of intentionality, objectivity, or conventional understanding.

Could the principle of genetic assimilation be used in some other way to help
explain cognitive change? This is a possibility. However, in order to do so, one would
have to question the assumptions Piaget makes in applying it. For example, the fact
that he uses genetic assimilation as a theory-constitutive metaphor strongly suggests
that he finds it appropriate to think of cognitive change as cognitive development.
Given this assumption, he can proceed to draw out the parallels between cognitive
and embryological change. One could question the assumption, draw the negative
conclusion, and not use the principle as a basis for a developmental account.

But one might well find the principle of genetic assimilation of little interest in this case. Models are borrowed from one science by another when their features appear applicable in the new domain. If cognitive change is not to be explained as a process of development, the principle of genetic assimilation might appear totally irrelevant. Indeed, the appeal of the equilibrium principle might drastically diminish.

The third conclusion is this. I have argued that Piaget makes highly problematic use of genetic assimilation and he does so because he assumes RTM. Even more fundamental than the utility of the equilibrium principle is the utility of this model of the mind. Should that be abandoned?

This may seem a preposterous question given our Kantian tradition. Is it possible to abandon it, one wonders. Whether it is possible to abandon RTM, it seems to me, is precisely the question that both philosophers and psychologists must face. Hamlyn (Note 3) maintains that one need not suppose a model of the mind at all. Toulmin (in press) shows that by focusing on a different notion of representation—representation as *internalization* rather than *stellen . . . dar* (setting forth)—it is possible to reenvision the process by which our understanding changes. Dennett (1978) argues that an intentional view of behavior—one which concentrates on the conditions under which we attribute change in behavior rather than on what happens inside the head so that behavior changes—is more fruitful. The implication of the foregoing analysis is that those who would do psychological theorizing can no longer afford to ignore these arguments.

With regard to the equilibrium principle, the argument in this book has its limits. I have analyzed but one case where its application proves highly unsatisfactory. I am not concluding, as a consequence of my analysis, that the equilibrium concept has no place in psychological theorizing. Rather, I maintain that psychology should seriously question its use of this popular idea as an explanatory device. The version of equilibrium that is chosen, the way it is applied, and the phenomena to be explained must be carefully evaluated if serious limitations are to be avoided in the account. Piaget's failures provide a basis for examining both shortcomings in other psychological explanations and the general appropriateness of the equilibrium principle for accounts across the discipline.

Paul had raised his eyes above her to the gaslight. He stared into its white glow, elevated with his voice above the little waiting-room. Then he looked down again at Ada—and for a moment, in the dark flicker left on his eyes by the previous brilliance he thought he saw in Ada the shape of understanding. But this could only have been the shape of his hope. As his eyes grew accustomed again to the room, as the glare dissolved, he saw that Ada was no longer there. He was alone. (Sansom, p. 45)

Reference Notes

1. Wood, G. D. *Triggering, or how concepts aren't acquired.* Paper presented at the meeting of the Midwest Cognitive Science Study Group, 1982. Manuscript submitted for publication.
2. Hamlyn, D. W. *Addendum.* Unpublished manuscript, 1979.
3. Hamlyn, D. W. Personal communication, summer, 1982.
4. Toulmin, S. *Human understanding, Vol. II: The individual acquisition and grasp of concepts.* Princeton, N.J.: Princeton University Press, in press.

References

Anscombe, G. E. M. *Intention* (2nd ed.). Ithaca, N.Y.: Cornell University Press, 1953.

Apostel, L., Mandelbrot, M., & Piaget, J. *L'explication dans les sciences*. Paris: Flammarion, 1973.

Baldwin, J. M. A new factor in evolution. *The American Naturalist,* 1896, *30*, 354.

Baldwin, J. M. *Mental development in the child and the race* (3rd ed., rev.). New York: Macmillan, 1915.

Beilin, H. The development of physical concepts. In T. Mischel (Ed.), *Cognitive development and epistemology*. New York: Academic Press, 1971.

Biro, J. I., & Shahan, R. W. (Eds.). *Mind, brain, and function: essays in the philosophy of mind*. Norman, Oklahoma: University of Oklahoma Press, 1982. (Reprinted from *Philosophical Topics,* Spring, 1981.)

Black, M. *Models and metaphors: Studies in language and philosophy*. Ithaca, N. Y.: Cornell University Press, 1962.

Boyd, R. Metaphor and theory change: What is "metaphor" a metaphor for? In A. Ortony (Ed.), *Metaphor and thought*. Cambridge: Cambridge University Press, 1979.

Brainerd, C. J. The stage question in cognitive-developmental theory. *The Behavioral and Brain Sciences,* 1978, *2*, 173-213.

Broughton, J. M. Piaget's structural developmental psychology II: Logic and psychology. *Human Development,* 1981, *24*, 195-224. (a)

Broughton, J. M. Piaget's structural developmental psychology III: Function and the problem of knowledge. *Human Development,* 1981, *24*, 257-285. (b)

Brown, R. How shall a thing be called? *Psychological Review,* 1958, *65*, 14-21.

Bruner, J. Inhelder and Piaget's growth of logical thinking I: A psychologist's viewpoint. *British Journal of Psychology,* 1959, *50*, 363-370.

Cannon, W. B. *The wisdom of the body*. New York: Norton, 1939.

Cellérier, G., Papert, S., & Voyat, G. *Cybernétique et épistémologie*. Etudes d'épisté-mologie génétique (Vol. 22). Paris: Presses Universitaires de France, 1968.

Chomsky, N. *Aspects of the theory of syntax*. Cambridge, Mass.: M.I.T. Press, 1965.

Chomsky, N. On cognitive structures and their development: A reply to Piaget. In M. Piattelli-Palmarini (Ed.), *Language and learning: The debate between Jean Piaget and Noam Chomsky*. Cambridge, Mass.: Harvard University Press, 1980. (a)

Chomsky, N. *Rules and representations*. New York: Columbia University Press, 1980. (b)

Chomsky, N. Rules and representations. *Brain and Behavioral Sciences*, 1980, *3*(1), 1-15, 42-61. (c)

Cunningham, M. *Intelligence: Its organization and development*. New York: Academic Press, 1972.

Dennett, D. C. *Brainstorms: Philosophical essays on mind and psychology*. Cambridge, Mass.: M.I.T. Press (A Bradford Book), 1978.

Dennett, D. C., Artificial intelligence as philosophy and psychology. In M. D. Ringle (Ed.), *Philosophical perspectives in artificial intelligence*. New York: Humanities Press, 1979.

Dennett, D. C. The milk of human intentionality. *The Behavioral and Brain Sciences*, 1980, *3*(3), 428-430. (a)

Dennett, D. C. Passing the buck to biology. *The Behavioral and Brain Sciences*, 1980, *3*(1), 19. (b)

Dewey, J. *How we think*. New York: D. C. Heath, 1933.

Dobzhansky, T. *Mankind evolving: The evolution of the human species*. New Haven: Yale University Press, 1962.

Dobzhansky, T. *Genetics of the evolutionary process*. New York: Columbia University Press, 1970.

Dreyfus, H. L. *What computers can't do: The limits of artificial intelligence* (2nd ed.). New York: Harper & Row, 1979.

Dummett, M. *Truth and other enigmas*. Cambridge, Mass.: Harvard University Press, 1978.

Erikson, E. *Insight and responsibility: Lectures on the ethical implications of psychoanalytic insight*. New York: Norton, 1964.

Feldman, C. F., & Toulmin, S. Logic and the theory of mind. In J. K. Cole & W. J. Arnold (Eds.), *Nebraska Symposium on Motivation* (Vol. 23). Lincoln: University of Nebraska Press, 1976.

Festinger, L. *A theory of cognitive dissonance*. Stanford: Stanford University Press, 1957.

Flavell, J. H. *The developmental psychology of Jean Piaget*. Princeton, N. J.: Van Nostrand, 1963.

Fodor, J. A. *The language of thought*, The language and thought series. New York: Thomas Y. Crowell Company, 1975.

Fodor, J. A. Fixation of belief and concept acquisition. In M. Piattelli-Palmarini (Ed.), *Language and learning: The debate between Jean Piaget and Noam Chomsky*. Cambridge, Mass.: Harvard University Press, 1980. (a)

Fodor, J. A. Methodological solipsism considered as a research strategy in cognitive psychology. *The Behavioral and Brain Sciences*, 1980, *3*(1), 63-73, 99-109. (b)

Fodor, J. A. *Representations: Philosophical essays on the foundations of cognitive science*. Cambridge, Mass.: M.I.T. Press (A Bradford Book), 1981.

Frege, G. [On sense and nominatum]. In H. Feigl (Ed. and trans.) & W. Sellars (Ed.), *Readings in philosophical analysis*. New York: Appleton-Century-Crofts, 1949.

Freud, S. [*The ego and the id*] (Joan Riviere, Trans., & J. Strachey, Ed). New York: Norton, 1960. (Originally published 1923.)

Goodman, N. *Fact, fiction and forecast* (3rd ed.). New York: Bobbs-Merrill, 1973.

Goodman, N. *Ways of worldmaking*. Indianapolis, Ind.: Hackett Publishing Company, 1978.

Hamlyn, D. W. Review of *The explanation of behavior*, by C. Taylor. *Mind*, 1967, *76*(301), 127-136.

Hamlyn, D. W. *The theory of knowledge*. Garden City, N. Y.: Doubleday, 1970.

Hamlyn, D. W. Objectivity, In Dearden, R. F., Hirst, P. H., & Petters, R. S. (Eds.), *Education and the development of reason*. London: Routledge & Kegan Paul, 1972.

Hamlyn, D. W. The concept of development. *Proceedings, Philosophy of Education Society of Great Britain*, Vol. 9, 1975, 26-39.

Hamlyn, D. W. *Experience and the growth of understanding*, International library of the philosopy of education. London: Routledge and Kegan Paul, 1978.

Hamlyn, D. W. What exactly is social about the origins of understanding? In P. Light & G. Butterworth (Eds.), *The individual and the social in cognitive development*. Brighton, England: Harvester Press, 1981.

Hamlyn, D. W. The concept of social reality. In P. Secord (Ed.), *Consciousness, behavior and social structure*. Sage, 1982.

Hamlyn, D. W. *Perception, learning and the self: Essays in the philosophy of psychology*. London: Routledge and Kegan Paul, 1983.

Haroutunian, S. Piaget's explanation of "stage" transition. *The Monist*, 1978, *64*(1), 622-635.

Haroutunian, S. Review of *Biology and knowledge: An essay on the relations between organic regulations and cognitive processes*, by J. Piaget. *Harvard Educational Review*, 1979, *49*(1), 93-100.

Haroutunian, S. Conceptual change: The nativist-constructivist debate. In D. DeNicola (Ed.), *Proceedings, Philosophy of Education Society*, 1981, pp. 49-58.

Heider, F. Attitudes and cognitive organization. In M. Fishbein (Ed.), *Readings in attitude theory and measurement*. New York: Wiley, 1967. (Reprinted from *Journal of Psychology*, 1946, *21*, 107-112.)

Hesse, M. *The structure of scientific inference*. Berkeley: University of California Press, 1974.

Inhelder, B., & Piaget, J. [*The growth of logical thinking from childhood to adolescence.*] (A. Parsons & S. Milgram, trans.). New York: Basic Books, 1958. Originally published, 1955.)

Inhelder, B., Garcia R. and Vonèche, J. (Eds.). *Épistémologie génétique et équilibration: Hommage à Jean Piaget*. Neuchâtel: Delachaux & Niestle, 1977.

James, W. *The principles of psychology* (2 vols.). New York: H. Holt and Company, 1890.

Kant, I. [*Critique of pure reason*] (N. K. Smith, trans.). Toronto, Canada: Macmillan and Co., Ltd., 1929. (Originally published 1781, version A, and 1787, version B.)

Kaye, K. *The mental and social life of babies: How parents create persons*. Chicago: University of Chicago Press, 1982.

Kessen, W. Stage and structure in the study of children. Thought in the young child: Report of a conference on intellectual development with particular attention to the work of Jean Piaget, 1967. *Monographs of the Society for Research in Child Development, 27*, Serial 83. New York: Kraus Report Co., 1970.

Kripke, S. Naming and necessity. In G. Harman and D. Davidson (Eds.), *The semantics of natural language*, Synthese Library, Vol. 40. Dordrecht, Holland: D. Reidel Publishing Co., 1972.

Lakoff, M., & Johnson, M. *Metaphors we live by*. Chicago: University of Chicago Press, 1980.

Lorenz, K. *Evolution and modification of behavior*. Chicago: University of Chicago Press, 1965.

Lorenz, K. [*Studies in animal and human behavior*, Vol. 1] (R. Martin, trans.). Cambridge, Mass.: Harvard University Press, 1970. (Originally published, 1970.)

Macnamara, J. Stomachs assimilate and accommodate, don't they? *Canadian Psychological Review*, 1976, *17*(3), 167-173.

Mischel, T. Scientific and philosophical psychology. In T. Mischel (Ed.), *Human action: Conceptual and empirical issues*. New York: Academic Press, 1969.

Mischel, T. Piaget: Cognitive conflict and the motivation of thought. In T. Mischel (Ed.), *Cognitive development and epistemology*. New York: Academic Press, 1971.

Nagel, E. Determinism and development. In D. B. Harris (Ed.), *The concept of development: An issue in the study of human behavior*. Minneapolis: University of Minnesota Press, 1957.

Papert, S. The role of artificial intelligence in psychology. In M. Piattelli-Palmarini (Ed.), *Language and learning: The debate between Jean Piaget and Noam Chomsky*. Cambridge, Mass.: Harvard University Press, 1980.

Pascual-Leone, J. A mathematical model for the transition rule in Piaget's developmental stages. *Acta Psychologica*, 1970, *32*(4), 301-345.

Peters, R. S. Education and human development. In R. F. Dearden, P. H. Hirst, & R. S. Peters (Eds.), *Education and the development of reason*. London: Routledge and Kegan Paul, 1972.

Peters, R. S. The development of reason. In R. S. Peters (collected papers), *Psychology and ethical development*. London: Allen and Unwin, 1974. (Reprinted from S. I. Benn and G. Mortimore (Eds.), *Rationality and the social sciences*. London: Routledge and Kegan Paul, 1974.

Phillips, D. C., & Kelley, M. Hierarchical theories of development in education and psychology. *Harvard Educational Review*, 1975, *45*(3), 351-375.

Piaget, J. [*The origins of intelligence in children*] (M. Cook, trans.). New York: Norton, 1952. (Originally published, 1936.)

Piaget, J. [*The construction of reality in the child*] (M. Cook, trans.). New York: Basic Books, 1954. (Originally published, 1937.)

Piaget, J. The general problems of the psycho-biological development of the child. In J. M. Tanner & B. Inhelder (Eds.), *Discussions on child development* (Vol. IV). New York: International Universities Press, 1956.

Piaget, J. Logique et équilibre dans les comportements du sujet. Logique et équilibre. In L. Apostel, M. Mandelbrot, and J. Piaget (Eds.), *Etudes d'épistémologie génétique*. Paris: Presses Universitaires de France, 1957, *2*, 27-117.

Piaget, J. [*Play, dreams and imitation*] (C. Gattegno & F. M. Hodgson, trans.). New York: Norton, 1962. (Originally published, 1945.)

Piaget, J. [*Six psychological studies*] (A. Tenzer, trans.). New York: Vintage, 1968. (Originally published, 1964.)

Piaget, J. [*Biology and knowledge: An essay on the relations between organic regulations and cognitive processes*] (B. Walsh, trans.). Chicago: University of Chicago Press, 1971. (Originally published, 1967.)

✳ Piaget, J. [*The principles of genetic epistemology*] (W. Mays, trans.). New York: Basic Books, 1972. (Originally published, 1970.)

✳ Piaget, J. [*The development of thought: Equilibration of cognitive structures*] (A. Rosin, trans.). New York: Viking Press, 1977. (Originally published, 1975.)

Piaget, J. [*Behavior and evolution*] (D. Nicholson-Smith, trans.). New York: Pantheon, 1978. (Originally published, 1976.)

Piaget, J. [*Adaptation and intelligence: Organic selection and phenocopy*] (S. Eames, trans.). Chicago: University of Chicago Press, 1980. (Originally published, 1974.) (a)

Piaget, J. The psychogenesis of knowledge and its epistemological significance. In M. Piattelli-Palmarini (Ed.), *Language and learning: The debate between Jean Piaget and Noam Chomsky*. Cambridge, Mass.: Harvard University Press, 1980. (b)

Piattelli-Palmarini, M. (Ed.). *Language and learning: The debate between Jean Piaget and Noam Chomsky*. Cambridge, Mass.: Harvard University Press, 1980.

Putnam, H. *Mind, language and reality: Philosophical papers* (Vol. 2). Cambridge: Cambridge University Press, 1975.

✳ Putnam, H. What is innate and why: Comments on the debate. In M. Piattelli-Palmarini (Ed.), *Language and learning: The debate between Jean Piaget and Noam Chomsky*. Cambridge, Mass.: Harvard University Press, 1980.

Quine, W. V. O. *From a logical point of view: Logico-philosophical essays* (2nd rev. ed.). Cambridge, Mass.: Harvard University Press, 1961.

Ringle, M. D. (Ed.), *Philosophical perspectives in artificial intelligence*. New York: Humanities Press, 1979.

Rosch E., Mervis, C. B., Gray, W. D., Johnson, D. M., & Boyes-Braem, P. Basic objects in natural categories. *Cognitive Psychology*, 1976, *8*, 382-439.

Rotman, B. *Jean Piaget. Psychologist of the real.* Ithaca, N.Y.: Cornell University Press, 1977.

Russell, J. *The acquisition of knowledge*. London: Macmillan, 1978.

Sansom, W. *The equilibriad*. London: The Hogarth Press, 1948.

Scheffler, I. *Beyond the letter: A philosophical inquiry into ambiguity, vagueness and metaphor in language*. London: Routledge and Kegan Paul, 1979.

Searle, J. *Speech acts: An essay in the philosophy of language*. Cambridge: Cambridge University Press, 1969.

Searle, Minds, brains and programs. *The Behavioral and Brain Sciences*, 1980, *3*(3), 417-424, 450-457. (a)

Searle, J. Rules and causation. *The Behavioral and Brain Sciences*, 1980, *3*(1), 37-38. (b)

Searle, J. Two objections to methodological solipsism. *The behavioral and brain sciences*, 1980, *3*(1), 93-94. (c)

Searle, J. *Intentionality: An essay in the philosophy of mind*. Cambridge: Cambridge University Press, 1983.

✳ Siegel, L., & Brainerd, C. (Eds.). *Alternatives to Piaget: Critical essays on the theory*. New York: Academic Press, 1978.

Simpson, G. On the Baldwin effect. *Evolution*. 1953, *7*(4), 110-117.

Spencer, H. *The principles of psychology* (2 vols.). New York: D. Appleton & Company, 1892.

Stich, S. Introduction: The idea of innateness. In S. Stich (Ed.), *Innate ideas.* Berkeley: University of California Press, 1975.

Strawson, P. F. *The bounds of sense: An essay on Kant's Critique of Pure Reason.* London: Methuen, 1966.

Taylor, C. *The explanation of behavior.* London: Routledge & Kegan Paul, 1964.

Toulmin, S. The concept of "stages" in psychological development. In T. Mischel (Ed.), *Cognitive development and epistemology.* New York: Academic Press, 1971.

Toulmin, S. *Human understanding: General introduction and part I.* Princeton, N.J.: Princeton University Press, 1972.

Vonèche, J., & Gruber, H. (Eds.). *The essential Piaget.* London: Routledge & Kegan Paul, 1977.

Von Foerster, H. On self-organizing systems and their environments. In M. C. Yovits & S. Cameron (Eds.), *Self-organizing systems.* Proceedings of an interdisciplinary conference, 1959. New York: Pergamon Press, 1960.

Waddington, C. H. The assimilation of acquired character. *Evolution,* 1953, 7(7) 118-125.

Waddington, C. H. The 'Baldwin effect,' 'genetic assimilation' and 'homeostasis.' *Evolution,* 1953, 7(4), 386-387.

Waddington, C. H. *The strategy of the genes.* London: Allen and Unwin, 1957.

Waddington, C. H. Evolutionary adaptation. In S. Tax (Ed.), *Evolution after Darwin: Vol. 1, The evolution of life.* The University of Chicago Centennial. Chicago: University of Chicago Press, 1960.

Waddington, C. H. *Principles of development and differentiation.* New York: Macmillan, 1966.

Waddington, C. H. Paradigms for an evolutionary process. In C. H. Waddington (Ed.), *Towards a theoretical biology: Vol. 2, Sketches.* Chicago: Aldine, 1969.

Waddington, C. H. *The evolution of an evolutionist.* Ithaca, N. Y.: Cornell University Press, 1975.

Waddington, C. H. (Ed.). *Towards a theoretical biology* (5 vols.). Chicago: Aldine Publishing Company, 1968-1972.

Wartofsky, M. *Conceptual foundations of scientific thought: An introduction to the philosophy of science.* New York: Macmillan, 1968.

Wartofsky, M. The model muddle: Proposals for an immodest realism. In M. Wartofsky & R. S. Cohen (Eds.), *Models: Representation and the scientific understanding.* Boston studies in the philosophy of science, Vol. 48. Dordrecht, Holland: D. Reidel Publishing Co., 1979.

Watson, J. B. *Psychology from the standpoint of a behaviorist.* London: Lippincott, 1929.

Weiss, P. A. *Principles of development: A text in experimental embryology* (2nd ed.). New York: Hafner Publishing Co., 1969.

Weiss, P. A. The basic concept of hierarchic systems. In P. Weiss (Ed.), *Hierarchically organized systems in theory and practice.* New York: Hafner Publishing Co., 1971.

Wilden, A. Piaget and the structure as law and order. In K. F. Riegel & G. C. Rosenwald (Eds.), *Structure and transformation: Developmental and historical aspects.* New York: Wiley, 1975.

Wilson, E. O., & Bossert, W. H. *A primer of population biology*. Stamford, Conn.: Sinauer Associates, Inc., 1971.

Wimsatt, W. C. Some problems with the concept of "feedback." In R. C. Buch & R. S. Cohen (Eds.), *Boston studies in the philosophy of science* (Vol. 8, 1970). Synthese Library. New York: Humanities Press, 1971.

Wimsatt, W. C. Randomness and perceived randomness in evolutionary biology. *Synthese*, 1980, *43*, 287-329.

Wimsatt, W. C. The unites of selection and the structure of the multi-level genome. In R. N. Giere & P. D. Asquith (Eds.), *Proceedings, Philosophy of Science Association*, PSA-1980, Vol. 2. East Lansing: Michigan State University, 1981.

Wittgenstein, L. [*Philosophical investigations*] (3rd ed.). (G. E. M. Anscombe, trans.). New York: Macmillan, 1958.

Wohlwill, J. F. Piaget's theory of development of intelligence in the concrete-operations period. Supplement to *The American Journal of Mental Deficiency*, 1966, *70*(4), 57-83.

Woodfield, A. *Teleology*. Cambridge: Cambridge University Press, 1976.

Author Index

Subject Index